Textures of Irish America

SANFORD STERNLICHT, Series Editor

TEXTURES

of

Irish America

LAWRENCE J. McCAFFREY

 SYRACUSE UNIVERSITY PRESS

First Paperback Edition 1998
98 99 00 01 02 03   6 5 4 3 2 1

Permission to quote from the following sources is gratefully acknowledged:

"The Recent Irish Diaspora in America," in *Contemporary American Immigration*, ed. Dennis Laurence Cuddy. Copyright © 1982 and reprinted with the permission of Twayne Publishers, a division of G. K. Hall and Co., Boston.

"Irish America," *The Wilson Quarterly* 9 (Spring, 1985). Copyright © 1985 by the Woodrow Wilson International Center for Scholars.

The paper used in this publication meets the minimum requirements of American National Standard for Information Sciences—Permanence of Paper for Printed Library Materials, ANSI Z39.48-1984. ∞™

Library of Congress Cataloging-in-Publication Data
McCaffrey, Lawrence John, 1925–
    Textures of Irish America / Lawrence J. McCaffrey.
        p. cm. — (Irish studies)
    Includes bibliographical references and index.
    ISBN 0-8156-0267-7   ISBN 0-8156-0521-8 (pbk.: alk. paper)
    1. Irish Americans—History.   I. Title.   II. Series: Irish studies (Syracuse, N.Y.)
E184.I6M36   1992
973'.049162—dc20   91-41159

Manufactured in the United States of America

To the Fourth Generation
Sean, Emily, and
Brian Luft McCaffrey, Kathleen McCaffrey,
and Alex McCaffrey-Trigoso

Lawrence J. McCaffrey is a professor emeritus of history at Loyola University of Chicago. He has published nine books, including *The Irish Experience* and *The Irish Diaspora in America,* and numerous articles about Irish and Irish-American history and literature. He is cofounder of the American Conference of Irish Studies and spends many of his summers in Ireland researching and teaching.

Contents

Illustrations

Preface

In this book, as in my previous examinations of the Irish-American experience, I interpret the Irish journey in the United States from the unskilled working-class ghettos to the middle-class suburbs as a success story in acquisition of material prosperity if not necessarily a spiritual or intellectual achievement. Most other historians who have analyzed Irish America in regional or national studies agree with this interpretation. Kerby Miller, however, is the most articulate and prominent of a small community of historians who propose a different point of view. In his critique of "The Irish-American Dimension" in *The Irish in Chicago*, Miller takes exception to my thesis that with some individual and geographical exceptions, the American Irish have been assimilated and have earned a comfortable standard of living and respectability in the United States as relatively contented citizens. Miller argues that I and two other contributors to the volume, Ellen Skerrett and Michael Funchion, place an "ahistorical overemphasis on the ultimate suburbanization and embourgeosiement of the Irish that trivialize the immigrant and even the second generation experiences." He complains that we pass over "the pain of exile; poverty, exploitation, and conflict (both inter- and intraethnic); the strains and disappointments of assimilation; and what Farrell (James T.) called the 'tragedy of the worker' " (*American Historical Review* 93, Dec. 1988, pp. 1393–94).

In his comprehensive, informative, exceptionally well written, and provocative *Emigrants and Exiles: Ireland and the Irish Exodus to North America* (1985), Miller does not laud the Irish-American story as one of economic and social progress and integration. Instead, having discerned feelings of loneliness, a sense of exile, and an insuperable longing for the familiar ways of home in letters to friends and relatives in Ireland, Miller concludes that Irish emigrants, particularly those with origins in the Gaelic West, had difficulty coping with Anglo-Protestant America's individualism and competitiveness and did not experience social mobility or achieve political power until late in the nineteenth century. Until then, life for many of the Irish in the United States was characterized by failure exhibited in alcoholism, crime, and neuroses. According to Miller, Irish Catholicism spiritually and psychologically comforted the Irish in America, and by emphasizing moral order and respectability it encouraged economic and social progress. But by stressing religious uniqueness, Catholicism fostered social isolation and obstructed the process of assimilation. In addition, the Irish-American nationalist concentration on Ireland worked against a melding into American society. The priorities and message of nationalism represented the frustrations and failures of Irish America, echoing the theme of exile, crying out for vengeance on the source of its misery: Britain.

In this volume I agree with Miller that life was extremely difficult and painful for Irish pioneers of the American urban ghetto. They were the first victims of the anti-Catholic core of American nativism. Those who came later also found existence in urban America a constant struggle for dignity and survival. Nevertheless, Miller exaggerates Irish-American misery. His main source—emigrants' letters—and his dominant interest—nationalism—distort his view of the American Irish. The Irish in the United States were more interested in Catholicism and politics, both of which had strong American focuses and purposes, than in bitter, Ireland-centered nationalism. Irish-American nationalism was not only a force toward estrangement; it included admiration for the United States and a desire to belong. According to nationalist propaganda, the achievements of emigrant exiles in the United States demonstrated that the Irish were noble people who flourished in a free environment, and American liberal democratic republicanism was a model for Ireland's future. Thomas N. Brown has suggested that the effort to liberate Ireland, thus providing a dignified, free homeland, reflected an Irish-American nationalistic attempt to make the Irish respectable in the United States.

Emigrants' letters are a dubious source for judging how the Irish accommodated to life in the United States. Many emigrants seldom, if ever, wrote home. It is reasonable to assume that those who were unhappy were more likely to send messages of despair than were the contented to articulate joy. And it was only natural for people communicating with parents and siblings in Ireland to express feelings of loneliness. Furthermore, these normal emotions did not necessarily mean that they were willing to exchange their new life for the old.

In his *Emigrants and Exiles* Miller does not offer a clear or comparative measure of alienation. All newcomers to cities in the United States, including rural Anglo-Americans, have been cultural strangers in their new setting. The Brahmins in Boston and the Anglo-Protestant elite in other cities felt bitter and alienated when they witnessed the conquest of their turf by "foreigners." Just how unusual was the experience of Irish Americans? They adjusted to the United States more quickly than did most European immigrants. They became citizens and, despite their religious and cultural isolation, easily conformed to and participated in American politics. By the end of the nineteenth century they dominated American sports, particularly the national game, baseball, and were prominent in the entertainment business. The Irish were more reluctant to return to their homeland than other European immigrants. For them, the journey to the United States was a one-way trip.

Miller and some other scholars who take a negative view of Irish progress in the United States matured at a time when few people born in Ireland inhabited American cities. Their academic approach to Irish America has not been leavened by personal experiences. Miller and his supporters were in college or university in the late 1960s and early 1970s when it was intellectually fashionable for students, offended by the American involvement in Vietnam and the presidencies of Lyndon Johnson and Richard Nixon, to feel bitter and detached. And they still are not comfortable in the land of Ronald Reagan, George Bush, and Dan Quayle. In describing Irish-American alienation in the past, they are expressing more of their own present-day ambivalences about their country than the sentiments of the Irish in the United States.

In contrast to Miller and other doubters of the Irish-American success story, I experienced boyhood and adolescence at a time when Irish America still had a vital existence, when a large number of streetcar motormen and conductors, subway drivers and maintenance personnel, railroad men, policeman, firemen, priests, nuns, and brothers spoke with Irish brogues. Irish-born parents who talked with their children about the Old Sod, and many preferred never to mention the place, told them that as much as they loved the land of their birth, the United States was the greatest country in the world and they loved it even more than Ireland. Very few immigrants, even if they experienced discrimination in America and had to work hard to maintain marginal levels of comfort, ever expressed a desire to return to Ireland. For them, the United States was the land of promise. Although it might have fallen short of original expectations, it offered much more freedom and opportunity than did Ireland. The Irish came to the United States to escape poverty and limited prospects. They expected the United States to give them, and even more so their children, employment choices and opportunities, economic security, influence, and respectability. It took time, but in large part they realized their dreams. Guided by their religious-ethnic heritage and their traumatic historical experiences on both sides of the Atlantic, most Irish Catholics in the United States know that there are no perfect places, people, or situations in this world. Still, they share Peggy Noonan's view of America: "This is the fairest place there ever was, it's wide open, and no one has cause for bitterness."[1]

Lawrence J. McCaffrey

Evanston, Illinois
December 1991

Acknowledgments

Portions of this book have appeared in "Irish Nationalism and Irish Catholicism: A Study in Cultural Identity," *Church History* 42 (Dec. 1973); "The Recent Irish Diaspora in America," in *Contemporary American Immigration*, ed. Dennis Laurence Cuddy (Boston: Twayne, 1982); "Irish America," *The Wilson Quarterly* 9 (Spring, 1985); "Ghetto to Suburbs: Irish Occupational and Social Mobility," in *Ethnicity and the Work Force*, ed. Winston A. Van Horne and Thomas V. Tonneson (Madison: Univ. of Wisconsin System American Ethnic Studies Coordinating Committee/Urban Corridor Consortium, 1985); "Irish-American Politics: Power with or Without Purpose?" in *The Irish in America: Emigration, Assimilation and Impact*, ed. P. J. Drudy (New York: Cambridge University Press, 1985); "Fictional Images of Irish-America," in *The Writer as Witness: Literature as Historical Evidence*, ed. Tom Dunne (Cork: Cork Univ. Press, 1987); "The Irish-American Dimension," in Lawrence J. McCaffrey, Ellen Skerrett, Michael F. Funchion, and Charles Fanning, *The Irish in Chicago* (Urbana: Univ. of Illinois Press, 1987), and "Irish Textures in American Catholicism," *The Catholic Historical Review*, 58 (Jan. 1992). My "Recommended Reading" section is a revised and updated version of a similar section in *The Irish Diaspora in America* (Washington, D.C.: The Catholic Univ. of America Press, 1984). I thank the editors and publishers of the books and periodicals listed above for permission to present previously published material in revised form and in a new context. I am grateful to Loyola University of Chicago for the semester leave of absence that gave me time to write the first draft and to the Research Board at Loyola for a grant to purchase pictures and permissions to use them. My graduate research assistant at Loyola, Collette Bliss, was kind enough to check my manuscript for typing mistakes.

xvi   *Acknowledgments*

Many good friends helped me during the process of writing *Textures of Irish-America*. Lisa Meloy read some of my chapters and made valuable suggestions for style and content changes. I learned a great deal and sharpened my ideas in conversations with Lisa Meloy, Ellen Skerrett, Maureen O'Rourke Murphy, Mary Helen Thuente, Jane McIver, Emmet Larkin, Joe Curran, Tom Flanagan, Charley Fanning, Tom Hachey, Alf MacLochlainn, and Tom Brown, who remains the most perceptive observer of Irish America. I treasure his advice and friendship. In my search for pictures I received valuable assistance from John and Selma Appel, Tom Brown, R. Vincent Comerford, Anne Siewers Coyne and John Coyne, Michael Grace, S.J., Sister Pat Illing, Dan Lydon, Alf and Fionnuala MacLochlainn, Joe Marcy, Sister Mary Consilii Reynolds, Tom Sheridan, Ellen Skerrett, and Joel Wells.

Textures of Irish America

The Irish-American Experience

Tugged up from their home roots, taken and going will-
ingly from the sea smell and the peat smells. . . . Shoved
into a boat with sweating and cursing and stinking and
praying, with deaths and births, with old age and youth,
they landed and a shovel was placed in their hands or a
hammer or a spade and they built Boston and New York
and Chicago and Philadelphia. And in the evening they
walked home in the leaning shadows of the gray stone to
their one room or two rooms and fell into bewildered
sleep.

—Jack Dunphy, "Prologue," *John Fury*

American urban ethnic history begins with Irish Catholic immigrants. They established its precedents and set its patterns. Fleeing
from poverty, Protestant ascendancy, British colonialism, and turbulence in their own country, large numbers of Irish Catholics began to
enter the United States in the 1820s. A steady stream became a flood
during the years of the Great Famine, 1845–49, when more than a
million refugees from hunger, disease, and despair found their way to
America. Irish emigration became institutionalized in the dreadful
1840s. To avoid a repeat of disaster and to establish and retain a reasonable standard of living in rural Ireland, most young men and
women had to leave the country.

Although the overwhelming majority of emigrants came from
rural Ireland, few tried their hand at farming in the United States.
Tilling the soil in Ireland had not been a secure or pleasant experience. Landlordism and small tenant holdings had not taught the necessary skills for large-scale agriculture in the United States. In
addition, the social isolation of rural America was not congenial to

1

the Irish Catholic communal personality. But Irish immigrants had no more technological skills for urban than rural living. Although the basement, attic, and tar-paper urban dwellings were bleak and depressing, at least American cities provided the company of their own misery-sharing people.

The emigrants' early encounters with urban America recalled the mental agonies of a nightmarish Irish history and opened a new set of psychological wounds. Anglo-American Protestants did not welcome Irish Catholics, who were the first group to create social problems in American cities. The Irish lived in vermin-infested tenements, on streets that were open sewers, in slovenly neighborhoods, and manifested drunkenness, violence, family disputes and breakups, crime, disease, and mental disorders. Anglo-Americans saw Irish Catholics as a social plague destroying their cities, filling their jails, hospitals, and asylums, and overburdening their limited social welfare system.

Much worse than Irish filth, health problems, and antisocial behavior was their religion. Anglo-American Protestants inherited the anti-Catholicism of British nativism and considered Catholicism as a superstitious and tyrannical danger to American culture and institutions. Until Irish Catholics began to arrive in large numbers, American fears of Romanism were mostly paranoid fantasies. During the early years of the republic, there were only about thirty thousand Catholics in the whole country. They were a quiet, private, deferential group served by a small number of priests. But the arrival of the aggressively and self-consciously Catholic Irish in large numbers convinced most Anglo-American Protestants that the curse of popery had reached their shores. Even the Enlightenment tradition was hostile to Irish Catholic immigration. Its rationality frowned on all organized religion, but Catholicism's dogmas, liturgies, and hierarchical authority structures were especially offensive to the advocates of individual liberty and the unfettered mind. Both the Protestant and Enlightenment traditions envisaged the United States as an essentially rural nation whose ideal citizen was the sturdy yeoman farmer. Urban Irish Catholics dependent on an expanding industrial economy violated this ideal.

Nativist contempt and harassment shattered already fragile Irish egos, creating mental as well as physical ghettos. In their struggle to survive an unfriendly American environment, Irish Catholics relied on their religious faith for spiritual comfort and psychological security, employed politics to defend their interests and to acquire power, and finally turned to Irish nationalism to cultivate ethnic pride and dignity.

In the nineteenth century, nationalism became for many people a substitute for a Christianity that failed to adapt to the impact of both urban industrialism and the intellectual and political revolutions of the eighteenth century. It provided the sense of community, destiny, and purpose that Christian beliefs and practices once gave to their lives. In an Ireland oppressed by British Protestant colonialism and Anglo-Irish Protestant ascendancy, Catholicism was nationality and culture as well as religion. It was the cohesive force that enabled the Irish Catholic majority to withstand centuries of defeat, persecution, imposed ignorance, and poverty. In the 1820s the central tenet of modern Irish nationalism—the determination to achieve a sovereign state—emerged in the agitation for Catholic emancipation.

In the United States, as in Ireland, Catholics were targets of scorn and prejudice from Anglo-Protestants. But in the New World, as in the Old, their religion preserved their community and gave them spiritual solace. By offering a sense of the familiar in strange surroundings, the Catholic church provided Irish immigrants with a comfort station, a sort of halfway house in an unfriendly urban America. Catholic educational and social welfare services that made up for the indifference of the Anglo-American Protestant establishment to urban misery prepared them first to survive and then to prosper. Parochial schools and the introverted nature of Catholic parish communities fostered cultural and institutional separateness and fed the claims of nativist propaganda that the Irish were unassimilable, but they did preserve an essential ethnicity. Institutional independence soothed damaged Irish egos, and Catholic schools taught American patriotism as well as religious doctrine. Parochial schools also gave their students the knowledge and skills necessary in the American economy.

Politics was the second most important instrument of Irish-American progress. Although the Irish initially lacked technological skills, they did have political experience. Along with Andrew Jackson, Daniel O'Connell, the founding father of Irish nationalism, was one of the architects of modern liberal democracy. In his massive agitations for Catholic emancipation and repeal of the Union with Britain, he mobilized, organized, and politically educated the Irish Catholic masses. O'Connell differentiated Ireland from most of Catholic Europe. He rejected Continental Catholicism's defense of the Old Regime and its aristocratic power and privilege. Although he was a devout, often scrupulous, Catholic, O'Connell committed Irish nationalism to popular sovereignty, social egalitarianism, the separation of church and state, and the freedom of the private conscience. Its alliance with Irish nationalism made Irish Catholicism politically civilized, accepting the principles of liberal democracy, which in turn helped Irish Catholics adjust to the American political consensus. Rather quickly, they established a leadership role in their own neighborhoods, and by the end of the nineteenth century they controlled the urban wing of the Democratic party and most of the major cities in the United States.

Although the Irish early displayed a genius when organizing for positions of power, too often their politics were circumscribed by Catholic peasant provincialism and narrow self-interest. And their obsession with politics as the road to affluence and influence limited their economic and intellectual horizons. But on balance, the Irish contribution to American government has been constructive. They have fused the Anglo-Saxon and Roman Catholic aspects of their ethnic cultural personality to lead the Democratic party and American government away from a system of selfish laissez-faire to one of communal liberalism. Although Irish politicians were more concerned with advancing the interest of their own people than sharing the benefits of power, they did provide significant services to all branches of the Democratic ethnic coalition. Along with Irish priests and labor leaders, they helped other Catholic nationality groups adjust to the American political consensus.[1] Perhaps for their long-range good, Irish Americans focused on politics to the neglect of other things, but they had little choice. Because of the Anglo-American Protestant monopoly of business and professional opportunities, ambitious Irish youth determined on success turned to religion and politics. Although political incomes often had the taint of graft, and political jobs circumscribed rather than enhanced class mobility, they satisfied the Irish hunger for security. Changes in American society, particularly following World War II, offered Irish Americans plentiful occupational opportunities, lessening their dependence on politically connected employment.

Although nationalism was not as prominent a feature of Irish-American life as Catholicism or politics, it was a unifying force, encouraging ethnic pride, providing an avenue for social mobilization. As they did in Ireland, nationalist organizations supplied entertainment and activities that helped distract members and participants from the tribulations of working-class life. Conditions in urban America nourished Irish-American nationalism. Pooled misery and Anglo-Protestant nativism forced the Irish to subordinate Old Country county, parish, and clan loyalties to a common protective nationality. Feelings of inferiority necessitated a search for "racial myths" that could buttress a positive and unique sense of identity. The cultural nationalism created by Young Ireland in the 1840s fed this need. Irish Americans found inspiration in the works of Thomas Osborne Davis, Charles Gavan Duffy, James Clarence Mangan, and John Mitchel. Later in the nineteenth century, T. D. Sullivan's edited collection *Speeches from the Dock* fired Irish-American blood with the brave words of young Irish martyrs facing death. Robert Emmet's 1803 courtroom defiance of Lord Norberry was the most popular piece of oratory in Sullivan's volume. Emmet was Irish America's favorite martyr-hero. Like Willie McDermott in Edward McSorley's excellent 1946 novel *Our Own Kind*, many American-born boys and girls listened attentively while their immigrant father or grandfather recited Emmet's address: "When my country takes her place among the nations of the earth, then, and not till then, let my epitaph be written."[2] In parish halls Irish Americans attended concerts featuring Thomas Moore's *Melodies*, and Charles Kickham's loving and romanticized description of rural life in Tipperary, *Knocknagow*, was their favorite novel about Ireland. They cheered when Matt "the Thrasher" Donovan bested Captain French of the Protestant ascendancy in a sledge-throwing contest, and they wept when beautiful Norah Lacy slowly died with the joy and patience of a saint.[3]

Early Irish-American nationalism expressed much bitterness over misery in Ireland and failure in America and hatred for the hereditary English enemy who had conquered and then misgoverned the homeland, driving large numbers of its people to a strange land where

they again suffered hard times and persecution. Elements of alienation, anger, insecurity, defensiveness, and a whining paranoia continued and still remain in Irish-American nationalism, but a search
for respectability also motivated many seeking to liberate Ireland.
When the Irish began to achieve economic and social mobility,
climbing from the ranks of unskilled to skilled labor and even into the
lower middle class, they could not understand why other segments of
American society continued to treat them as less than social equals.
They failed to comprehend that their control of an expanding, increasingly powerful American Catholicism sustained prejudice against
them, and many decided that their inferior position reflected the servitude they had experienced in their homeland. They believed that if
they could free Ireland from the yoke of British tyranny and place it in
the family of nations, they would liberate themselves socially.

Leaders of Irish-American nationalism wanted to use the political influence and voting power of their people to turn American foreign policy toward opposition to Britain. They also hoped to employ
the United States as a dollar, arms, and morale arsenal for liberation
efforts in Ireland. Occasionally Irish Americans did succeed in embit-
tering Anglo-American relations, but in general they had little impact on the pro-British establishment in charge of national affairs.
Although foiled in its campaign to redirect American foreign policy,
Irish-American nationalism did fuel the freedom movement in Ireland. Without Irish America, nationalism in Ireland might not have
survived. The Irish diaspora in America provided both the physical
force and constitutional nationalist movements in Ireland with the essential funds and passion that enabled them to force British governments to make major concessions regarding Irish religious, social, and
economic grievances. The democratic, egalitarian, and republican
contents of Fenianism were manifestations of the Irish-American
spirit and political value system. Irish Americans authored the New
Departure strategy that Michael Davitt and Charles Stewart Parnell
directed in the land war, which produced tenant rights and eventually
peasant proprietorship. Dollars from the United States financed the
Home Rule movement and the Irish parliamentary party. Irish-
American money and arms supplied the Irish Republican Army
(IRA) in the 1919–21 War of Independence, and Irish-American
opinion, joined by voices demanding justice from all over the world,

persuaded the British government to offer dominion status to a twenty-six-county Free State that evolved into the present Irish Republic.

Catholicism, politics, and nationalism furnished the ethnic pride and solidarity that enabled Irish Americans to survive poverty and prejudice and to find a secure place in the United States. But success diminished the need for these qualities; affluence, education, and respectability altered and lessened the religious, communal-liberal, and patriotic features of the Irish-American ethnic profile. Immigration laws, the Great Depression of the late 1920s and 1930s, and World War II reduced Irish immigration to a trickle. Furthermore, the achievement of the sovereign twenty-six-county Irish Free State and later the republic as well as the social mobility of the Irish in the United States combined to direct Irish-American attention away from Ireland and toward domestic concerns. The alliance between the United States and Britain that began in World War I, revived in World War II, and persisted through the Cold War significantly reduced Irish-American Anglophobia. Although American dollars help subsidize the Provisional Irish Republican Army's campaign against British military forces and the Royal Ulster Constabulary in Northern Ireland, the proportion of the Irish in the United States contributing to the IRA war chest is relatively small. Though sympathetic to the issue of Catholic civil rights in the Six Counties and to their idea of a united Ireland, most Irish Americans reject violence as an instrument of change. There is another reason for their lack of enthusiasm for the IRA: they have become very American. Like the rest of their fellow citizens, they are short on historical memories and consciousness, and they are appalled by terrorism. Americanization has also turned Irish Americans against the addictive losing-cause martyrology that is inherent in the nationalism associated with Northern Ireland. After centuries of losing in Ireland, the Irish in the United States finally became winners. Therefore, it is difficult for them to understand the IRA's enthusiasm for dying for Ireland. They share with other Americans the conviction that it is better to live for one's country than to die for it.[4]

Although their nationalism has subsided, Irish Americans remain highly visible in politics. Population shifts from city to suburbs and more cosmopolitan interests have made their political presence more national than local. Although most prominent Irish politicians continue to serve the liberal wing of the Democratic party, many Irish-American voters have been attracted to Republican conservatism. This shift represents middle-class self-interest, but, like retreating nationalism, it also suggests a disappearing Irish historical memory and ethnic self-consciousness.

Vanishing Irish ethnicity is more significant in its religious than in its nationalist or political aspects. Unlike former urban neighborhoods, in suburban melting pots the Catholic parish is no longer the social as well as religious and educational nucleus of Irish life. In suburbia and affluent pockets of cities, parishes are multiethnic in composition and have minimal social purposes. Catholics, Protestants, Jews, and nonbelievers fraternize in a variety of organizations and clubs.

Even the religious aspect of parish life has less attraction or urgency than in former times. Vatican II reforms and responses to ecumenism have altered the liturgy of American Catholicism. Much of the formality is gone; priests face the congregation and say mass in English, and laypeople play prominent roles at mass and other services. Church leaders believed these changes would appeal to the laity, but falling attendance at Sunday mass and devotions, as well as a decline in the use of the sacraments, indicates that people are not very impressed with liturgical innovations. They seem to miss the history and the mystery of the old liturgy that added enchantment to their lives and linked the present with the past. But modernization is not the only aspect of contemporary Catholicism offensive to many members of the faith. Beginning with their quarrel with the 1968 papal anti-birth-control encyclical *Humanae Vitae*, American Catholics have disagreed with clerical authorities on many issues, including the exclusion of divorced people from full participation in the rites of the church, the insistence that priests cannot marry, the prohibition against women clergy, and even the absolute ban on abortion.

Apparently, most Catholics prefer a liturgy more conservative and traditional, more aesthetically and emotionally pleasing, and a liberal stance on dogma, rules, and regulations. This last demand reflects both their assimilation into the American mainstream and their advanced level of material comfort and education. As fully integrated citizens, rather than members of an oppressed minority, they are taking a more objective and intellectual view of their church. Before John F. Kennedy's presidency, Irish Americans desperately wanted acceptance, but they needed their religion as a psychological shelter and a source of ethnic cultural solidarity. Mentally segregating religion and politics as well as church and state, they ignored the contradictions inherent in their allegiance to the most politically liberal and religiously authoritarian systems in the Western world. As the memories of persecution disappeared and the Irish became confident in their Americanism, they began to demand that their church be as supportive as their country of individual liberties, freedom of conscience, and shared power.

The inflexibility of Rome and the impact of the American environment on the Irish made quarrels with church authority and defections from Catholicism inevitable. But is a sense of Irishness separate from Catholicism possible in the United States? Catholicism became the bedrock of Irish-American identity by instilling into Irish culture, not a lofty intellectual or aesthetic sense, but a unique sense of values and attitudes. It embodied the Irish-American historical experience, signifying both persecution and preservation and providing a sense of community, nationality, and identity. What can take its place? Without it will the Irish portion of the American ethnic mosaic disappear? Will Irish Americans continue to possess a unique personality or will they increase the blandness and uniformity that threatens the continued adventure of American pluralism?

2

From Ghetto to Suburb

GOING AND COMING

From 1820 to 1920 about five million mostly young, Catholic, and single Irish immigrants entered the United States. They formed the latest phase of their country's long refugee tradition. Sixteenth- and seventeenth-century English conquests, occupations, and plantations, followed by punitive legislation, deprived members of the Catholic aristocracy and gentry of property, power, and status, leaving them with the choices of remaining quietly and humbly at home, turning Protestant, or going to Catholic Continental countries to seek fame, fortune, and social standing. During the eighteenth and nineteenth centuries, Ireland dispatched a new breed of exiles. Resentments against the established Protestant church and British mercantile restrictions on the Irish economy drove hundreds of thousands of Ulster Presbyterians to North America, where they contributed their talents and energy to the birth and development of a new nation.[1]

As the most debased people in western Europe, Catholics had better reasons than Presbyterians to leave Ireland. Most were agricultural laborers striving to rent tiny mud-walled, dirt-floored, thatch-roofed cottages to house and small potato patches (conacres) to feed large families. Next to laborers, tenant farmers were the most numerous class of Catholics. Some, perhaps two hundred thousand, rented enough land to be ranked as a rural bourgeosie, but the overwhelming majority occupied smallholdings, about five acres on the average, and did not live much better than laborers. By the late seventeenth century a population increase began to reduce the already perilous living standard of rural Irish Catholics. From 1687 to 1725 the population escalated from 2,167,000 to 3,042,000. Fifty years later 4,019,000 people occupied the island. From 1821 to 1841 the population jumped from 6,802,000 to 8,175,000.[2] This multitude resided in a country smaller than the present American state of Indiana, had no significant industrial alternative to a primitive agrarian economy, and was increasingly dependent on a single food source, the potato.[3] In 1835 a British government-appointed commission of Irish bishops, both Catholic and Protestant, and prominent laymen investigated poverty in their country and concluded that at least one-third of the people were paupers.[4]

Despite poverty, oppression, and lack of basic civil liberties, Catholics were reluctant to cross the Atlantic. Demoralization, the expense of the voyage, ignorance, and the fatalism inherent in their Gaelic and religious values discouraged such a long and arduous journey. In the eighteenth century, however, some of the Catholic poor found their way to England, Scotland, and Wales, where they worked the harvest or provided unskilled labor for the British transportation and industrial revolutions. Seasonal agricultural laborers moved back and forth between two islands, but canal diggers, layers of railroad track, and factory workers stayed in Britain. Irishtown ghettos became a bleak aspect of the British urban landscape, previewing the early Irish-American experience.[5]

Although they feared the Atlantic crossing, Catholics were not complete strangers to eighteenth-century America. Some with ambition and skills had joined Ulster Presbyterians in the New World. They achieved respectability and occasionally distinction, especially in Philadelphia. Most of the indentured servants and convicts who arrived in British North America from Ireland were Catholics. After servitude or sentences, both usually for seven years, spent in the plantation economy of the South, they moved to the Appalachian frontier. Because the majority of servants and convicts did not leave Ireland as informed or devout Catholics and the American church lacked the personnel and facilities to minister to people on the outer geographic and social edges of society, they melded into evangelical Protestant or Ulster Presbyterian communities.[6]

Events and changes in Ireland during the 1820s initiated a large Catholic emigration. Anglicization and modernization diminished Gaelic-Catholic thought patterns binding the Irish to their homeland. Losses from potato diseases began a series of famines that climaxed in

the Great Hunger of the 1840s. An agricultural depression that followed the Napoleonic Wars encouraged a shift in agriculture from tillage to grazing, forcing people off the land and decreasing needs for
labor. Because of famine, evictions, and unemployment many joined
secret agrarian societies, touching off violent protests against high
rents for farms or conacre potato patches, tithe payments to the Protestant church, and fees demanded by Catholic priests for baptisms,
weddings, and funerals. Daniel O'Connell's agitation for Catholic
emancipation resulted in a bill in 1829 that opened political and professional doors to upper- and middle-class Catholics but did little to
relieve the misery of the masses.[7]

The Great Famine (1845–49) was the most decisive event in
modern Irish history. Hunger and fever claimed at least one-and-a-
half-million lives, forced another million or so to flee Ireland, and institutionalized emigration as a safety valve to relieve pressure on a
static agrarian economy.[8] After the Famine, some rural young people
found employment in cities or towns, a few young men joined the British armed services, the Royal Irish Constabulary, or the Dublin Metropolitan Police, and the Catholic church welcomed potential priests,
nuns, and brothers. But parents raised most of their children for export. Surplus sons who could not inherit the farm or shop or secure
jobs as tradesmen, or did not want to enter the church or become soldiers or policemen, and daughters without dowries for marriage or religious vocations or unable or unwilling to become servants in the big
houses left for the United States.

According to Janet Nolan's *Ourselves Alone,* because the Famine
radically changed Irish marriage patterns, women had more reason to
leave Ireland than men. Before the catastrophe of the 1840s, the Irish,
trusting in God and the potato, married relatively young and had
many children. After the Famine, families remained large, but young
people hesitated to wed. Throughout the country there was a growing
conviction that imprudent marriages had created overpopulation that
resulted in the casualties of the 1840s. To avoid a repetition of those
grim years, people postponed marriage until they felt economically secure through the possession of a farm. This new outlook meant that
many young men and women would never be able to wed. The desire
to hold and pass on the farm replaced romance as the main motiva-

tion for marriage. Rural families no longer subdivided holdings among their sons. Only one, usually but not necessarily the oldest, inherited the farm. Only one daughter received a dowry. Gender segregation and Catholic puritanism supplemented and provided religious justification for a socioeconomic situation that resulted in late marriage and often permanent celibacy. With fewer local employment prospects than men and doomed to lives of insignificance and boredom, Irish women were anxious to emigrate to the United States to seek economic and marriage opportunities denied them at home. By 1880 more Irish women than men were entering America.[9]

Even a religious vocation did not exclude emigration. Many young people entering the church eventually left Ireland to serve expanding Irish Catholic communities throughout the English-speaking world. By 1880 two-thirds of the people born in Ireland were living someplace else, usually in the United States.

The American Irish, particularly servant girls, sent passage money or ship tickets to siblings back home. Although Irish Americans funded the exodus, some joined with priests and journalists in warning prospective emigrants that the United States was far from a paradise, that gold did not lie in its streets, jobs were scarce, work was hard, the climate was harsh, American materialism and competitiveness contrasted with Irish Catholic values, and Protestants in America despised Irish Catholics with at least the same intensity as those in the United Kingdom.

The journey to America in the early nineteenth century was a torturous ordeal. Most emigrants left from Liverpool after crossing the Irish Sea packed on the decks of small boats from Dublin. Liverpool runners grabbed their grubby luggage and took them to overcrowded, filthy boardinghouses. Like the runners, boardinghouse keepers were often Irish themselves. They exploited emigrants by overcharging them for food, cheap grog, rent, and ship tickets.

Sick from rolling seas, the stench below deck, hunger, and disease, Irish passengers found the sea journey a dreadful experience. Brutal ship captains and crews beat and robbed many of them. Emigrants often began voyages with few provisions, sailed in vessels lacking adequate space, food, or toilet facilities (American ships were cleaner and the crews were more humane than British vessels), and many died en route and were consigned to watery graves. During the Famine years, when many passengers embarked with fever, ship deaths were common.

In American ports, naïve Irish travelers again encountered shifty runners, cheating boardinghouse keepers, and unscrupulous grog house operators. In addition, they were duped by sellers of counterfeit canal, railroad, and riverboat tickets.[10] Some Famine immigrants, especially these who came through landlord-sponsored emigration projects, arrived literally naked in the New World. They carried Famine fever with them, and large numbers died shortly after landing. In 1847, perhaps as many as thirty thousand ended their journey in graves in Grosse Isle near Quebec.[11] Down the St. Lawrence, six thousand more Famine refugees are buried in Montreal.

Irish Catholics entered the United States in a variety of ways. Some sailed directly to New York, New Orleans, or Boston. Others took the less expensive route to Canada as ballast in lumber and flax ships returning from the United Kingdom. Those who landed in New Brunswick often walked south into Maine. Those who disembarked in Quebec or Montreal could make their way on foot or by riverboat to Vermont or New York. And then there were the "two-boaters" who first went to Newfoundland and earned enough money in the fisheries to continue on to Boston.

Settling in America involved difficult adjustments for Irish immigrants. In *Hibernia America: The Irish and Regional Cultures*, Dennis Clark points out that the Irish played a variety of roles on the American frontier as riverboat gamblers, fur trappers and traders, cowboys, outlaws, peace officers, soldiers, ranchers, and farmers, but most of them became involved in the transportation and industrial economies and settled in towns and cities.[12] Such a life was a radical change from their rural, peasant Irish origins. Although Irish and Irish-American Catholic bishops joined with many journalists in a plea to emigrants planning on going to the United States to avoid wicked and worldly cities that would imperil their religious beliefs and values, the Irish gravitated toward the emerging American urban industrial economy.[13] More compelling reasons than unfortunate agrarian experiences in Ireland and money shortages restricting them to arrival ports determined the choice of city and town residences. American urbanization reflected Irish economic liabilities and Catholic personalities.

British colonialism and Irish landlordism retarded development of the peasants' agricultural skills, sapped their energies, and diminished their ambitions to cultivate the land with intelligence or enthusiasm. Subsistence farmers who worked with spade, hoe, and scythe lacked the expertise or the enterprise to till efficiently the vast, fertile fields of America.

Contrasts between social life in rural Ireland and that of the agrarian United States also steered the Catholic Irish toward American towns and cities. Working in the tiny fields of Irish farms, men conversed with neighbors across ditches, hedges, and stone walls. A short evening stroll brought them to a neighbor's cottage for visits that lasted long into the night. Irish settlers in rural America were overwhelmed by its spaciousness and its torrid summers and frigid winters. Blizzards, vast prairies, and the individualistic Protestant culture often meant social isolation and loneliness for gregarious Irish Catholics. Most of them preferred towns and cities, where the company and comfort of their own kind compensated for the crime and disease that infested their tenement and tar-paper shack neighborhoods.[14]

Former Irish farmers and agricultural laborers chose not to cultivate American soil, but their skill limitations also restricted urban economic opportunities. They had to accept casual, unskilled, difficult, dirty, unhealthy, and low-paying jobs working in stables or driving horses as draymen or cabbies; loading, unloading, and crewing ships, riverboats, and barges; sweeping out factories and saloons; digging foundations and carrying hod on construction sites; serving people in restaurants and bars; and mining coal in Pennsylvania, gold in California, and copper in Montana.

New Orleans was second to New York as the Irish port of entry. In that southern city, they competed with slave and free African Americans for work as servants, cabbies, and stevedores. They loaded, unloaded, and crewed Mississippi River boats, often sweating below deck "screwing" down cotton bales or in engine rooms, risking loss of life and limb from frequent explosions. In Louisiana many Irish perished while draining malaria-infested swamps for tillage or road construction. Managers of these projects preferred employing the cheap and apparently inexhaustible supply of Irish immigrant workers to risking high-investment African-American slave labor.

When the American transportation revolution began, "Paddies" dug canals and then cut railroad trails through forests and mountains before laying track. Canal digging and railroad development brought the Irish to the urban frontier. They began the westward movement working on the Erie Canal, completed in 1825, which connected the Hudson River at Troy with Buffalo on Lake Erie. In 1836, some of the Irish navvies who had worked on the Erie and other canals came to Chicago to dig the Illinois and Michigan Canal, which was to link the Great Lakes with the Mississippi and thus eastern and midwestern cities with New Orleans. Graveyards along canal and railroad routes testify to the Irish contribution and sacrifice to the effort to shape a continent into a nation through improved transportation.[15]

Although Irish women employed in eastern textile mills and shoe factories also were a significant segment of America's early industrial work force, they were even more important as domestic servants. Anglo-Protestant women considered employment as servants degrading. Parents of non-Irish urban ethnics (except Swedes) hesitated to send their daughters to work in the homes of strangers. But because the overwhelming majority of Irish women came to the United States on their own without social snobbery, there were no barriers excluding them from domestic service. Such work offered rooms in comfortable homes, nourishing food, clean clothing, a taste for civilized living, and salaries that compared favorably with those in factories and mills.

If Irish women married in the United States and if their spouses did not die young from dangerous work or disease, they were less likely to seek employment outside the home than were women of other nationalities. Instead, they concentrated their attention on directing their husbands and children toward middle-class respectability. Widowed or abandoned Irish wives frequently worked in mills or factories, but many supported themselves and their children by taking in boarders. Even some with working mates took in roomers to supplement family incomes. In Irish families it was common for husbands and working children living at home to turn over their paychecks to wives and mothers, who gave them an allowance. Combined incomes managed by matriarchs made it possible for Irish-American families to buy houses.[16] At home the Irish had been propertyless, and owning a house of their own symbolized dignity and liberty.

Many young Irishmen had been attracted to the British armed forces by colorful uniforms, adventure, a little money, three meals a day, reasonably clean places to sleep, comradeship, and pensions. Love of country and a determination to demonstrate it added to the same inducements to inspire the Irish to enlist in various branches of the American military. They contributed to American and Union victories in the Mexican and Civil wars. Those who lived in the South were loyal to the Confederacy. After Appomattox, Irish soldiers were among those who guarded and expanded the western frontier. Many lost their lives in the Seventh Cavalry under the command of General George Armstrong Custer at the 1876 Battle of the Little Big Horn.

ALIENS

The contributions of Irish Catholics to America's industrial growth and transportation expansion and their defense of the country did not win the friendship or respect of Anglo-Protestants, who considered them a "massive lump in the community, undigested, undigestible."[17] Their culture of poverty combined with the traumatic psychological adjustment to urban America resulted in a massive social problem. Dreary ghettos nurtured crime, vice, and disease. Well into the twentieth century tuberculosis afflicted the Irish on both sides of the Atlantic. Depressing living conditions and economic hardships increased in Irish fondness for drink that often led to violence and poverty.

Contemporary Irish Americans take pride in their family life, but through much of the nineteenth century the phenomena of widowed or abandoned working mothers and unemployed, underemployed, or absent fathers, many laboring on canals or railroads, further eroded family structures weakened by emigration from a more socially cohesive rural society. Wife battering and desertion were not uncommon male responses to hard times in the United States. Feeling defeated and degraded in America, both men and women reacted with antisocial behavior. The Irish seemed a gigantic human urban social blight as they filled jails, sanitariums, hospitals, almshouses, and insane asylums.

Convinced that Irish poverty, slovenliness, alcoholism, crime, violence, improvidence, and mental and physical disorders were polluting the United States, Anglo-American Protestants resented their presence. They also objected to the financial burdens of police and institutional responses to the Irish social problem. Even more irritating to Anglo-Protestants than Irish Catholic behavior was their religion. Anti-Catholicism was at the heart of American as well as British nativism. Many early settlers in British North America left England because they thought the established church was corrupted by popery. In the New World they hoped to create a pure Protestant commonwealth. Most of the American colonies legislated anti-Catholic penal laws like those of Britain and Ireland. Resentment against the 1774 Quebec Act, which gave French Canadian Catholics religious freedom, was a factor in the American rebellion against British rule. Afraid of offending America's Bourbon allies, General George Washington ordered his troops to stop hanging the pope in effigy on November 5, Guy Fawkes Day.[18] After independence some states retained anti-Catholic codes until well into the nineteenth century. New York did not nullify them until 1806, Connecticut in 1818, Massachusetts in 1833, and North Carolina in 1835.

In the early days of the republic American Catholics were few in number and weak in organization, and anti-Catholicism was more paranoia than reaction to a genuine threat. The Irish immigration, however, gave nativist anxieties a more realistic and frantic tone.

Enlightenment rationalism complemented the Protestant nucleus of American nativism to produce a view of Catholicism as a superstitious, anti-intellectual, authoritarian monster that was challenging American values and institutions. The theory of Jeffersonian democracy, a product of the Enlightenment, insisted that the nation's liberties could survive only in an agrarian environment that emphasized citizen ownership of small farms as a symbol of and protection for individual dignity and freedom. Consequently, poverty-afflicted Irish Catholics were a contradiction of the rural, liberal individualism that Anglo-American Protestants interpreted as the spirit of their country. The anti-Catholic nativist conception of the Irish presence as an urban social plague and a cultural tumor eating away at the heart and soul of the nation persuaded Ulster Presbyterians in America to avoid association with Irish Catholics. Their cultivation of a separate Scots-

Irish ethnic identity ensured that the Irish-American image and personality would be Catholic.

In the United States, as in Britain and Ireland, Anglo-Protestants and Scots-Irish Presbyterians included racial prejudice in their objections to Irish poverty and Catholicism. They argued that indigence and disorderly conduct were inherent in Irish Catholics. Nativists insisted that the Irish religious choice of Rome signified an inferior intellect and that Catholicism locked the Irish into ignorance, superstition, shiftlessness, and treason. A September 9, 1868 *Chicago Evening Post* editorial complained of the large Irish population in jails, reform schools, hospitals, and charitable institutions: "Scratch a convict or a pauper and the chances are that you tickle the skin of an Irish Catholic, an Irish Catholic made a criminal or a pauper by the priest and politician who have deceived him and kept him in ignorance, in a word, a savage, as he was born."[19]

Working-class Protestants, fearing the Irish as cheap and sometimes scab labor competition, often were more nativist than their more affluent coreligionists. Unlike many English and northern European immigrants who had urban experience and manufacturing skills, peasants from Ireland had little familiarity with or appreciation for trade unionism. Their willingness to toil for long hours in less than human conditions for barely subsistence wages hindered the progress of the American labor movement and limited the potential of the strike as an effective weapon against unjust employers.[20]

American nativism was expressed in propaganda, mob violence, and political action. Such 1830s newspapers as the *American Protestant Vindicator and the Defender of Civil and Religious Liberty Against the Inroads of Popery* waged a constant war against imagined Jesuit subversion in the United States. The Protestant press panicked readers with reports that the pope and European despots, particularly Prince von Metternich, chief minister of the Hapsburg monarchy and prime champion of the Old Regime, were planning to destroy the United States and had already started operations in the Mississippi Valley. Eastern Protestants sent rifles and Bibles to save the western frontier from Roman intrigue. Real and bogus former priests and nuns horrified and titillated Protestant minds with lectures, pamphlets, and books about Catholic depravity. A former priest, Samuel B. Smith, in *The Downfall of Babylon*, and a prostitute, Maria Monk, who falsely claimed that she had been a nun, in *Awful Disclosures of the Hotel Dieu Nunnery of Montreal,* told lurid tales of sex orgies between priests and nuns. Monk spoke of priests seducing young women in the confessional and described lust tunnels connecting convents and rectories, which also served as burial grounds for the baptized and then strangled babies born of clerical copulation. Rumors of the evil that took place behind convent walls and of young women being held captive in nunneries against their will, triggered the 1831 burning of the Ursuline convent in Charleston, Massachusetts.

Massive Irish immigration in the 1840s and 1850s inflated Protestant anger and anxiety. In 1844 mobs invaded the Irish ghetto in Philadelphia, burning houses and dynamiting Catholic churches. Nativists justified attacks on churches by claiming they were arsenals containing weapons for Irish traitors determined on destroying American liberty. In the early 1850s, Protestants burned Irish sections of Lawrence, Massachusetts. In 1855, many wealthy Boston families fired Irish domestic servants following a rumor that they were instruments of a Vatican plot to poison Massachusetts Protestant leaders.

Many American politicians used anti-Catholic rhetoric, and both Federalists and Whigs encouraged nativism to attract votes. In 1854, an anti-Catholic secret society, the Order of the Star Spangled Banner, became the American party. Its members pleaded ignorance of the party's objectives and thus were called Know-Nothings. The Know-Nothing program included limiting immigration, prolonging the naturalization process before conferring citizenship, and restricting political office to the native-born. Although the American party opposed all foreign influences, Catholics, particularly the Irish, were its main focus. Nativism enrolled not only the ignorant but respectable reformers intent on purging the Irish urban social blight. In New Orleans, French Catholics, hostile to the poor Irish immigrants in their city, voted for American party candidates.[21]

In 1854 and 1855, Know-Nothings enjoyed spectacular election successes in Massachusetts, Pennsylvania, Delaware, New Hampshire, Rhode Island, Connecticut, Maryland, Kentucky, New York, and California. The greatest triumph occurred in Massachusetts where the American Party captured the governorship and both houses of the legislature. Following their victory, Know-Nothings formed the Join Special Committee of the Inspection of Nunneries and enacted a strict residency requirement for naturalization. Its political victories in 1854 and 1855 gave the American party hope of winning the White House the following year. But its candidate, former president Millard Fillmore, who was also supported by the Whigs, carried only one state and finished third to Republican John C. Frémont and the winner, Democrat James Buchanan. By 1856, anti-Catholicism was receding, superseded by sectional tensions between North and South.[22]

Nativists discovered that the Irish were tough enemies. Because history had linked their religion, culture, and nationality, they reacted aggressively to persecution. In Ireland, St. Patrick's Day was a religious occasion; in the United States, it began as a demonstration of Irish pride and defiance. In 1844, after nativists had burned Catholic churches in Philadelphia and threatened to do the same in New York, Archbishop John Hughes surrounded them with armed Irish guards. He also warned that he would have his Irish followers torch New York if the nativists desecrated even one Catholic church. Anti-Catholics heeded his message.[23] In 1854, during the heyday of Know-Nothingism, in Massachusetts, Yankees in Lowell, protesting Catholic schools and an Irish militia company, marched on the Irish ghetto. Both men and women parishioners successfully defended St. Patrick's Church and the convent of the Notre Dame sisters. One Irish matron threw a leader of the invading Yankee mob off a bridge into the Merrimac River.[24] On job sites, Irish Catholics often battled Protestants who resented their presence.

Although the Irish stood up to their enemies, nativist prejudice increased the insecurities that originated in the poverty and oppression of Ireland and continued in the hardships of America. Nativism created mental as well as physical ghettos. Charges that they did not belong and could never become real Americans convinced many Irish that they would always be displaced people in the United States.

Nativist attacks plus such perceived American cultural threats as secularism, materialism, and the Protestant-oriented public school system convinced Irish Catholic leaders that they needed to create a self-contained cultural community. Bishops successfully appealed to the generosity and religious enthusiasm as well as the historical memory of Irish Americans. In the New World as in the Old, the Irish were asked to use their meager resources to support the church. In building an alternative institutional complex of schools, hospitals, asylums, and orphanages, the hierarchy and clergy responded to real fears and served authentic needs. They also fed the nativist appetite for evidence that Catholicism was alien, divisive, and subversive.

Unfortunately, the Irish did not convert their experiences with bigotry into empathy for its other victims. Instead, they responded to prejudice with prejudice. Compensating for the psychological wounds inflicted by nativism and for their unskilled working-class status, the Irish took out their frustrations and low self-esteem on African Americans. Ignoring the counsel they received from Daniel O'Connell, liberator of Catholics in the United Kingdom and architect of modern Irish political nationalism, Irish Americans refused to equate the miserable condition of African-American slaves with their own unfortunate historical experience.[25] Prominent Protestant abolitionists such as Reverend Lyman Beecher, who were anti-Catholic nativists, irritated Irish Americans by demanding emancipation and full civil rights for African Americans in the South while ignoring the plight of the urban Irish in the North. Adopting the same negative attitude that Protestant workers had toward them, the Irish categorized free African Americans as cheap and scab labor competition. They feared that the end of slavery would increase the number of unskilled African-American job seekers, further delaying Irish achievement of economic security.[26]

Racial bigotry and Irish anger over the draft act, which imposed an unfair burden on their community, merged in July 1863 to erupt in urban riots. The worst of these took place in New York, where mobs of Irish, many deranged with drink, roamed the city streets, murdering, burning, and looting. They killed eleven African Americans and an American Indian whose skin color was mistaken for black, incinerated an African-American orphanage, and, altogether, destroyed about $3 million worth of property. When the police were unable to curb the mayhem, authorities summoned soldiers from Gettysburg. Archbishop Hughes helped disperse the rioters by telling them to get off the streets and back to their homes. During the five days of arson, pillage, and violence, policemen and soldiers killed over a hundred rioters. Mobs took the lives of three policemen and injured many others. Most of the police and many of the soldiers were as Irish as the rioters.[27]

MOVING UP

The draft riot notwithstanding, Irish soldiers fought bravely and well for the Union and the Confederacy. Irish priests courageously served as army chaplains. Irish nuns selflessly nursed the wounded and dying. For a time Irish-American patriotism diminished nativism; the postwar acceleration of industrialization had the same effect. Demands for unskilled labor in the factories offered a welcome to immigrants. In many fashionable circles economic needs substituted an inclusive or melting pot for an exclusive vision of the American destiny and purpose. In the late nineteenth century, southern and eastern European immigrants pushed the Irish up the working-class occupational ladder in the same way that Irish Catholics had advanced Anglo-Protestants earlier in the century.

Famine-related changes in Ireland improved the quality of post-1850 emigrants, enhancing their prospects for social mobility. By radically reducing the Irish population, especially among the economically and culturally deprived agricultural laboring class, the Famine brutally but effectively raised the survivors' standard of living. The number of landholders and the size of farms increased proportionally. Gifts of money from children in the United States, rising prices for agricultural products, and stable rents also improved conditions in rural Ireland. Peasant families dwelled in more comfortable cottages, wore better clothing, and enjoyed a more varied and nourishing diet.[28]

People in Ireland began to feel better mentally as well as physically. Daniel O'Connell's successful agitation for Catholic emancipation in the 1820s and his unsuccessful mass movement to repeal the Union with Britain the the 1840s created an effective Irish political nationalism, which lessened the inferiority complex and the serf mentality that had inhibited Irish progress. O'Connell's nationalist mobilizations taught the Irish political skills that they could apply in the United States as well as in the United Kingdom.[29] Starting in the 1840s, Young Ireland's cultural Irishness augmented O'Connell's political nationalism. The Young Irelanders' historical perspective was more mythical than real, but it countered the passivity and fatalism in the Gaelic and Catholic traditions. Cultural nationalism taught that the Irish were a noble race with a glorious past and a promising future, a message that lifted spirits at home and abroad.[30]

Mass education also enhanced morale and the quality of life in Ireland. In 1831, two years after Ireland's Catholic majority achieved legal political equality, the British government created an Irish national elementary school system. No doubt Westminster politicians wanted to Anglicize Irish Catholics now that they had political power. National schools did speed the transition from the Irish to the English language, but by creating a reading public for nationalist propaganda, they also advanced the values of Young Ireland and elevated the cultural level of the population. From 1850 to 1910, the national schools raised the literacy rate from 75 to about 97 percent. Although Irish immigrants at the turn of the century still were deficient in technological skills, they could read and write better than most Americans and had the intellectual background to learn what they needed to know in the cities of the United States.[31]

While material comforts, nationalism, and education were increasing Irish confidence and sophistication, a reformed Catholicism was disciplining character. In many parts of pre-Famine Ireland, superstition competed successfully with Catholic doctrine. Many laypeople knew little about the official teachings of their church and were not strict in religious observances. Clerical education and discipline were far from exemplary, and the hierarchy was divided into factions that quarreled publicly.[32] By exterminating the most impoverished, and therefore the most ignorant, portion of the population, the Famine made it easier for priests to instruct survivors. The growing power and spread of nationalist ideology, with its emphasis on history, also helped to effect Catholic reform by making people conscious of the links between their Catholic and Irish heritages. Consequently, many in Ireland considered a strong belief in and conscientious practice of their faith a statement of nationality. Even British Victorian values helped change the Irish religious mood. Such values defined respectability in Ireland as well as in Britain, adding fuel to the drive for a more rigid Catholicism.

From 1849 to 1875 guided by Paul Cardinal Cullen, the church built chapels, rectories, convents, and schools, improved clerical education and discipline, and harmonized differences within the hierarchy in a public display of almost complete unanimity. In matters of faith and morals, Irish bishops and priests were extraordinarily loyal to Rome. Irish laypeople became the most pious and orthodox Catholics in western Europe. They were diligent in attending mass and receiving the sacraments. Irish Catholics participated in a myriad of devotions, including Benediction of the Blessed Sacrament, the Rosary, Stations of the Cross, and Forty Hours. They frequented parish missions and generously contributed their short supply of pennies, shillings, and pounds to support the church at home, in Rome, and in foreign missions.[33] Ireland's zealous and devotional Catholicism spread throughout the Irish spiritual empire in the English-speaking world. Post-Famine Catholicism encouraged the Irish already in the United States and those about to come to be more sober, industrious, and respectable.

In addition to declining nativism in the United States, an improvement in the quality of Irish immigrants and an expanding American economy, politics helped some Irish-Americans achieve increased economic security. Through O'Connell's Catholic and repeal agitations and later Charles Stewart Parnell's Home Rule movement of the 1880s, the Irish learned the techniques of democratic politics. It was the only skill they brought with them to the United States, and they used it to become the major ethnic group active in American politics. By 1890 they were a powerful force in a large number of American cities. Urban governments spent money for roads, bridges, and public buildings, and Irish politicians were in a position to award construction contracts to their own people, creating entrepreneurs and jobs. Political influence was a major reason for the plentiful number of first-, second-, and third-generation Irish-American contractors. In 1870, 17 percent of American contractors were born in Ireland, three times as many as those who came from Germany or England.[34] Politicians selling or awarding utility contracts and transportation franchises put pressure on public service companies to employ Irish workers. Politics also produced desk jobs at city hall and appointments to police and fire departments. As Steven P. Erie explains in *Rainbow's End Irish-Americans and the Dilemmas of Urban Machine Politics, 1840–1985*, however, state controls over urban taxing powers and finances limited the economic potential of Irish politicians in the late nineteenth-century. Fiscally conservative Irish bosses were reluctant to alienate the middle class by enacting high property taxes.

Limited resources restricted patronage. Therefore, in the period 1880 to 1900, few Irish workers were politically connected, and most of them were unskilled.[35] Still, politics did provide some jobs and had the potential to produce more.

Like politics, sports and entertainment offered the Irish an ego lift as well as ways out of poverty and insignificance. During the nineteenth century, the Irish dominated American prizefighting. The sport was so thoroughly associated with them that non-Irish boxers often assumed Irish names. But the barbarity of prizefighting and the brutality and coarseness of the men who fought in the ring (there were not many "Gentleman Jim" Corbetts) did not enhance the Irish image. Football, associated with Ivy League universities, was a gentleman's game, and not many Irish attended Harvard, Yale, or Princeton, or, for that matter, any university. It was not until Notre Dame began to emerge as a football power around the turn of the century that the Irish had the opportunity to achieve recognition on the gridiron. They were, however, stars in track and field before that time.

If boxing seemed to confirm nativist prejudices that the Irish were somewhat less than human, baseball, a skill sport that projected a pastoral mythical image, gave them a better profile. Although the green fields of baseball diamonds represented the rural romanticism of the American spirit, Steve Allen Riess in *Touching Base: Professional Baseball and American Culture in the Progressive Era* estimates that more than 90 percent of professional players of the game in the early 1900s were Irish or German.[36] "Casey at the Bat," Ernest L. Thayer's 1888 epic baseball poem, represents the Irish impact on the game. In addition to "Mighty Casey," Cooney, Flynn, and Jimmy Blake played for the Mudville nine.

In a paper presented at the 1989 American Conference for Irish Studies at Syracuse, New York, Dennis Clark pointed out the benefits that baseball brought to Irish America. In the ghetto it provided a constructive alternative to crime and vice. It also offered opportunities for male bonding in a Victorian gender-segregated milieu. Clark argued that Irish stardom in baseball, America's most popular game until it was challenged by professional football in the 1950s, made them national heroes, speeding their acceptance by the general public. Irish fascination with baseball, the most quintessential of American sports, and the skills they brought to it, were signs of their adjustment to life and values in the United States, contradicting the view that they were an alienated people on the western shore of the Atlantic.[37]

Like religion and politics, sports offered possibilities to the Irish, who were excluded from business and the professions by the Anglo-Protestant establishment. And athletics provided the Irish community with badly needed heroes. But the Irish role in sports expressed alienation as well as assimilation. Athletic competition unleashed bottled-up anger and resentment. In the games they played, the Irish were able to challenge enemies inside and outside their neighborhoods. To them, sports often resembled war. In Chicago, for example, baseball, football, basketball, and boxing involved competition among Catholic ethnics. They enjoyed beating each other but took even more pleasure in routing Protestant foes. Until recently, the Southside White Sox, founded by Irish American Charles Comiskey, was the Catholic team; the Northside Cubs was the Protestant team. Many Chicago Catholics believed the bogus story that Philip K. Wrigley, the Cubs owner, was a member of the Ku Klux Klan[38] and that entering Wrigley Field to watch the Cubs play was equivalent to attending a Protestant church. In other cities as well, athletic loyalties were as religious and ethnic as they were territorial. All of Catholic America cheered for Notre Dame against secular and Protestant colleges and universities. In 1937 and 1941, Irish Americans rooted for Jimmy Braddock and Billy Conn when they fought Joe Louis, not only because they were white and he was black but also because they were the last important Irish champions in a sport they once dominated. Irish victories on baseball diamonds, football gridirons, basketball courts, and in boxing rings helped compensate for the defeat of the Armada, the loss at Kinsale, Wellington's victory over Napoleon at Waterloo, the rout of Young Ireland in 1848, the Fenian disaster in 1867, and the years of Anglo-American nativism.

Beginning with Irish pioneers of the ghetto, sports had negative as well as positive impacts on ethnic, racial, and religious minorities. Athletics provided celebrities and heroes but at the same time confirmed negative "racial" stereotypes, suggesting that physical superiority equaled intellectual inferiority—strong backs indicated weak minds. The association of Irish Americans with baseball, the great national game, indicates that they accepted the United States more than it did them.

In addition to projecting negative stereotypes, athletics can also establish false priorities in minority communities. Instead of becoming a means for mobility, success in sports is often an end in itself. In many instances, Irish-influenced Catholic education has concentrated on athletic programs and victories to the neglect of academic achievement.

Along with another nativist target group, Jews, the Irish have been prominent in show business as singers, dancers, acrobats, actors, and comedians. Role-playing on the stage camouflages misery while sublimating or exorcising ghetto neuroses and anxieties. More than any other entertainer, singer, dancer, composer, playwright, and actor, George M. Cohan epitomized the multifaceted talent, insecurities, sentimentality, and patriotism of the American Irish.

Despite their prominence as theater performers, the early nineteenth-century American theater was not kind to Irish Americans. Irish stage characters were crude and rude, figures of menace as well as of fun. On stage "Paddy and Biddy" were ignorant, lazy, unreliable, emotionally unstable, hard drinking, often violent, improvident buffoons. Beginning in the 1850s, Dion Boucicault, Irish actor and playwright, gave Americans a more sympathetic view of the Irish in his romantic melodramas. His plots contained comical people and funny situations, but his characters were not stupid or menacing. Boucicault presented Ireland as a land of romance and the Irish as pure and gentle, simple and naïve rather than foolish. In musical comedy, Edward Harrigan, an Irish American, portrayed his people and their life in the cities in the same spirit that Boucicault did Ireland and the Irish.[39] American cinema before 1910 copied theater in portraying the Irish as an inferior species—good to laugh at, bad to trust.[40]

By the turn of the century, Irish-American audiences, desiring social mobility and respectability, did not want to see themselves portrayed as comic figures. They even resented Boucicault's plays and the musicals of Harrigan and his partner, Tony Hart, as too stage Irish. They were incensed when the Abbey Theatre brought John Millington Synge's *Playboy of the Western World* to American cities. Like Dublin audiences, the Irish in the United States complained that

Synge did not properly respect Irish Catholic virtues. They joined Anglo-Protestant progressives to force a more favorable image of the Irish in films. Their defensiveness hindered the development of plays and motion pictures by Irish-American writers about their own people.[41]

Although slightly more than 20 percent of employed Irish Americans in 1900 were unskilled, poorly paid laborers, three-quarters of those in blue-collar occupations were skilled or semiskilled.[42] In mines, factories, mills, packing houses, foundries, and on the docks, the Irish were foremen of work crews. On railroads their numbers declined in section gangs and increased as engineers, firemen, switchmen, levermen, clerks, and telegraphers. Irish masons, steamfitters, carpenters, plasterers, plumbers, roofers, and, after the turn of the century, electricians, outnumbered diggers and hod carriers on construction sites. Politics put young Irish men into city halls as clerks and on police forces and fire departments. Many urban transport workers on streetcars, elevated railroads, and subways had Irish brogues. Irish families sent their best and brightest sons and daughters into the church as priests and nuns. Connections between law and politics drew the Irish into the legal profession. Irish communities needed doctors as well as lawyers, attracting young people into medicine, where they eventually established themselves as dedicated general practitioners and talented specialists. Considering the associations between the Irish and alcoholic beverages, it is not surprising that many were saloon proprietors. But a large number owned more respectable small businesses.

Curiosity, writing skill, and a love of excitement made natural journalists of the Irish. They were numerous on city newspapers as editors and crime, political, and sports reporters. Irish-American literature evolved out of journalism. Early Irish Catholic emigrants left Ireland culturally as well as technologically impoverished. Irish America began its existence and shaped its personality long before there was a late nineteenth-century literary renaissance in Ireland. And rural Catholic peasants, who populated Irish America, had little contact with or understanding of the prose and poetry of the Anglo-Protestant geniuses at the heart of the literary movement in Dublin.

Irish immigrants received their education in Irish cultural nationality from journalists such as Thomas Davis of the 1840s Young

Ireland weekly the *Nation* and Charles Kickham and his colleagues on the 1860s Fenian voice the *Irish People*.[43] Kickham's *Knocknagow* (1879) was the favorite immigrant novel. It inspired their nationalism and reinforced their image of Ireland as a Garden of Eden lost to British colonialism.

Following the Irish precedent, Irish-American literature emerged from newspaper offices. Starting in the 1870s, John Boyle O'Reilly and his *Boston Pilot* protégés, including Katherine E. Conway, James Jeffrey Roche, and Louise Imogen Guiney, "the first significant literary coterie in Irish-America," authored a quantity of and occasionally high-quality prose and poetry. But as Charles Fanning, the leading scholar of Irish-American literature, observes, their work was flawed by imitating the romanticism of the *Nation* and the idealism of the New England literary establishment.[44]

Fanning credits Chicago journalist Finley Peter Dunne with creating the first authentic ethnic community in American literature. Dunne's sports, police, and political reporting gave his writing a direct and realistic sharpness. Dunne's Mr. Dooley essays in the *Chicago Evening Post* of the 1890s were a social history of the Irish neighborhood on the south branch of the Chicago River. Bridgeport, originally named Hardscrabble, was first settled in the 1830s by navvies digging the Illinois and Michigan Canal. In Dunne's time it was full of Irish factory, mill, and stockyard workers; policemen and firemen; priests and politicians; housewives, widows, and servant girls; Clan na Gael nationalists; and toughs and criminals. In conversations with McKenna and Hennessey, patrons of his Archey Road (Archer Avenue) saloon, Martin Dooley, a County Roscommon expatriate, described and analyzed the joys and tribulations of Bridgeport's blue-collar workers.

Dunne both empathized with Irish efforts to survive in urban America and understood how they calloused their personalities and pragmatized their principles. He also witnessed the disintegration of an Irish neighborhood. Ambitious mothers insisting on education and Americanization for their children, high school and a few college graduate sons and daughters growing apart from their immigrant parents, and newcomers from southern and eastern Europe, who pushed the Irish up the occupational ladder and out to new parts of the city, phased out working-class Irish Bridgeport.[45]

The Irish in the United States started out culturally and technologically far behind other European immigrants, and at the turn of the century they were not as economically prosperous or as socially respectable as Anglo, German, or Scandinavian Americans. Since the 1840s, however, they had traveled a considerable distance from their impoverished beginnings. By 1900, Irish Americans were enjoying relative economic security and exhibited self-confidence. But depending on region and gender, there were variations in their rate of progress.

For various reasons, the Irish on the urban frontier advanced more quickly than those in eastern cities. Common sense suggests that emigration and migration are selective processes. Frequently, emigrants journeying to the United States were more adventurous and energetic than their siblings who remained at home. And the Irish who moved on to the Midwest and Far West were likely to be more ambitious and enterprising than those who stayed mired in the bleak ghettos of the East. Urban frontier cities profited from the post-Famine emigration from Ireland as well as the migration of energetic Irish Americans from New England and the Mid-Atlantic States.[46]

Social structures in the Midwest and Far West were more fluid and anti-Catholicism less focused and intense than in the East. Economies were dynamic and varied, offering an abundance of employment prospects. Production and profit took precedence over prejudice. Job opportunities and hard work propelled Irish on the urban frontier toward economic and social mobility. In new cities the progress of recent Irish immigrants often surpassed that of third- and fourth-generation New England Irish Americans.[47]

Eastern Irish Americans continued to exhibit paranoia while their counterparts on the urban frontier were growing up comfortably with their cities. Familiarity and frequently friendships with people from other religions and nationalities gave them broader perspectives than those on the Atlantic seaboard. In the long run, urban frontier experiences translated into a more liberal Catholicism and politics than in the East.

The progress of Irish Americans owed a great deal to the women in their communities. Not only did they nourish and civilize family life and subsidize most of the emigration from Ireland, they also nurtured each other. Catholic bishops and priests were inclined to ignore

the problems of women in urban American such as births out of wed-
lock, abusive husbands, widowhood, and lonely spinsterhood, but
nuns sheltered the poor and afflicted of their sex. The Sisters of
Mercy, the Presentation Sisters, and the Sisters of Charity of the
Blessed Virgin Mary originated in Ireland and served Irish America in
their schools and hospitals and charitable institutions. They and
other orders recruited heavily among Irish-American women. Because
the charters of some orders prevented nuns from teaching boys or
young men, they concentrated their educational mission on women.
After the American hierarchy in 1884 commanded parents to send
their children to parochial schools, charters were altered and nuns
taught both sexes.

Education placed the Irish in the vanguard of American women
marching toward economic independence and professional status.
Early twentieth-century Irish women entered business as office help or
as trained typists and shorthand secretaries. When telephones became a common means of communication, many operators were Irish.
More significantly, Irish women became prominent in the nursing and
teaching professions. They were essential to public as well as Catholic
education and health. In 1890, daughters of Irish immigrants exceeded "the combined total of all female teachers with English or German parents."[48] Before other Americans of their sex, Irish nuns and
lay women reached leadership positions as school principals, college
presidents, and hospital directors.

Despite their accomplishments, self-reliance, and economic sovereignty, Irish women were not interested in feminism. They were not
intimidated by the indifference of male religious and lay leaders to
their unique concerns and problems, but they did accept the main
current of opinion that the sexes had and should have different
spheres of interests and influence. But they were secure in the conviction that theirs were at least as important as the politics and sports
that seemed to obsess Irish men.[49]

Better jobs and the acquisition of new houses in nicer parts of
the city did not always ease Irish insecurities. Lingering nativism and
competition for urban employment and neighborhood turf convinced
many in the Irish community that their enemies came in many
shades, yellow and Anglo-Protestant white, as well as black. During

the 1880s, Patrick Ford, editor and publisher of the most influential Irish-American newspaper, the New York–based *Irish World*, preached a militant anticapitalism, but it echoed much of the anti-Semitic American populism of the time.[50] One of Ford's contemporaries, San Francisco's Denis Kearney, another Irish-American champion of the workers, wanted to halt Chinese immigration.[51] Often the Irish did not welcome coreligionist immigrants from eastern and southern Europe, viewing them as labor competition, ridiculing their customs and difficulties with English, and deriding the quality of their Catholicism.

Irish Americans were convinced that they were the best Catholics in the world and demanded that others emulate their devotionalism. Irish-American religious arrogance is featured in J. F. Power's prize-winning 1962 novel, *Morte D'Urban*. Its main character, Father Urban, tells Father Wilf, the retreat director at St. Clement's Hill, that he is unwisely catering to "ham and sausage" Teutonic and central Europeans instead of the Irish, who "ecclesiastically speaking were the master race, and had the saints, and still had the bishops to prove it."[52]

Circumstances gradually forced Irish-American labor concerns, like their politics, to expand beyond the ethnic enclave. A few Irish violently expressed their hostility to laissez-faire capitalism. The Molly Maguires, named after a secret agrarian society in Ireland, killed nine people in the Pennsylvania coal fields in the late 1870s. Mythology has exaggerated the Mollies as gallant foes of oppression, but their anger was directed as much against hereditary ethnic rivals, English, Scottish, and Welsh mine owners and bosses, as it was against low wages, high prices in company stores, exorbitant rents for company houses, and health risks in the mines.[53]

Some Irish were more genuine radicals than the Mollies. Cork-born Chicagoan Mary Harris "Mother" Jones of the Industrial Workers of the World (IWW, or "Wobblies") served several jail sentences for organizing miners. In 1914, James Larkin, founder of Ireland's Transport and General Workers Union, came to the United States after his failed Dublin general strike the year before. He collaborated with the IWW, organized Montana copper miners, helped found the American Communist party, and served time in Sing Sing prison during the "red scare" of the 1920s. Elizabeth Gurley Flynn, William Z. Foster, and "Big Bill" Haywood were other prominent Wobblie or communist Irish Americans.[54]

Contrary to the opinion held by many Americans that the labor movement revealed the violent nature of Irish and other foreign influences, most Irish-American men and women labor leaders were proponents of collective bargaining rather than bloody battles with owners and bosses. They agitated for higher wages, shorter workdays, and a safer employment environment for union members. In 1879, Terence V. Powderly, a prominent Irish-American nationalist, became grand master of the Knights of Labor, the first significant effort to organize workers all over the United States in one union. When the American Federation of Labor (AFL) came into existence in 1881, the Irish were numerous among its leaders. In the first decade of the twentieth century, 50 of 110 AFL presidents were Irish.[55]

Folklore of the labor movement features its struggles against irresponsible, unbridled capitalism and its role in the march toward social justice. Historian Herbert Hill questions this self-glorification, arguing that before the 1930s Irish and Jewish forces in the American Federation of Labor, in protecting the interests of white ethnics, neglected African, Asian, and Hispanic Americans.[56]

In the late nineteenth century, melting pot ideology did not reflect the reality of social or economic America. While Irish and Jewish labor leaders ignored nonwhites, Anglo-Protestant nativism resurfaced in expressions of militant antagonism toward Catholics and Jews. Economic instability after 1880 persuaded many Americans that resources and opportunities in the United States should be reserved for the native-born. Recessions, depressions, and unemployment provoked labor unrest, strikes, and lockouts. Sometimes confrontations between labor and capital were violent, especially when employers replaced striking union workers with scabs. At times, state governors mobilized their national guard units to break strikes and to protect industrial property. Many Americans blamed economic and class conflict on ideas that European immigrants supposedly brought to the United States. And they associated trade unionism with alien sedition.

Social Darwinism provided a racial dimension to late nineteenth- and early twentieth-century nativism. Jews and Latin and

Slavic Catholics joined the Irish as the targets of such organizations as the American Protective Association and the Ku Klux Klan.[57] Although the Irish were light-skinned, frequently blue-eyed, fluent in English, and, by this time, generally socially well-adjusted, Anglo Saxons on both sides of the Atlantic had a long tradition of expressing anti-Catholicism in racist rhetoric.[58] And in defending capitalism against the invading hordes of Europe and attempting to preserve the racial purity of Anglo-Saxon America, nativists retained their anti-Catholicism. Fears of the Roman church as mysterious, superstitious, authoritarian, and culturally and politically alien remained as strong in intellectual and academic circles as in the main streets of small-town America or down on the farm.[59] Anti-Catholicism focused on the Irish because they led an ever-growing, increasingly powerful American Catholicism concentrated in large cities. No matter what their country of origin, Catholic immigrants entered a church dominated by an Irish hierarchy and clergy, joined Irish-led labor unions, and voted for Irish political machines. Every increase in the population of Catholic America enhanced Irish power, intensifying nativist reactions to its existence.

Many Irish Americans approaching or passing the economic borders of the middle class were puzzled by their continued social ostracism. Some concluded that they were degraded in America because of the colonial status of Ireland and that as long as it remained a captive of Britain, other Americans would consider them an inferior people. Therefore, to create a national homeland and erase the stigma of inferiority, many of the Irish in the United States supported constitutional and revolutionary movements to liberate the homeland.[60] Their nationalism, however, increased rather than diminished Anglo-American contempt for them. Before the United States entered World War I in April 1917, Anglophiles railed against neutralist Irish and German Americans. They supported the British position that Dublin's 1916 Easter Week rebellion was engineered by Germany. Following the armistice, many Anglo-Americans resented Irish America's pressure on Woodrow Wilson and Congress to support the declared Irish Republic during the 1919–21 Anglo-Irish War. Like the president, many criticized hyphenated Americanism and were furious when the Irish responded to Wilson's pro-British policy by opposing the League of Nations.[61]

RESPECTABILITY

Despite their bad start in the United States and the antagonism of Anglo-American nativism, by the 1920s a large number of Irish Americans had joined the middle class. Among those of college age, 25 percent; mostly women studying to be teachers or nurses, were receiving higher education.[62] Upper working- and middle-class families were moving from their original neighborhoods, most to better locations in the city, some to the suburbs. Occupational and residential mobility are themes in the novels of James T. Farrell, Irish America's first literary star. Mostly written in the 1930s and 1940s about the 1920s, the Studs Lonigan and Danny O'Neill novels are Farrell's best and most important creative endeavors. His Chicago Washington Park Irish are the sons and daughters of Finley Peter Dunne's Bridgeport residents. Reaching the semiskilled, skilled working, and lower middle classes (Studs's father is a paint contractor, Danny's Uncle Al a shoe salesman), they have moved from cold-water to steam-heat flats near the southside's lakefront. Impressive-looking, expensive-to-build Catholic churches and schools are neighborhood focal points and monuments to Irish affluence. But appearances are deceiving. Farrell's Irish are still insecure. Like their immigrant grandparents or parents, they remain rootless refugees. They push farther and farther south in the city to avoid an expanding black ghetto.[63]

In the 1920s, the Irish often obtained employment through political connections. After 1900, Irish political machines were able to use patronage power through alliances with state governments and by heavily taxing business properties. According to Stephen P. Erie, "Machines directly and indirectly controlled more than 20 percent of post-1900 urban job growth, double their pre-1900 share." Most politically related employment went to the Irish. In such places as New York, Albany, and Jersey City "the Irish were rewarded with more than 60 percent of this newly created patronage."[64]

Erie argues that political jobs retarded rather than speeded Irish economic and social mobility. Working for the city locked them into blue-collar and marginal middle-class occupations such as policemen, firemen, and lower-level urban bureaucrats. Erie's thesis assumes that the Irish had other employment possibilities. But this was not true. Anglo-Protestant American businesses excluded them from management positions, and their historical experience limited their ambition. Memories of religious persecution, famine, poverty, evictions, and exile made them obsessed with security. Jobs that offered a decent standard of living and the opportunity to own a home satisfied the expectations of most Irish Americans. Referring to Edward Levine's 1966 study of Irish-American politics, *The Irish and Irish Politicians: A Study of Cultural and Social Alienation,* Erie acknowledges that the Irish "were alienated from Protestant values and institutions." In the working-class shelters of the Catholic church and the Democratic party, they settled for "power and security, not money or status."[65] In comparison to their past, power and security seemed like progress and provided a base upon which to construct a future.

Although Erie concedes that the Irish were motivated primarily by a desire for security, he questions whether they found it in political employment. He points out that the Great Depression that began in 1929 forced urban government to restrict spending and reduce patronage positions.[66] No doubt the economic decline that began with the Wall Street collapse and lasted until World War II took its toll on Irish Americans, but they probably weathered hard times better than did many other ethnic groups. City jobs were likely to be more secure than factory work. And because so many Irish Americans were involved in urban transport and railroad work and the medical and teaching professions, portions of the American economy that operated during the Depression, their families continued to enjoy an income. Therefore, though the pace of mobility slowed in the 1930s, it was not halted, and they remained in relatively good economic condition.

As the Irish began to feel comfortable and secure in the United States, they became less preoccupied with Ireland and more interested in things American. Throughout the nineteenth century, Irish-American anger and money sustained the forces of constitutional and physical force nationalism in Ireland. During the 1919–21 Anglo-Irish War, their support for Republican rebels helped persuade the British government to make concessions to Irish nationalism. The Anglo-Irish Treaty was not completely popular in Ireland. It confirmed the 1920 partition of the country into an overwhelmingly Catholic, twenty-six-county Free State and a two-thirds-Protestant six-county, home-rule Northern Ireland. The oath of allegiance to the British monarch triggered a civil war between Free Staters and Republicans who considered it a betrayal of the separatist principles of Patrick Pearse, James Connolly, and other martyrs of the 1916 Easter Week rebellion. Despite the oath and partition issues, most Irish Americans were satisfied that Britain had granted Ireland a respectable degree of independence on which to expand its sovereignty. And the fratricide of civil war disgusted many others, further diminishing their concern for the Old Country.

Modifications in the spirit of Irish nationalism added to the cleavage between the Irish at home and those of the diaspora. Starting in the 1880s, many champions of Irish independence demanded a Gaelic as well as a free Ireland. This objective inspired Pearse and many other 1916 heroes. It also was an important objective in the Anglo-Irish War, and Irish Free State and later Republican governments encouraged and financed efforts to restore Irish as a vernacular language. An Irish nationalism inspired by the purpose of restoring the ancient tongue had little meaning for Irish people in the English-speaking world, who saw it as the substitution of provincial exclusiveness for an inclusive brand of Irishness. Beginning in 1924, U.S. legislation restricting immigration also reduced personal and cultural contacts and interests between the Irish in Ireland and those in the United States.

Just when things were going well for the American Irish, their collective ego was shattered in 1928, when Al Smith, the first Irish Catholic presidential candidate, lost to his Republican opponent, Herbert Hoover. Many Irish and other Catholics in the United States did not understand that a booming economy guaranteed that the Republican party would retain the White House. Instead, they blamed Smith's defeat on a barrage of anti-Catholic propaganda and Ku Klux Klan intimidation.[67] At the time, few people realized that Smith's defeat created the urban ethnic coalition that would become the key constituency of the Democratic party well into the 1960s. In the 1930s, Franklin D. Roosevelt's New Deal restored some if not all of the psychological security of Catholic America.[68] FDR rewarded Catholics for their loyal support to the Democratic party throughout the years by appointing them to about one-fourth of government positions. The Irish were the greatest beneficiaries of the president's generosity, and in Congress and the bureaucracy they were important agents in creating the American welfare state.

Reflecting social mobility and power, Irish politics and Catholicism in the 1930s and 1940s became more cosmopolitan and less provincial, more inclusive and less exclusive, and more altruistic and less self-centered.[69] The labor movement also revealed an expanding Irish social conscience. Irish Americans were at the forefront of the Congress of Industrial Organization's (CIO) mobilization of unskilled workers in mines, steel mills, and automobile plants, people hitherto ignored by the American Federation of Labor, which included only skilled trades. The esteemed second president of the CIO, Philip Murray, was a liberal democrat and Irish Catholic who stood for social justice. Another Irishman, George Meany, became the first president of the merged AFL-CIO in 1955 and held that post until shortly before he died in 1979. Both Murray and Meany rejected racism in their working-class solidarity appeals.

In places such as Boston and New York, the Depression increased job competition and intensified ethnic and racial strife. Both cities displayed Irish anti-Semitism.[70] But in many parts of the United States, the economic crisis followed by World War II speeded the Irish approach to acceptability and respectability by uniting Americans in common misery and common cause, banking the fires of nativism. Popular entertainment, especially its most frequented form, the movies, did much to improve the Irish-American image. The Depression fostered public resentment against the Anglo-Protestant financial establishment. James Cagney's films for Warner Brothers appealed to the angry, disillusioned masses. Cagney was a rough, tough, but brave, witty, charismatic movie gangster with a sense of street justice and humor. Audiences loved it when this quintessential urban Irish antihero defied the system and spit in the eyes of big shots. Films were full of other Irish urban types such as politicians and policemen. But the most important Irish cinema role was that of the priest, played by some of America's favorite actors. Spencer Tracy was Father Tim Mullin in *San Francisco* (1936) and Father Edward Flanagan in *Boy's Town* (1938) and *Men of Boy's Town* (1941). Pat O'Brien was Father Jerry Connolly in *Angels with Dirty Faces* (1938); Father Francis Duffy in *The Fighting 69th* (1940); and Father Dunne, a real St. Louis priest champion of newsboys in *Fighting Father Dunne* (1948). The most popular of all the priest movies was *Going My Way* (1944), starring Bing Crosby as Father Chuck O'Malley, Barry Fitzgerald as Father

Fitzgibbon, and Frank McHugh as Father Timmy O'Dowd. Crosby played Father O'Malley again in *The Bells of St. Mary's* (1945), co-starring Ingrid Bergman as the mother superior and principal of the parochial school. Movie priests were social problem solvers rather than advocates of Catholic theology or ministers of Catholic liturgy. Father Connolly, a boyhood friend of gangster Rocky Sullivan (James Cagney), tries to save New York East Side kids from a life of crime like Rocky's. The Father Flanagan films were intended as a biography of a real cleric who did not believe that there was such thing as a bad boy. Flanagan established Boy's Town near Omaha, Nebraska, to take poor urban boys out of environments of crime and poverty and teach them to be useful citizens. Father O'Malley manages to save two parishes from financial collapse and, at the same time, straighten out the lives of young boys by getting them interested in baseball and choir singing. The image of the priest as a civilizing influence in urban America diminished popular conceptions of Catholicism as mysterious and alien. As evidence of its impact and popularity, *Going My Way* won seven Academy Awards. Crosby was selected as best actor, Fitzgerald as best supporting actor, and Leo McCarey won awards for direction and story writing.[71]

Movies also celebrated the patriotism of Irish Americans. *The Fighting 69th* was made after World War II had started and America's intervention was a possibility. *Yankee Doodle Dandy* (1942) went into production shortly after the Japanese attack on Pearl Harbor. It is a glorified film portrait of George M. Cohan, emphasizing his love of country and the contribution of his songs to the American spirit. In giving the Congressional Medal of Honor to Cohan (James Cagney), Franklin D. Roosevelt (Captain Jack Young) remarks: "That's one thing I've always admired about you Irish-Americans. You carry your love of country like a flag, right out in the open. It's a great quality."[72]

By the close of World War I, Irish America was a familiar and generally likable segment of the American ethnic landscape. St. Patrick's Day no longer symbolized alienation and defiance. For the Irish and other Catholics it was a festive interlude in the sober season of Lent. For all Americans it was the harbinger of spring at the close of a bleak winter.

After World War II, the GI Bill of Rights helped Irish Americans complete their evolution from members of the unskilled working class to an essentially middle-class status. Large numbers of honorably discharged Irish-American veterans, many well prepared for higher education in Catholic high schools, took advantage of the government's generosity by attending colleges and universities. By 1950, for the first time, more Irish-American men than women were receiving higher educations. Among American ethnics, including Anglo-Protestants, only Jews sent more of their young people to college than did the Irish.[73] A considerable portion of Irish Americans who earned bachelor degrees went on to attend graduate and professional schools. When they completed their educations, they became leaders in academic life, medicine, business, and law.

Irish-American occupational mobility lessened their urban visibility. They were packing up their university degrees and middle-class respectability and heading for the suburbs. Irish migration from the cities became a mass exodus in the 1960s, when large numbers of African Americans, fleeing from poverty and oppression in the South, entered northern urban centers. Their presence panicked whites into leaving old neighborhoods. As the most successful Catholic ethnics, the Irish were the first to abandon city parishes.

Although Irish success was shaded by some failures and continued anxiety about their place in America, as witnessed by their support of Senator Joseph McCarthy's Red witch-hunting of the early 1950s, a 1963 National Opinion Research Center survey indicated that they were the most advanced American Catholics in education, occupations, and income. They also measured highest on general knowledge, religious and racial tolerance, and self-content.[74]

Most symbolic of Irish America's rise from ghetto poverty to middle-class respectability was the election of John F. Kennedy as thirty-fifth president of the United States in 1960. Although we now know that Kennedy's White House resembled *The Arabian Nights* more than Camelot, he captured the American imagination and the respect of the world community. The young president's charm, good looks, and self-deprecating wit and the energy of his New Frontier lieutenants obscured the less-than-promised accomplishments of his administration. More important, he made Americans feel good about themselves and take pride in their country as the civilized bastion of liberal democracy, emotions and convictions that they have not experienced in quite the same generous and idealistic way since

Kennedy's life was claimed by rifle shots in November 1963. After Dallas, in a novel, *Fogarty and Company*, Joe Flaherty wrote: "What was lost with Kennedy was not so much substance as style. . . . The truth was that America could ill-afford to squander its stylish sons. . . . Kennedy had been a relief, a pleasure to have your cocktail with as he appeared on the evening news, a respite from all those goddam Grant Wood people who have been running the country for years."[75]

Although Kennedy was far less culturally Irish Catholic than his name or public image suggested, his national and international popularity transferred to all Irish Americans.[76] His election and his standing enabled them to shed any last doubts about their acceptability. John Ford, perhaps the greatest of all film directors, expressed Irish America's reaction to Kennedy's triumph. After the 1960 election, he wrote a friend that for the first time in his life he felt like a first-class citizen.[77]

Because he confirmed and represented their success story, no group mourned the assassination of Kennedy more than Irish Americans. Some who retained remnants of ghetto paranoia believed his death was another example of history's curse on the Irish. But more were sure that they were on top to stay and that their fellow Americans never again could or would doubt their loyalty or question their contribution to the United States.

Certainly the image of Irish America has continued to improve since the 1960s. Occasionally, however, anti-Irish stereotypes have reappeared in popular entertainment. Compared to the portrayal of African, Hispanic, Jewish, and Polish Americans, the popular television situation comedy "Barney Miller" shows New York Irish policemen in a negative light. Kelly, who returns to the eleventh precinct as a replacement, is a racially prejudiced coward. Bigoted, sexually neurotic, crooked Lieutenant Scanlan from Internal Affairs is always snooping around attempting to prove that Barney and his colleagues are as corrupt as he is. Two characters in films, Joe Curran in *Joe* (1970) and Willie Conklin, captain of the Emerald Isle Volunteer Fire Company, in *Ragtime* (1981), are obnoxious bigots with all the traits despised by American liberals.[78]

Conklin, Curran, Kelly, and Scanlan are exceptions to the way literature and the entertainment, information, and advertising media presents Irish Americans. In Tom Wolfe's best-selling *Bonfire of the Vanities* (1988), New York's Irish policemen are extraordinarily courageous, the most admirable and heroic characters in the novel.[79] The hard-drinking, ignorant, and brawling Greenhorns of early American fiction, theater, and cinema have been replaced by charismatic urban antiheroes and social worker priests and finally by America's beautiful people. Grace Kelly and Gene Kelly became the "American dream girl" and the "All-American boy."[80] On today's television screens, the comic and irresponsible Paddies and Biddies of former times have been replaced by handsome or beautiful Patricks, Seans, Brians, Kevins, Bridgets, Sheilas, Deirdres, and Eileens wearing Irish-knit sweaters and selling soap, beer, and automobiles.

Despite the middle-class status of the general community and its public image as America's favorite ethnics, not all of the Irish in the United States exemplify achievement, assimilation, confidence, or contentment. The paranoids, drunks, wife-beaters, bigots, and religious and sexual neurotics inhabiting the novels of Jimmy Breslin, James Carroll, Elizabeth Cullinan, Ellen Currie, John Gregory Dunne, Joe Flaherty, Thomas J. Fleming, Mary Gordon, and Pete Hamill exist in real life, as do bleak urban Irish ghettos of mind and place. T. J. English's *Westies* discusses Irish mobs and gangs in New York City's Hell's Kitchen. They murdered, were in the juice rackets, sold numbers, intimidated witnesses, and formed alliances with the Mafia well into the 1980s. Sadly, many Irish residents of the neighborhood regarded them as folk heroes.[81] In the mid-1970s, television viewers all over the United States and in Europe saw angry Irish faces and heard hate-filled Irish voices shouting obscenities and racial insults at frightened African-American teenagers exiting buses that had transported them from the South End and Roxbury to schools in Charleston and South Boston. They also observed Irish gangs assaulting blacks and lines of Irish women marching with religious banners, praying the rosary, and beseeching the Blessed Virgin to protect their neighborhoods and schools from African Americans. Boston's Irish response to school integration through busing revealed the frustrations of people with the same psychological afflictions as African Americans. They had little self-esteem and were left behind in Irish America's march to middle-class status, their psyches victims of economic and social prejudices.[82] Irish-American inferiority and persecution complexes, inarticulate rage, and self-pity are not confined to the Boston area. They are also evident in sections of the Bronx, Queens, Manhattan, and Brooklyn as well as in Philadelphia and in southwestern and northwestern Chicago.

In these places, members of the Irish working and lower middle classes have joined other Catholic ethnics in resisting African-American efforts to leave depressing, crime-ridden ghettos for more attractive neighborhoods with better schools.[83] Urban white racism involves more than resentment of skin color. Economic and social factors and cultural differences between evangelical African-American Protestants and white Catholics are also important. Protective of traditional family and sexual mores and standards as well as worried about bungalow and property values, the safety of their streets, and good education for their children, white Catholic ethnics who have struggled so long to acquire economic security and social respectability in the United States do not want to assimilate with the southern Protestant poverty culture represented by African Americans. They interpret integrated neighborhoods and schools as the beginning of reverse social mobility. Because few want or can afford to abandon old neighborhoods for the suburbs or to buy costly condominiums or houses in gentrified sections of the city, they vocally and sometimes physically resist racial mixing.[84]

The Boston school busing crisis and white ethnic reactions to integration in other cities have reinforced a long-held liberal opinion that the Irish and other Catholic ethnics constitute an entrenched working-class barrier of bigotry and ignorance against racial integration and harmony in the urban North.[85] This notion, however, distorts reality. Irish America is not essentially working class nor is it dominated by bigotry and ignorance. According to National Opinion Research Center (NORC) findings, reported by Andrew M. Greeley in 1981, 71 percent of the Irish in Chicago and Minneapolis were in white-collar occupations. In Chicago, 39 percent were in the professional or managerial levels of the middle class; in Minneapolis, the figure was 38 percent. Fifty percent of the Chicago Irish earned more than $25,000 annually.[86] A large number of Irish-American blue-collar workers, especially those in the building trades, enjoy middle-class incomes. NORC evidence indicated that the Irish in Chicago and Minneapolis were not unique. Its 1977 and 1978 General Opinion Social Survey revealed that "in terms of education, occupation, and income, Irish Catholics are notably above the national average for other whites. In education and occupation they are now even with the British Protestant group and substantially ahead of that group in income. Finally, while they lag somewhat behind Jews in occupational prestige and education, their average income in the years from 1975 to 1978 is slightly ahead of both the British Protestants and Jews."[87] NORC figures also show that Irish Catholics are more likely "to attend graduate school and choose academic careers" than are white Protestants.[88]

Money, education, and high-level occupations do not necessarily determine sensitivity to injustice or tolerance to others, but in the case of the Irish they seem to. Research evidence indicates that American Catholics, particularly those educated in Catholic schools, colleges, and universities, are more compassionate than American Protestants on such issues as civil rights, social justice, racial equality, peace, and disarmament and that the Irish are the most liberal of Catholics.[89]

THE NEW IRISH AMERICANS

Because immigrant quotas set in the 1960s discriminate against northern Europeans, over the last twenty years or so only a few hundred Irish annually have legally entered the United States. Some represent a "brain drain" of university and professional school graduates. Most, however, resemble those who came before them: sons with no prospects of inheriting the family farm, daughters without attractive marriage prospects or employment hopes, young people from farms, towns, and cities searching for excitement and opportunity. Many new Irish immigrants feel uncomfortable with and somewhat resentful toward the well-educated, middle-class majority in the general Irish-American community, yet they experience comparatively rapid occupational and social mobility. Because their numbers are small, they seldom remain isolated from the general mainstream. They take advantage of Irish political power and economic influence and are more fortunate in finding steady, well-paying jobs, especially in construction work, than other European Catholic immigrants or African- and

Hispanic-American entrants into urban, industrial America. Recent Irish immigrants invest a considerably portion of their incomes in educating their children. After attending college or university, sons and daughters of Irish-born parents reach the middle class. Consequently, the contrast between old and new Irish America tends to fade within a generation.

Beginning in the 1980s, a new type of Irish immigrant arrived in the United States. Many thousands, escaping a collapsing Irish economy, illegally entered the country.[90] Quite a few of these newcomers are university educated and could make a significant contribution to the American economy. But because visibility would lead to deportation, they have to take unskilled jobs as waiters and waitresses, housekeepers, baby-sitters, and handymen repairing homes and maintaining yards. Because these Irish immigrants arrived after the new amnesty law deadline, they cannot be legalized. Many Irish Americans, including politicians such as Senator Edward M. Kennedy of Massachusetts, are striving to create avenues to legitimize the existence of young Irish people living under cover in urban America. Considering the contribution the Irish already have made to the development of the United States and the talent they again are prepared to offer, the government in Washington could properly and beneficially afford to be generous to those forced to leave Ireland by economic circumstances. Legalizing the new wave of Irish exiles and expanding the Irish immigration quota will cost much less than bailing out an impoverished Ireland at some future date and will do much to support the stability of a friendly liberal democracy.

On sentimental occasions, new immigrants, like the old, shed tears for and sing sentimental songs about "that dear land across the sea," but for the Irish who have chosen to come to the Untied States, it always has been their land of opportunity and primary loyalty, and their journey to America has been a one-way trip. They have demonstrated their affection for and commitment to the United States with hard work, patriotism, military service, and, when possible, rapid citizenship and active political participation. Their lingering devotion to Ireland pales in comparison with their passionate love for America.

3

Religion as Culture and Community

The three main textures of Irish America—Catholicism, politics, and nationalism—defined, mobilized, and articulated Irish-American ethnicity. Of the three, Catholicism is the most important. Religion gave Catholics in Ireland an identity, a cohesiveness, and a sense of purpose that enabled them to survive the ravages of history. Catholicism was the most precious possession the Irish brought to America, where again it served and comforted them in adversity.

THE PRE-IRISH AMERICAN CATHOLIC CHURCH

In 1632, King Charles I awarded George Calvert, Lord Baltimore, a charter to settle land in North America between the Potomac River and the fortieth parallel. Calvert died before the charter received the great seal, and his son Cecil inherited the grant. Catholic Lord Baltimore intended the Maryland colony to be a refuge for his coreligionists suffering persecution in England. The Calverts, however, did not want Maryland to be exclusively Catholic. They encouraged Protestants to settle in the colony and granted religious freedom to all residents. Despite Calvert's example of tolerance, Protestants did not welcome Catholics to British North America. They insisted that popery was a malignancy eating away at the religious, political, and social health of Europe, and they did not want its evil on the western shores of the Atlantic. Many early colonists, particularly New Englanders, left their homeland to escape an established Protestant church which they considered corrupted by such papish features as bishops, decorated churches, candles, and vestments. Their Nonconformist friends

47

and relatives in England were the core of the opposition to the Stuart monarchy, which some considered secretly Catholic and others as at least pro-papist.

Anti-Catholicism was a major factor in the muster of parliamentary forces in two successful revolutionary efforts against the Stuarts, one in the 1640s, the other in 1688. After the latter, the Glorious Revolution, the British and Irish parliaments passed laws outlawing Catholic religious practices, forbidding Catholic seminaries, banning Catholic bishops, and prohibiting priests from entering the country. They also denied laymen opportunities to inherit or purchase property or to attend school; refused them the right to vote, to hold political office, or to bear arms; and barred them from the professions. This denial of civil liberties and religious freedom reduced Catholics to less than second-class citizens. Because the majority of British people were Protestant while 75 percent of the Irish were Catholic, penal laws had a much greater effect in Ireland than in Britain.

Most of English anti-Catholicism turned on the Irish as the leading subversive threat to the security of the British Isles. The Irish seemed to confirm this view by their stubborn resistance to the Elizabethan conquest, their encouragement of the Spanish intervention at Kinsale in 1601, their opposition to English parliamentary rebels and Oliver Cromwell in the 1640s, and their rallying around King James II. The revolution of 1688 was not glorious in Ireland, where Catholics and their French allies futilely if bravely fought the armies of William II for three years.

Britain's and Ireland's anti-Catholic penal laws seemed a contradiction to the antityranny arguments raised against alleged Stuart oppression. The same people who had denounced French and Spanish Catholicism as unenlightened and bigoted enforced in Ireland barbaric acts of repression equaling those of the Inquisition and much worse than the revocation of the Edict of Nantes. They justified their persecution of Catholics with the claim that popery was subversive to English culture and liberties and that to permit its existence was to endanger true religion, the state, and society.

Colonial legislatures in North America followed the Irish and British Protestant examples and passed penal laws against Catholics. Quaker Pennsylvania was an exception to this extreme form of religious prejudice, but in Maryland the Protestant majority outlawed the religion of its founders.

The American Enlightenment combined with Protestant prejudices to reinforce the anti-Catholic core of American nativism. Eighteenth-century liberal intellectuals were hostile to all forms of organized religion as contrary to reason and freedom, but they believed Catholicism to be much more blighted by superstition and authoritarianism than Protestantism.

Despite the liberal principles of the Declaration of Independence, the Constitution, and the Bill of Rights, religious freedom emerged slowly in the United States. The federal government disestablished Protestant churches, but some state legislatures retained anti-Catholic penal laws until well into the nineteenth century.

Living in a hostile environment, early American Catholics tended to be passive and obsequious. To avoid persecution, they practiced their religion as privately as possible with very little ceremony. Their chapels had an austere, almost Protestant appearance. Priests did not wear clerical garb and people referred to them as "mister" rather than "reverend" or "father." American Catholicism's humble and subdued character indicated more than fear. It also expressed a desire to assimilate and belong.

In 1784, Rome appointed John Carroll, a member of an old Maryland Catholic family with distant Irish roots, the cousin of Charles, a signer of the Declaration of Independence, as head of the first Catholic mission in the United States. In this position, he attempted to create an American Catholicism with weak connections to Rome, lay trustee control of parishes, an English-language liturgy, and a theology much more in tune with the rationalism of the American Enlightenment than with the mysticism, sentimentality, and emotionalism of European Catholicism.[1]

Carroll began to take a more Roman view when he was chosen in 1788 and consecrated in 1790 as the first Roman Catholic bishop in the United States and primate of the American church. In addition to his responsibilities as primate, his conservatism was shaped by negative American Catholic upper-class reactions to Jeffersonian democracy as Jacobinism; the antiliberal influence of clerical refugees from the French Revolution serving the American church; and Rome's insistence on hierarchical structure, obedience to authority, and devotionalism. The influx of Irish immigrants reinforced the primate's leadership position, speeding the Romanization of American Catholicism.

IRISH CATHOLICISM

Irish immigrants brought with them an aggressive and combative Catholicism shaped by centuries of conflict with English and Anglo-Irish Protestants and Scotch-Irish Presbyterians. The Reformation in England and the effort to expand it to Ireland, plus the Irish dimension of the sixteenth- and seventeenth-century European wars of religion, made Catholic versus Protestant the most significant ideological component in the Irish struggle for survival. Protestantism was the cultural thrust of Anglo-Saxon colonialism. Catholicism represented a besieged Gaelic way of life. It was also the religious faith of the descendants of the Norman English who invaded Ireland in the twelfth century. This Old English colony refused to surrender property, status, and political power to new English Protestants.

Even with Spanish assistance, Ireland could not resist Elizabeth's military forces. Her successor, James I, took revenge on Ulster, the most culturally Irish province and the last to hold out against the queen's army, by appropriating and planting the estates of its clan chieftains with a colony of English Protestants and Scots Presbyterians.

Twice in the seventeenth century, Gaelic Irish and Old English Catholics tried to exploit conflicts between king and Parliament in England to reverse the Elizabethan settlement and the Stuart plantations. The first effort provoked the wrath of Cromwell; the second, the dreadful penal laws. Both resulted in the merger of Old English and Gaelic communities into the depressed and disposed Irish Catholic nation. To maintain dignity and to find opportunity, many members of the Catholic aristocracy and gentry became exiles on the Continent. Most of those who remained in Ireland joined the Protestant church to retain their property, social status, and political influence. The masses remained Catholic but existed as the most wretched people in western Europe. The penal laws divided Ireland into two distinct communities: Protestant and Catholic, conqueror and conquered, powerful and impotent, prosperous and poor. In the eighteenth century, England's Protestant planter garrison in Ireland controlled over 90 percent of the island's property and all of its political power. With most of their leaders in exile or intimidated into silent subservience or turning Protestant, the Catholic masses were reduced to the level of dehumanized, demoralized, impoverished serfs. Nonconformists were not the social or economic equals of Anglicans, but they were much better off than Catholics, and their Calvinist zeal, plus their Ulster encounters with a large embittered Catholic community, made them more zealous enemies of popery than were the Anglicans.[2]

In Ireland, Catholicism distinguished the oppressed natives from the Anglo-Irish conquerors and planters and the Scots-Irish farmers and artisans. Catholicism was the only meaningful symbol and expression of identity, the only real consolation for the common folk. It brought some beauty into wretched lives, some hope in desperate situations. Rejecting Daniel Corkery's thesis in *Hidden Ireland* (1924) that the Gaelic tradition predominated in the culture of Irish Catholics during the eighteenth century, Sean O'Faolain in the "Proem" of his 1938 biography of Daniel O'Connell, *King of the Beggars*, insisted that Catholicism emerged as the most important element in the Irish personality. He described it as "not an inconsiderable possession." The Irish had "in a word, with that one exception of their faith, nothing, neither a present, nor a past, nor a future."[3] Catholicism nourished their long march toward freedom and dignity.

In the course of the eighteenth century, Protestants, increasingly secure in their conquest and resentful of British political and economic controls, cultivated an Irish consciousness projected in the Whig rhetoric of the Glorious Revolution. Like Anglo-Americans, they borrowed the ideas of John Locke to protest British tyranny. Irish Protestant patriots exploited Britain's preoccupation with the American Revolution to form a volunteer army, ostensibly to protect Ireland from a feared Bourbon invasion, actually to extort concessions from a beleaguered British Parliament. Protestant patriots did achieve free trade and more legislative scope for their Dublin Parliament, but they excluded Irish Catholics from their concept of the Irish nation.

Despite some late eighteenth-century mitigation of the penal laws providing benefits for the Catholic aristocracy, gentry, and middle class, the Irish masses remained "hewers of wood and drawers of water." But not all Protestants wanted to keep Catholics down. Henry Grattan, the leading patriot in the struggle for Irish sovereignty, told his coreligionists that as long as Catholics were slaves they could not really be free. And some of the United Irishmen, especially Theobald Wolfe Tone, wanted to incorporate Catholics in the Irish nation.

Founded in 1791, the United Irishmen tried to forge an alliance between Protestant middle-class radicals, Catholic gentry and middle-class seekers of civil liberties, and Catholic peasants (the Defenders) demanding an end to manorialism. The United Irishmen began as political reformers advocating an Irish Parliament subject to the influence of public opinion rather than property. Frustrated by government oppression and inspired by the democratic and republican opinions of the American founding fathers and the French Jacobins, they moved from reform to revolution. Irish insurrections in 1798 exhibited more sectarian hatred and suspicion than mutual cooperation. In Wexford, Catholic peasants, inflamed by economic and social grievances and religious antagonism, killed some Protestant landlords and wanted to do the same to others. In Mayo, they joined General Jean R. M. Humbert's French invaders, not to fight for "liberty, equality, and fraternity" but for the pope and the Blessed Virgin. Ulster Protestant United Irishmen, suspicious of armed papists, refused to cooperate with Catholic Defenders. Orange yeomen from the North put down the Catholic peasant revolt in Wexford. In Antrim and Down, the British and Irish governments employed Catholic militiamen from the South to defeat Protestant United Irishmen. Many Catholics fought in Charles Cornwallis's army that forced the surrender of General Humbert.[4]

Even before the disturbances of 1798, a significant number of Protestants abandoned patriotism to endorse a union with Britain. They wanted a shield to protect Protestant ascendancy from the threat of an alliance between Protestant middle-class radicalism, Catholic discontent, and the armies of the French Revolution. The events of 1798 and the French intervention solidified their ranks and purpose. Many of the Protestants opposing the union were as selfishly motivated as those pushing the British connection. They were convinced that a Protestant Irish Parliament would be more vigilant in suppressing Catholic protest than a remote, perhaps unconcerned, legislature in the United Kingdom.

The events of 1798 persuaded William Pitt the Younger, the British prime minister, that Catholic discontent in Ireland endangered British security during its struggle for survival against the armies of the French Revolution. Exploiting Irish Protestant anxieties, Pitt either persuaded or bribed an Irish parliamentary majority to vote for an Act of Union with Britain. He could not, however, convince either non-Catholics in Ireland or the British Parliament, people, or monarchy to combine the Union with Catholic emancipation. Consequently, in 1801 Irish Catholics entered the United Kingdom as an oppressed minority.

Irish nationalist mythology has enshrined the period of the Irish Protestant nation as a golden age destroyed by British duplicity. Throughout the nineteenth and into the twentieth centuries constitutional nationalists were attempting to restore the Irish parliament in College Green. Sean O'Faolain, however, was skeptical about the quality of eighteenth-century Anglo-Irish patriotism, arguing that it was more Protestant than Irish. In *The Irish,* he described the Anglo-Irish as a separate enclave: "They resided in Ireland—their country never their nation—so that their achievements were, for the most part, so remote from the life of the native Irish (now utterly suppressed) that they ultimately became part of the English rather than the Irish cultural record."[5]

Without Catholic equality, the Union between Britain and Ireland was destined to fail. In the 1820s, Daniel O'Connell created modern Irish political nationalism around the Catholic issue. During his mass agitation for Catholic emancipation, he recruited priests as his mobilizing lieutenants, cementing and highlighting the historical associations between Catholic and Irish. The alliance between Irish Catholicism and Irish nationalism politically civilized the former because O'Connell's movement insisted on the principles of liberal democracy, including the right of private conscience and the separation of church and state. Therefore, the Irish, the most religiously loyal and obedient Catholics, departed from Rome's political and social conservatism.[6]

Unlike Continental clerics, priests in Ireland were not part of the establishment. Their church survived through the financial

generosity of impoverished serfs, not from state subsidies or the contributions of landed aristocrats. As leaders of the people, the clergy
participated in movements connected with political and economic
grievances. When Gustave de Beaumont and Alexis de Tocqueville
visited Ireland in the early nineteenth century, they were amazed to
hear priests say that the people were the source of sovereignty and that
they preferred the political ideas of British radicals and Whigs to those
of Continental Catholic philosophers.[7]

Catholic emancipation in 1829 convinced Protestants that Irish
nationalism was not only a camouflage for Catholic power ambitions
but that it also contained the potential for the triumph of a peasant
democracy. Many former Protestant patriots now became Unionists;
those who already were emotionally attached to the British connection became even more loyal. In giving Catholics hope for the future,
emancipation also strengthened the bonds between religion, culture,
and nationality in Ireland. According to Patrick O'Farrell, "There is
much more to Irish Catholicism than the official pronouncements of
the hierarchy: it is a set of values, a culture, a historical tradition, a
view on the world, a disposition of mind and heart, a loyalty, an emo-
tion, a psychology—and a nationalism."[8]

No-popery in England, Scotland, and Wales contributed as
much if not more to the linkage of Irish and Catholic, British and
Protestant than the siege mentality of Irish Anglicans and Nonconformists. The progress of Irish nationalism made the Irish question the
most emotional issue in British politics: the Union became the rallying point for aristocratic privilege, property rights, the empire, and
the Protestant constitution. British politicians, mostly Conservatives,
exploited British public opinion's antipathy toward things Catholic to
gain or maintain office or to preserve the status quo.[9] They insisted
that Irish nationalism and Irish Catholicism were inseparable threats
to the United Kingdom and the empire. In a desperate effort to defeat
Liberal reform through its alliance with Irish nationalism, Conservatives inflamed the irrational prejudices of British and Irish Protestants, particularly in northeast Ulster. They played the "Orange
Card"—"Ulster will fight and Ulster will be right"—even to the prec-
ipice of civil war in 1914.

Although O'Connell developed the potential of the historical
bonds between religion and nationality to build the foundations of

Irish nationalism, for a time the connection fostered nationality more than religion. Recent examinations of the pre-Famine Catholic church reveal a quarreling hierarchy, a poorly educated and undisciplined clergy, and a superstitious laity, casual in religious practices.[10] The need for reform was particularly evident in the Gaelic, economically underdeveloped western and mountainous regions of the country, where there were serious shortages of priests and chapels. Although there was room for improvement, Ireland, even on its Gaelic, pre-Tridentine fringes, was more Catholic in faith and worship than other parts of western Europe.[11]

Beginning with relaxation of the penal laws in the late eighteenth century, Catholic reform began in cities, towns, and prosperous Anglicized rural sections of Ireland. Change was apparent in considerable construction and repair of chapels, in increased enthusiasm for such devotions as the Rosary and the Stations of the Cross, and in the rising number of parishioners attending missions. O'Connell's agitation for Catholic emancipation added to the momentum of religious renewal by encouraging Catholic assertiveness and confidence. As an instrument of population control, even the cruel Famine speeded religious reform. Starvation and emigration devastated the poorest, most ignorant, and least devout portion of the population, leaving Ireland with a more pious, better-informed Catholicism. Because the population decline resulted in a more favorable balance of priests and laity, the church was better able to take care of the spiritual needs of the people. Eighteenth-century improvements in the condition of the church, the confidence and energy that flowed from emancipation, and the Famine-induced population reduction prepared the way for the era of Paul Cullen in Irish Catholicism.[12]

In 1849, Pius IX appointed his friend and adviser on Irish affairs Paul Cullen, head of the Irish College in Rome, archbishop of Armagh, primate, and papal envoy in Ireland. In 1852, Cullen succeeded Daniel Murray as archbishop of Dublin. In 1866, the pope named him the first Irish cardinal. At the 1870 Vatican Council, Cullen drafted the formula defining papal infallibility. As an ultramontane enemy of British and Anglo-Irish Protestantism and Gallican Catholic nationalism, Cullen was determined to bring the Irish church under Roman discipline and into full harmony with its doctrine and practices. Until his death in 1878, he dominated Irish

Catholicism. Except for Connacht and parts of Ulster, Cullen managed to fill Irish bishoprics with his choices. Under his guidance, the hierarchy presented a harmonious public profile. He also improved clerical education and discipline; successfully encouraged the recruitment of large numbers of priests, nuns, and brothers, sending many of them off to the United States and throughout the British empire as missionaries; and built churches and schools and filled them with the most loyal, devout, and generous Catholics in the Roman fold. [13]

Catholicism in Ireland was more fervent and pastoral but also more legalistic and less theological or aesthetic than the Continental version. It measured religiosity by conformity to the letter rather than the spirit of the law. In practice, Catholicism in Ireland was more puritanical as well. Some trace an obsession with sins of the flesh to the early Irish church, pointing to St. Kevin in the seventh century as an example. According to legend, he dispatched a young woman off a stone cliff into the lake below when she invaded his monastery cell at Glendalough. By the eleventh century, Irish monasticism had lost its unworldly reputation. Monks, including abbots, had concubines and mistresses and fathered children. Such misconduct gave Adrian IV (Nicholas Breakespear), the one and only English pope, a reason to ask Henry II to invade, conquer, and bring Ireland under Roman discipline. Territorial ambitions rather than the papal appeal sent the Anglo-Normans to Ireland in 1169. On arrival, however, they justified their presence by claiming an intention to purify Irish Catholicism.

Those lamenting Irish Catholic puritanism frequently trace it to Jansenism. They say it was passed on by French clerical professors, refugees from the Revolution, to Irish seminary students at Maynooth, County Kildare. [14] There is plausibility in the Jansenist thesis, but Irish puritanism is an emphasis on one aspect of Roman Catholicism rather than a heresy. Originally, its motivation was more economic and social than religious. Even before the Famine, Catholic and rural mores limited peasants' sexual activity. Unwed mothers were uncommon in Ireland. Pregnancy usually led to marriage, seldom to abortion or child abandonment. Comparatively chaste in conduct, the Irish, like the poor in many times and places, married young, often imprudently, and parented large families. Ribaldry in Irish folklore and the sexual games and conduct at wakes and holy wells indicate that they had a natural, exuberant view of sex. But the Great Hunger forced them to ponder the consequences of too many people on too little land with few industrial or commercial employment alternatives to agriculture. This reality forced emigration for most and delayed marriage or encouraged permanent celibacy for those who remained at home. Men postponed marriage until their fathers died and they came into possession of family farms, which often happened when they were in middle age. Some lived and died as bachelors. Irish marriages were negotiated matches rather than romantic responses to passion and usually wives were much younger than husbands so love and strong sexual desire were not significant aspects of Irish family life. Catholic condemnations of premarital sex and urgings to avoid sin reinforced more than they generated Irish puritanism. Catholic teachings helped provide the strength to endure the physical and psychological torments of sexual abstinence and solitary living. Therefore, the Irish, more than others, adhered to the Catholic premise that chastity was a priority virtue and celibacy the highest calling.[15]

Ireland was Anglicized as well as Romanized, and the Irish took rules and regulations, including the church's, on sex more seriously than did Latin Catholics. There were not many differences between the British Nonconformist and Irish Catholic consciences. Irish views on respectability had British models. Victorianism invaded and conquered Irish attitudes. Because of their inferiority complex, Irish Catholics were determined to prove that they were even more virtuous than British and Irish Protestants.[16] Their zeal in this regard led the hierarchy, clergy, and "respectable" middle and strong farmer classes in 1891 to condemn Charles Stewart Parnell and dethrone him as leader of the Home Rule movement after his involvement in a divorce scandal.[17]

Irish Catholics are as famous for their excessive drinking as for their sexual inhibitions. Perhaps the two are related. Unlike many other European Catholics, the Irish are deficient in the culinary arts. English influences have helped to make their cuisine range from boring to wretched. But Irish beer and whiskey are excellent. Heavy and hearty drinking has a long Irish tradition. Members of the eighteenth- and nineteenth-century Anglo-Irish Protestant aristocracy and gentry thought it a breach of hospitality to send guests home sober. No doubt, upper-class examples influenced peasant conduct. But the Catholic poor had other excuses to drink. Alcohol warmed the body in the damp and cold of the Irish climate and released the mind from torturous thoughts of poverty, hunger, and hopelessness.

Alcohol abuse (much of it involving illegally distilled poteen) and its disruption of work habits and family relations concerned many leaders, including Catholic bishops and priests, many of whom shared this vice with the laity. In the 1840s a Capuchin friar, Theobald Mathew, enrolled five million people in a temperance crusade. Coping with alcohol-related Irish social problems in the United Kingdom and the United States, English, Irish, and Anglo-American Protestants praised and contributed money to Father Mathew's movement. It was a remarkable event in 1851, at a peak period in anti-Irish American Catholic nativism, when Father Mathew spoke to a joint session of Congress in Washington. Although Mathew intended to keep temperance separate from politics, O'Connell saw great advantage in melding it with his effort to repeal the Act of Union. "Ireland Sober Is Ireland Free" became a slogan for his Loyal National Repeal Association in the 1840s. He told mass meetings that Ireland's independence would be secured by the efforts of teetotalers.[18] Temperance reading rooms and bands of musicians played important roles in O'Connell's massive agitation for repeal in 1843.

Father Mathew is honored by statues in Cork and on Dublin's O'Connell Street, but, like so many other positive features of life, his attempt to save Ireland from the curse of drink collapsed during the Famine. In improving times following the Famine, misery receded as a motive for drinking, and relief from sexual tensions became a more important reason. Late marriage, prolonged or permanent celibacy, and constant clerical warnings about sex discouraged social associations between men and women. Priests roamed the countryside, flailing away with blackthorn sticks at young couples courting in ditches or dancing at crossroads. Ireland's puritan atmosphere sent young men and women off to America, and it increased the importance of the public house as a male club. Drinking with the "lads" in the local became a substitute for the company of women. As men descended into alcoholic hazes, their sexual interests and desires decreased.[19]

A strict sexual morality that began as a way of avoiding poverty through the reduction of population and then evolved into a main feature of Irish Catholicism became an important dimension of the Irish religious and secular value systems. Men and women who could well afford to marry delayed or avoided such a commitment. Even today, the pub continues to serve as a substitute for the home. Priests still have a tendency to concentrate their sermons on adultery and fornication while tolerantly passing over alcohol abuse as a manly vice.

THE GREENING OF AMERICAN CATHOLICISM

American experiences strengthened the ties between Irish and Catholic. In urban ghettos, cut off from their traditional rural culture, the Irish in the United States felt lonely and isolated. Pressures from American nativism, technological and cultural poverty, psychological insecurity, and alienation combined to enhance the significance of Catholic faith and worship. Catholicism became the glue of the Irish community, the one familiar institution bridging rural Ireland and urban America. It consoled Irish misery, disciplined Irish conduct, and fused people from different provinces, counties, townlands, and villages in Ireland into an Irish-American ethnicity.

Early Irish Catholic immigrants entered a small, insecure American church. In 1789, it had only about thirty thousand members, one-tenth of them black slaves. Most American Catholics lived in Maryland and Pennsylvania. Catholic America had the services of only one bishop and thirty priests, mostly Anglo or Anglicized Americans and French Sulpicians.[20]

Expanding Irish America demanded its own clergy. John England, who in 1820 at age thirty-two became bishop of Charleston, South Carolina, was one of the first priests from Ireland to serve in the United States.[21] Unfortunately, few of the early Irish missionaries matched him in quality. Bishops in Ireland found the United States a convenient dumping ground for whiskey-drinking, womanizing, and rebellious priests. In America, these rejects usually continued their unruly ways. England and other American bishops improved the quality of priests by establishing seminaries to train a native clergy and by asking prelates in Ireland to send them better men. After Cullen took command, the Irish church developed a pride in the Irish spiritual empire in the English-speaking world and a determination to make the new Irish church as zealous as the ancient church of Colmcille and Columbanus in its Christianizing activities. Missionary zeal inspired a historical interpretation that gave religious meaning to the suffering of the Irish people. Their sorrows were a sign of God's love, not His indifference. He inflicted hunger, poverty, and oppression on them to test and strengthen their faith. Then He sent them into exile to carry His message of salvation to others and to save them from sin. Belief in Ireland's historical destiny to sanctify the world sent many good Irish priests to the United States.

By 1860, Irish and German immigration raised the number of American Catholics to about 3 million. They were divided among forty-three dioceses and two territories. Forty-five bishops and more than two thousand priests, mostly Irish or Irish American, ministered to American Catholics. Later in the century, Italians, Poles, Lithuanians, Czechs, Slovaks, Hungarians, Croatians, and other nationalities joined the Irish and Germans in a colorful American Catholic mosaic. By World War I, at least twenty thousand priests and many times that number of nuns served the spiritual, educational, and social needs of 20 million American Catholics. Today a pluralistic Catholic America of 60 million is enriched by Haitians and African Americans and a growing multiracial and ethnic Hispanic population. Soon Hispanics will be the largest segment of Catholic America, but at roughly 18 percent the Irish still have that distinction.[22] Their influence exceeds their numbers. The hierarchy remains close to 50 percent Irish, and Irish priests, nuns, and brothers continue to overrepresent the size of their ethnic community.

For many reasons the Irish became the dominant force in American Catholicism. They were the first large group of European Catholics to arrive in the United States. Once here, they were exceptionally aggressive in promoting their religious beliefs. More than other Catholic ethnics, the Irish sent their sons and daughters into religious life. The Irish also had an advantage in adjusting to American ways. Before leaving Ireland, they had been partially Anglicized culturally and almost totally in language. While German, Italian, Polish, and other Slavic Catholics isolated themselves through their retention of language and cultural uniqueness, the Irish were visible on the American scene. To Protestant, Jewish, and nonreligious Americans, the Catholic church was essentially Irish.

Irish Americans gave an urban working-class profile to American Catholicism. They also made it more Roman and aggressive. Irish influences produced a generous as well as a devotional laity. In Ireland, Catholicism, the religion of a 75 percent majority, had to fend for itself. Anglican Protestantism, serving only 13 percent of the people, was the established religion. Impoverished Catholic peasants not only supported their local parish, they also contributed large sums to Rome and financed foreign missions. In light of the principle of separation of church and state in the American Constitution, it was fortunate that the Irish, and not people from nations where religion was an appendage and an instrument of the state, were the first Catholic Europeans to enter the United States and take command of the church. Irish Americans began building the facilities necessary to house an expanding Catholicism and passed on their magnanimous spirit to others, enabling the church in the United States to carry out a wide spectrum of religious, social, and educational functions; to send large donations to Rome; and to finance missionary activities in Asia, Africa, and Latin America. The Irish tradition of giving and the example it set made the United States the most important financial reservoir of Roman Catholicism.

As a result of its long history as a persecuted religion closely associated with a peasant culture in Ireland and the urban working class in the United States and Britain, Irish Catholicism, at home and abroad, has been more pastoral than aesthetic or intellectual. And it has emphasized rules and regulations. In sermons, retreats, parish missions, devotional exercises, and parochial school religious instructions, American Catholicism has given more emphasis to attendance at mass on Sundays and Holy Days of Obligation, reception of the sacraments, not eating meat on Fridays, keeping Lent, public piety, and sexual purity than to the Christian spirit of charity.

In the United States, Irish Catholicism has been as prudish as in Ireland. Priests and nuns have been fanatic in their denunciations of dirty books, filthy movies, and short skirts and in their warnings of the consequences of keeping bad company, entertaining impure thoughts, masturbation, and even passionate kissing. Irish Catholic pressures were largely responsible for the creation of the Hays Office in 1922 to keep the movies clean. When the Hays Office proved an ineffective censor, the Motion Picture Producers and Distributors of

America adopted a production code in 1930. Daniel Lord, S.J., of St. Louis drafted the code, and Martin Quigley, editor and publisher of the *Motion Picture Herald*, another Irish-American Catholic, secured its passage. Still, Catholics were not satisfied with the contents of movies. They believed more vigilance against smut was necessary and in 1933 founded the Legion of Decency. Its rating system had a considerable impact on the film industry.[23]

Irish Americans also have followed the example of their brethren in Ireland in marrying late or not at all. Spinsters and bachelors living at home with their parents have been common in working- and middle-class Irish America. And as in Ireland, many Irish Americans have found alternatives to sex in the bottle.

Many Irish-American writers concur with those in Ireland that Irish Catholicism imposes an oppressive burden of peasant pietism, dogmatic authoritarianism, sexual frustration, and anti-intellectualism. Failing to understand that Irish Catholicism is obsessively Roman rather than unique, quite a few of them have endorsed Michael Novak's description of it as a "Celtic Heresy" and Philip Roth's observation that Jewish writers were fortunate to have escaped "an Old Country link and strangling church like Italians, or the Irish or the Poles."[24]

Irish-American literature's quarrel with the Catholic influence focuses on its puritanism. Writers argue that sexual inhibitions have made the Irish neurotic, emotionally cold, and alcoholic. They frequently treat Irish sexual neurosis in a humorous if satirical manner. In Tom MacHale's *Farragan's Retreat*, Arthur Farragan turns holy pictures and religious statues toward the bedroom wall while making love with his wife, Muriel. When John Fitzpatrick in Edward Hannibal's *Chocolate Days, Popsicle Weeks* is captivated by an attractive woman, Sister Mustentoucher invades his mind to say no! In John Powers's nonmalicious, funny *Last Catholic in America* and *Do Patent Leather Shoes Really Reflect Up?* and in Caryl Rivers's *Virgins*, nuns, priests, and brothers try to dampen the sexual fires of youth in Catholic secondary schools.[25]

In angry or sober as well as humorous prose, Irish-American writers describe the emotionally cold, introverted personalities resulting from sexual frustration. James T. Farrell's Chicago Irish have difficulty expressing aspirations and emotions, instead internalizing their feelings in daydreams and fantasies. Unable to communicate affection, desire, sadness, or loss, they explode in anger. Harry Sylvester's 1947 novel *Moon Gaffney* had a tremendous impact on Irish-American intellectuals, not for the quality of its writing but for its angry message. Sylvester's Brooklyn Irish of the 1930s are pious, churchgoing Catholics who think of themselves as the chosen people, the only real Catholics and patriots, but they hate African Americans and Jews, and they view social improvement efforts as communistic. They are so concerned with respectability and conformity that they canonize mediocrity. In *Moon Gaffney,* Irish charm and wit are frivolous and often cruel. Alcohol, a substitute for sex, fuels social activities. Men prefer crowded places with drinks in their hands to intimacy and privacy with women. Jimmy Breslin's 1973 novel *World Without End, Amen,* features a cold, loveless, double-fault marriage between Dermot and Phyllis Davey. Dermot cannot say "I love you" to the woman he has been seeing and sleeping with for four years.[26]

Irish-American playwrights also focus on the cold personal relationships among their subjects. Eugene O'Neill's work is loaded with sexual neurosis, guilt, and heavy drinking. The Tyrones in probably his and America's best play, *A Long Day's Journey into Night* (written in 1940, released in 1956), interact more easily in anger than in love. Frank Gilroy's prize-winning 1965 play, *The Subject Was Roses,* also examines the emotional strains in an Irish family. In explaining to her son, who has just returned from army duty in World War II, why she married John Cleary and why there is so much hostility in their union, Nettie says she was attracted by his Irish fun-loving, exuberant personality in large social settings, but once married she found that he could not be intimate and giving within the family. She also concedes that her Irish Catholic emotional coldness contributes to the failed marriage.[27]

Though not as puritanical, emotionally remote in personal and family relationships, or alcoholic as the Irish, other American Catholic ethnics have been touched by their aberrations. The pietism, legalism, and sexual obsessions of Irish priests, nuns, and brothers have permeated Catholic education from elementary school through college and university.

Positive Irish political values have helped to compensate for the negative puritanism and emotional frigidity in American Catholic culture. Contrasting with the reactionary Old Regime flavor of Continental Catholicism, the Irish version, politically civilized by its alliance with liberal democratic Irish nationalism, has advocated a popular sovereignty form of government and has insisted on the duties as well as the rights of property. Because Irish Catholicism accepted democratic principles, freedom of conscience (pragmatically if not ideally), and the separation of church and state, Irish immigrants were able to adjust speedily to the American political consensus and lead other Catholics into a similar accommodation.

Of course, there was a paradox in the Irish allegiance to the most authoritarian religious system in the Western world, Roman Catholicism, and its most liberal political expression, Anglo-Saxon and Anglo-American constitutionalism. In trying to reconcile conflicting Anglicized and Romanized facets of their ethnic personality, they denied their existence. As loyal Catholics and devoted Americans, they did not want to face the contrast between their two loves. They could not afford to make a choice between a religion that was their culture, nationality, and emotional security and a country that had saved them from poverty and humiliation. To solve the dilemma of where to place their loyalties, the Irish extended separation of church and state to segregate religion and politics mentally and emotionally. This compartmentalization helped them retain their Catholic-rooted ethnicity as well as their American patriotism. It also explains why Irish-American Catholicism is so devotional and pastoral and so minimally intellectual—the irreconcilable cannot be rationally reconciled. Isolating religion from politics also moved Irish-American liberalism in a pragmatic rather than an ideological direction, and perhaps it accounts for the nonchalant attitude toward graft in Irish-American politics.

Irish-American Catholic social and cultural adjustments, like their economic progress, reflected regional diversity. In eastern cities, where the working-class, nativist-pestered Irish huddled in ghettos of mind and place, bishops and priests were wary of American values. On the urban frontier, where the Irish were moving toward and sometimes reaching middle-class respectability and mingled with non-Catholics, the hierarchy and clergy favorably evaluated American culture. Unlike some Midwest prelates who wanted to settle Catholic immigrants in rural surroundings similar to those they came from, bishops in the East argued that the urban parishes were better shelters for their religious faith and culture. Churchmen in the East also regarded economic and social reform movements as dangerous because they could lead Catholics into Protestantism, secularism, or socialism. Fears of socialism caused many eastern bishops to oppose the labor movement. Their solution to the social problems rampant in urban Catholic America was religious acceptance of poverty as the will of God. They promised heavenly rewards to compensate for earthly injustices, defended property rights as the law of God and the church, and recommended private rather than public charity.[28] Bishops on the urban frontier advised Catholics to accept New World opportunities and to involve themselves in the totality of American life. Led by Archbishop John Ireland of St. Paul, Americanizers attempted to compromise with public education. In two towns within Ireland's jurisdiction, Faribault and Stillwater, Minnesota, Catholic schools joined with their public counterparts in a shared-time experiment. Catholic children attended parochial schools for religious instruction and then switched to public schools for secular learning.[29]

In Baltimore, the Irish experienced more success than in other eastern cities. Their archbishop, James Cardinal Gibbons, generally supported John Ireland. Both prelates and their episcopal allies criticized the injustices resulting from laissez-faire capitalism. They understood that the quickest way for the church in the United States to repeat the European loss of working-class support was to remain indifferent to social and economic problems and therefore supported the labor movement. Gibbons went to Rome and defeated an appeal by eastern bishops to have the pope condemn the Knights of Labor.[30]

At the same time that most bishops in the East wanted to preserve Catholic ghettoism, the Ireland-Gibbon faction insisted that American liberal democracy, with its separation of church and state, was totally compatible with Catholicism and gave it an opportunity to grow and prosper in a free environment. Liberals in the hierarchy believed that energized in the free American environment, Catholicism would eventually convert a majority of the nation's citizens.

Archbishop Michael Corrigan of New York and Bishop Bernard McQuaid of Rochester allied with midwestern German prelates to lead the opposition to Americanization. They championed Rome's antagonism to liberalism and modernism and its position that the ideal relationship between church and state was unity. They suspected lay intellectualism and leadership, insisting that Catholic education concentrate on preserving the faith. These attitudes prevented the Catholic University of America from achieving the academic distinction envisioned by its liberal sponsors.[31]

Religious orders joined the controversy between liberal and conservative bishops. The Paulists, founded in 1859 by Isaac Hecker, once a New England Transcendentalist, were intended to be an American urban mission. They joined with the Holy Cross fathers at Notre Dame, then a small college for men, in agreeing with Ireland and Gibbons that Catholicism needed to adjust to American conditions. The Jesuits, whose secondary schools and colleges catered to the sons of upper- and middle-class American Catholics, were strong advocates of Roman authoritarianism. They stood with Corrigan and McQuaid.

The debate over Americanism moved beyond the United States. Liberal Catholics in France argued the positions of Ireland and Gibbons in confrontations with conservatives and sometimes distorted their ideas into a modernist theology. Bishop Sebastian Messmer of Green Bay, Wisconsin, a German-American leader, and Corrigan and McQuaid endorsed a French conservative request that Leo XIII officially brand Americanism a heresy. In January 1899, the pope wrote Gibbons that the following positions were contrary to official church doctrine: action takes precedence over contemplation, natural virtues are more important than supernatural virtues, and the dictates of private conscience supersede the divinely inspired teachings of Holy Mother church.[32] Although the Gibbons-Ireland faction correctly replied that their version of Americanism was social, economic, political, and cultural, not theological, and the pope was condemning misrepresentations of their views, they had been censured, and their opponents were ecstatic and arrogant in victory. During the reign of Leo's successor, Pius X, Rome conducted a spiritual reign of terror against modernism, purging liberal theologians and further limiting the intellectual range and contents of Roman Catholicism.

Temporarily silenced intellectually, liberal Catholicism remained active in arenas of economic and social conflict. Many progressive Irish-American bishops and priests endorsed working-class demands. Two papal encyclicals, Leo XIII's *Rerum Novarum* (1891) and Pius XI's *Quadragesimo Anno* (1931), attacked industrial capitalism from a neomedieval distributist and corporate state ideology. In the United States, Catholic liberals constructed a social gospel by adapting papal pronouncements to the American industrial situation.[33] In the 1920s, as head of the National Catholic Welfare Conference, Monsignor John A. Ryan, a St. Paul protégé of Archbishop Ireland and an articulate advocate of the cause of labor, authored an agenda for social justice that anticipated the New Deal.[34]

Ryan was one example of how Catholic liberalism and conservatism continued to retain regional distinctions. Usually the archbishops of St. Paul and Chicago were more socially conscious and favorable in their estimates of American culture and society than were the archbishops of New York, Boston, and Philadelphia. The Midwest Irish, more economically successful and socially integrated than those in the East, were friendlier to American liberal ideas.

Although more in touch with general American culture, the Midwest Irish shared an Irish-American ambiguity concerning the place of Catholicism in the United States. Unlike German, French, Polish, and other Catholic ethnics, Irish Americans from all regions did not want their parishes and schools to function as obstacles to Catholic occupational mobility. Irish-American bishops intended the church in the United States to be a national institution, not a federation of ethnic enclaves. They frowned on the use of other languages than English in sermons and devotions or in the classroom. Many were unfriendly to national parishes, conceding them only in response to militant demands. Irish Catholic educators discouraged the presentation of the Catholic cultural and historical heritages in ethnic contexts, including their own. Their schools and colleges did not concentrate on Irish history and literature outside their relevance to Catholicism. Non-Catholic institutions of higher learning were much quicker to appreciate the significance of Irish literature than were Catholic colleges or universities.

Catholic education focused on the Middle Ages as the epoch best typifying the Catholic ethos and genius and the universality of the church as a great spiritual and intellectual empire embracing all western European people. Catholic colleges and universities presented philosophy and psychology as well as theology from a neoscholastic perspective. Theoretically, Thomistic theology was the "queen of the sciences" and all other academic disciplines were expected to acknowledge the superiority of its insights.

When teaching literature, Catholic educators preferred English and Continental to Irish writers. Educated Irish Americans were often totally oblivious to the Irish literary tradition, and if they were aware of it, many thought it too peasanty crude to satisfy American Catholic intellectual pretensions and yearning for respectability. The earthy, irreverent, often anticlerical works of such Irish and Irish-American Catholics (at least culturally) as James Joyce, Sean O'Faolain, Frank O'Connor, James T. Farrell, and Eugene O'Neill were too profane and rebellious for proponents of Irish-American Catholic pietism. It was not until the 1960s that Irish Americans began to appreciate their own significant cultural heritage.

Irish-American Catholic education began with two purposes, neither of which had much to do with intellectuality or creativity. One was the achievement of social mobility and respectability, the other the preservation of a Catholic subculture to protect against American materialism and secularism. In addition to catechism, Catholic elementary and secondary schools emphasized reading, writing, and arithmetic, the fundamentals that enabled their students to find respectable employment. But Catholic school experiences also encouraged them to retreat into parish neighborhoods for spiritual, social, and cultural sustenance. Catholic colleges and universities provided ethnic communities with teachers to shape souls and to train minds, doctors to heal bodies and to guard against birth control and abortion, and lawyers to support family structures by discouraging divorce.

Although Catholicism was more ghettoized in the East, Catholic education was more prevalent in the Midwest. Bishops at the 1884 Third Plenary Council in Baltimore decreed that parents should send their children to Catholic schools. By that time, however, large numbers of Catholics in eastern cities were taking advantage of secularized public education, and few parishes had the resources to build schools. But in the Midwest, where the church was rapidly expanding and Catholics were relatively affluent, parishes often constructed churches and schools at the same time. Because midwestern bishops and priests were so keen on Catholic education, occasionally the school came first and mass and devotions were held in its basement until a proper church could be built.

Because of lack of money and properly qualified teachers, Catholic schools at the beginning were not particularly good. But they had the advantage that parents were determined that their children would succeed and supported classroom discipline. And nuns, priests, and brothers who taught in Catholic schools were dedicated and increasingly better educated. As a result, Catholic education on all levels improved. In secular subjects, Catholic schools imitated the curriculum of public schools and in time often exceeded their quality, civilizing the sons and daughters of rough immigrants. The Irish journey from the unskilled working class to the middle class owed much to the discipline and learning effectiveness of Catholic education. Another such testimony is the present-day decision of many Catholic and non-Catholic black parents, determined to promote the mobility of their children, to enroll them in the same parish schools once attended by white ethnics.

Unfortunately, Catholic education infrequently has moved beyond the search for respectability. Catholic secondary schools can take pride in the large number of their graduates going on to college. Catholic colleges and universities produce a bevy of teachers, lawyers, doctors, dentists, social workers, and businessmen. But neither Catholic secondary nor higher education (some Catholic women's colleges such as St. Catherine's in St. Paul, Minnesota, are exceptions) have done much to encourage the creative imagination. They advise students to read books, not to write them, to appreciate art but not to create it, to listen to music but not to compose it. Too often Catholics leave their high schools and colleges educated but not intellectual, skilled but not creative.

In 1956, Monsignor John Tracy Ellis, supported by other prominent Catholics, complained that their American coreligionists had achieved social respectability but had failed to make a significant impact on the intellectual life of the United States. He quoted Denis W. Brogan, the British authority on American studies, who in 1941 wrote, "In no Western society is the intellectual prestige of Catholicism lower than in the country where, in such respects as wealth, numbers, and strength of organization it is so powerful."[35] Ellis's main concern was the lack of scholars emerging from Catholic schools. But when he published his indictment, the impact of the G.I. Bill of Rights on post–World War II America was not yet evident. Since the 1950s, the Irish, and to a lesser extent other Catholics, many trained in Catholic elementary and secondary schools and in Catholic colleges and universities, have produced an abundant supply of professionals, scholars, business men and women, and housewives with sophisticated cultural tastes. But the failure of Catholic education to encourage the creative arts is still disappointing. In present-day Catholic colleges and universities theoretical tribute is paid to the liberal arts, but the main concerns of administrators and boards of trustees are directed toward business and preprofessional training. Catholic campuses are saturated with a trade school mentality, discouraging intellectualism and artistic creativity.

Critics of the intellectual and imaginative limits of Catholic education in the 1950s blamed Irish authoritarian, rote memory approaches to teaching and learning. But there is no evidence that the Irish version of Catholicism is any more authoritarian or less intellectual than others. Everywhere post-Tridentine Roman Catholicism (except for a brief period between the reigns of John XXIII and John Paul II) has been dogmatically inflexible and inhospitable to intellectual speculation. The fascination with the medieval past that permeated Catholic education for so many years did not encourage its students to make a significant mark in the intellectual and artistic world of the twentieth century. To preserve the faith, it was safer to live in the past than the present and to prepare doctors, lawyers, and businessmen who seldom quarrel with church authority or teaching than artists and intellectuals who do.[36]

THE IRISH-AMERICAN COMMUNITY: PARISH, PRIEST, AND PEOPLE

For individual Catholics, the political and educational nuances of their religion were never as important as its personal and community significance. Many sophisticates in the American church, including some Irish, have scorned the peasant tone of Irish Catholicism: imitation gothic and baroque churches cluttered with statues of the sacred and bleeding heart of Jesus and the immaculate heart of Mary, trays of vigil lights, off-key organs accompanying sentimental hymns, mumbled and mispronounced Latin, and sermons designed to inculcate the fear rather than the love of God.

Irish pioneers of the American urban ghetto experienced their faith and worship quite differently than did its aesthetic critics. For them, it was a comfort station in an alien, urban industrial environment, a bridge of familiarity linking their past life in rural Ireland with their new existence in American cities. As in British oppressed Catholic Ireland, the church told the hungry, the wretched, the sick, the dispossessed, and the persecuted Irish in the United States that they were children of a loving God and that if His justice did not prevail in this world, it certainly would in the next. Built with meager savings from backbreaking labor, Irish churches manifested pride and confidence as well as an affirmation of strong religious faith and conviction. Under their roofs and inside their walls believers escaped the harshness of poverty and dreary urban lives in an atmosphere of history and mystery. They thought the statues, the stained glass windows, the music, the incense, and the Latin liturgy beautiful and uplifting. The mass and the sacraments provided them with spiritual strength and psychological consolation. More important, they brought the grace of salvation. Emotionally and spiritually, every Catholic was reborn in the confessional. In *Bare Ruined Choirs,* Garry Wills captures the emotional glow that came to so many from the sacraments of the church:

> There were moments when the weirdest things made a new and deep sense beyond sense—when Confession did not mean cleaning up oneself (the blackboard erased again) but cleansing a whole world, the first glimpse of sky or grass as one came out of church. When communion was not cannibalism but its reverse, body taken up in Spirit. Being inwardly shaken by unsummoned prayers, as by muffled explosions. Moments of purity remembered, when the world seemed fresh out of its maker's hands, trees washed by some rain sweeter than the world's own.[37]

As well as spiritual joy and comfort, Irish Catholicism in the United States continued to provide community, values, psychology, and ethnic identity.

According to anthropologist and archaeologist E. Estyn Evans, Irish Catholic culture is essentially rural.[38] In Ireland, towns and cities are monuments to the foreign invader and occupier. But in America, economic circumstances and communal personalities necessitated city living for the Irish. This environmental shift created serious social and psychological problems for the immigrants, but the Catholic parish was a buffer zone, functioning as a peasant village in an urban situation. Within its boundaries, people had a social and cultural as well as a religious ethnic community. They attended lectures, plays, dances, and socials in the parish hall, and they played on parish athletic teams. James Carroll's novel *Prince of Peace* describes how the Irish Catholic parish once was the focal point of Irish neighborhoods, the gathering place for devotions, educational, social, and athletic events.[39] As William Gibson depicts so well in *Mass for the Dead*, the Irish, like other Catholic ethnics, marked their pilgrimage through this world with rituals from the joyful christening service welcoming an infant into the Christian community to the requiem mass saying good-bye to a departed soul entering the Kingdom of God, with first confession and communion (childhood), confirmation (adolescence), and marriage (adulthood) in between, all in the parish church.[40]

Although anticlericalism is far more muted in Irish than in Continental Catholicism, priests have antagonized a large number of Irish and Irish-American writers. In James Joyce's *Portrait of the Artist as a Young Man*, Simon Dedalus tells his Christmas dinner guests during a discussion of the clergy's role in the fall of Parnell, "We are an unfortunate priest-ridden race and always were and always will be till the end of the chapter." In Irish-American fiction, many priests are fools or knaves. Edmund Farragan in Tom MacHale's *Farragan's Retreat* is a likable simpleton. Edmund is too stupid to participate in the family trucking business, and the Farragans buy his way into a religious order, the Tirungians, where he becomes father general. In William Kennedy's *Billy Phelan's Greatest Game*, Martin Daugherty worries that his seminary-bound son might become like some clerics he has known: "There was a suburban priest who kept a pet duck on a leash. One in Troy chased a nubile child around the parish house. Priests in their cups. Priests in their beggar robes. Priests in their eunuch suits."

Priests in *Moon Gaffney* are more knavish than clownish. "Bingo Bob-bie" Malone recruits for the profascist, Coughlinite Christian Front. Another ultraconservative bigot, Father O'Driscoll, a women's college chaplain, purposely provides wrong information to students on the rhythm method of birth control. He thinks it hilarious when they get pregnant on their honeymoons. Another unpleasant women's college chaplain is Father Denton Malone in Thomas Fleming's *Sandbox Tree*. He tortures students with his sexual puritanism, trying to drive them to choose the convent over marriage.[41]

Because of the importance of the sacraments, priests in Catholicism are more important than ministers are in Protestantism or rabbis in Judaism. Links between religion, culture, and nationality and their leadership in anti-British and other populist agitations gave priests more status and respect in Ireland than they had in other places. Unlike so many Catholic countries under the domination of aristocratic, reactionary regimes, where the church's defense of the political, economic, and social status quo bred anticlericalism, in Ireland the priest symbolized the condition of an exploited and oppressed majority victimized by foreign Protestant colonialism. He came from the people, serving them in efforts to secure civil liberties, economic justice, and national independence. Reverence and admiration for the priesthood carried over from Ireland to America. In the United States, Irish Catholics again suffered from discrimination and oppression, and the priest comforted them with the sacraments and spoke for their interests. An occasional priest might resemble the fools and knaves that sometimes appear in Irish and Irish-American fiction, but farmer and shopkeeper families in Ireland and working- and lower-middle-class families in Irish America have given their most talented sons to the church.

As in rural Ireland, the leadership role of priests in urban America gave them power and influence beyond the sphere of religion. Although Catholic seminaries in both countries have been trade schools, not universities, and their religious studies have been more apologetics than investigative theology, priests once were far better educated than the overwhelming majority of the laity. Believing them to be learned as well as divinely inspired, people visited the rectory to seek help on a multitude of problems: wayward children; delinquent adolescents; drunken, abusive, or philandering husbands; unfaithful wives; quarrels with neighbors; poverty; unemployment; and sickness. The priest did more than listen. He lectured or counseled parishioners, tried to find jobs for those out of work, wrote letters recommending young men and women for scholarships to Catholic secondary schools and colleges, organized and often coached athletic teams, and advised and sat through the meetings of such parish organizations as the Holy Name and Altar and Rosary societies. He did all of this in addition to saying mass, hearing confessions, baptizing infants, visiting parochial school classes, marrying young couples, anointing the sick and dying, and burying the dead. The 1944 movie *Going My Way* and its 1945 sequel, *The Bells of St. Mary's,* romanticized clerical life by omitting its frustrations, doubts, and loneliness, but there was considerable truth in their portrayal of Father Chuck O'Malley as a community leader and problem solver.

Why did such a complex, difficult, and time-consuming vocation as the priesthood attract so many young men? The status of the clergy in Ireland and Irish America and the fervor of Irish Catholicism are two good reasons. To the Irish, the privilege of saying mass, miraculously changing bread and wine into the body and blood of Christ, and serving as the sacramental mediator between God and man has been the highest calling in life.

In Irish America, as well as in Ireland, the priesthood not only infers sanctity, it also indicates respectability and social mobility. Because of both their religious and secular roles, priests have been men of power and influence. Parish priests, not required to take the vow of poverty, often have lived in fine houses, eaten well, drunk the best whiskey, and, with the advent of the automobile, driven expensive cars. Sometimes, through the generosity of parishioners, coupled with wise investments, they have accumulated small fortunes. Families of priests have shared their spiritual eminence, secular importance, and worldly abundance. A priest has been a treasured family possession. Irish fathers and mothers, for practical and spiritual reasons, have been proud to see their sons in clerical garb.

Because of its status, Irish families have contributed their best and brightest to the priesthood. From the time a boy exhibited above-average intelligence and an interest in religion, his mother began pushing him in the direction of the seminary. Sometimes the inclination followed rather than preceded parental urging. Few quick-minded Irish lads have not played priest on an orange crate altar, pretending to change grape juice and white bread into the Eucharist. At some stage of their boyhood or adolescence, probably most Irish young men have thought about the possibility of becoming a priest.

After ordination, young diocesan priests have gone into parishes, usually working for years as curates. Sometimes they have served under stern, insensitive, and inflexible pastors. The power and prestige of the clerical state and the respect, deference, and love the laity bestowed on it have helped young men to survive the rigors and the loneliness of chastity and celibacy.

Sexual temptations have not necessarily been the most difficult challenges to a priest's spirituality. His secular duties often have infringed on his religious obligations. Edwin O'Connor's Pulitzer Prize–winning 1961 novel, *The Edge of Sadness,* is a sensitive study of conflicting clerical roles. Father Hugh Kennedy is so involved with his middle-class parish, St. Stephen's, that he neglects to cultivate spirituality. Thus, when his father, also his best friend, dies, he turns for consolation to whiskey, not God. Alcoholism forces Hugh's removal from St. Stephen's to take a four-year rest cure in Colorado. When the bishop calls him back to the city, he is assigned to Old St. Paul's, a run-down inner-city parish. Hugh contentedly views St. Paul's as an interlude, a step on the way to another comfortable Irish parish. Because Hugh is indifferent to his shabby parish and its polyglot population, Stanley Danowski, the naïve, platitudinous, intellectually dense curate, ministers to St. Paul's urban outcasts. Hugh first patronizes the young Pole, then gradually realizes that his assistant is unconsciously giving him a lesson in true priestly deportment. Through associations with the Carmody family, Hugh resumes Irish social relationships. Charley, the eighty-one-year-old, cruel-tongued, emotionally cold, financial skinflint family patriarch has acquired a fortune from property, mostly apartment rentals. His children, John and Helen, were Hugh's childhood friends. John is pastor of St. Raymond's, Hugh's idea of the perfect parish, but is psychologically harassed by its nonreligious burdens: the demands of clubs and societies, interventions on his privacy, details of maintaining the physical plant. In desperation, he asks the bishop for permission to enter a monastery. His request is denied because the bishop insists that the contemplative life is not for those who want to escape the world and that priests should seek God in other men, not in isolation. When Hugh commiserates with his friend, John tells him that he also is guilty of shirking the obligations of his vocation. This rebuke leads to self-recognition. When John dies from ulcers caused by stress, the bishop offers Hugh St. Raymond's. Without hesitation, he says no, realizing that Catholicism should transcend ethnic tribalism and that priests must serve people in all conditions and places, even the most wretched of God's creatures.[42]

Monsignor Desmond Spellacy in John Gregory Dunne's 1977 novel, *True Confessions,* is another priest caught between the cities of God and men. As chancellor of the Los Angeles archdiocese, trouble-shooter and hatchet man for the cardinal, Desmond has to build cheaply and quickly the churches and schools needed in a rapidly ex-panding metropolitan area. To do this, he forms an alliance with Jack Amsterdam, vice lord turned contractor. In a vigilante raid on evil and hypocrisy, Desmond's homicide detective lieutenant brother Tom, formerly Amsterdam's bagman, pins a false murder charge on his ex-boss. The resulting scandal blocks Desmond's rise to auxiliary bishop. Instead, he ends his clerical career in a poor desert parish finding sat-isfaction and spiritual peace functioning as a priest rather than as a politician.[43]

Clerical frailties are main themes in the work of J. F. Powers. His highly regarded short stories and National Book Award novel, *Morte D'Urban,* satirize priests who invite money changers into the temple. They enjoy good food and drink, expensive cars, tailored clothes, and golf at the country club. Their font of wisdom is the *Reader's Digest.* Oblivious to poverty, social injustices, racism, and the messages of progressive papal encyclicals, they focus their wrath on fornication, adultery, contraception, sex in books and films, and communism.[44]

Generally priests have not been intellectuals, and many have fallen far short of sainthood. A few who were not suited for the church but were forced into the seminary by family or communal pressures or led there by neuroses and afraid to leave because of the contempt that many Irish Catholics have had for "spoiled priests" have succumbed to temptations of the flesh and bottle. The overwhelming majority, how-ever, have been intelligent, hardworking men and good shepherds to their flocks.

Irish families have offered their most talented daughters as well as their gifted sons to the church. Because of its semicloistered existence and its limited scope—teaching and nursing—the life and image of nuns has been more sacrificial and less prestigious than that of priests. Still, Irish-American fathers and mothers have had great respect for the sisterhood, and more of their daughters have entered it than those of other nationalities.

Irish-American nuns, like priests, have wanted to please and serve the Lord, but they have also derived more than spiritual benefits from their vocation. Today's Catholicism has fallen behind some other Christian communities in offering women leadership roles. But until recently, nuns were as close to clerical rank as women could get in either Christianity or Judaism. The sisterhood as well as the priesthood has provided career and social mobility. As teachers, nurses, and school and hospital administrators, nuns have been a successful community of professional women, respected by males for their secular competence and leadership when other women were not. For parents of parochial school children, for students in Catholic elementary and secondary schools and women's colleges, and for patients in Catholic hospitals, what "sister said" has been almost as commanding and infallible as what "father said."

American Catholics did not view the convent as a dreary place of drudgery and isolation. Instead, it was a pleasant and stimulating alternative to dismal, often loveless marriages to indifferent or abusive husbands and the care of many children. Sensitive, intelligent daughters of working-class parents, exposed to the sisterhood in parochial schools, saw new possibilities open to them in religious life: education, gentility, the companionship of other women, and the chance to be somebody. Nuns were role models for young women searching for achievement and respect beyond home and family.[45] Their example and their educational role assisted Irish-American women to become the most successful members of their sex in the United States. As educators, school administrators, union leaders, nurses, physicians, and lawyers, they added a women's leadership dimension to American society.[46]

Some Irish-American men have chosen to be brothers, most serving as teachers, a few as nurses. Although many teaching brothers are much better educated and more intellectual than diocesan priests, they never have had the same status in the Catholic community, and they have commanded less respect than nuns. The laity has had a hard time understanding why a bright, personable young man would settle for something less in the church than the priesthood. Their déclassé position suggests that brothers are exemplars of Christian humility and charity. In Ireland, however, the brotherhood can lead to social mobility. Unlike priests from the strong farming and middle classes, most, if not all, brothers have come from the ranks of the small farming and urban working classes. Their vocation has given them an education and a better social standing.[47] In the United States, however, Irish-American brothers come from the same social classes as priests. Most were inspired in their life choice by the dedication and piety they observed in the brothers who taught them in Catholic secondary schools and colleges.

THE TRIUMPH OF IRISH-AMERICAN CATHOLICISM

Following World War II, immigration restriction and assimilation reduced the European aspect of American Catholicism. During the prosperous 1920s, many Catholics, especially the Irish, continued on the road to affluence. Parishes and schools followed well-educated, prosperous Irish Americans into upper working- and middle-class city neighborhoods and out to the suburbs. Despite the social advances of the laity, many bishops and priests, especially in the East, still worrying that mainstream American values and culture threatened the faith, were uncertain as to the appropriate degree of Catholic involvement in national life. Manifestations of anti-Catholic nativism in the 1928 presidential election seemed to justify their apprehensions. Insecurity contributed to Irish and German working-class support for the isolationist, anti-Semitic populism of Father Charles Coughlin in the late 1930s.[48] It was also a reason for the endorsements that many clerics and a large portion of the Catholic press gave to General Francisco Franco during and after the Spanish civil war and to other dictators throughout the Latin Catholic world. The main body of Irish Americans, however, remained the key element in the urban ethnic Democratic coalition, which in 1932 put Franklin D. Roosevelt in the White House. When he rewarded Catholics, mostly Irish, for their allegiance to the Democratic party with a fair proportion of government offices, and when Americans banded together to resist economic depression, European fascism, and Japanese imperialism, anti-Catholic nativism became less popular and significant. A friendlier national environment and a growth of confidence among Irish Americans set the stage for their burst of energy and achievement following World War II.

Catholic clerical and newspaper praise of fascist regimes in the 1930s proved an embarrassment when the United States went to war against Germany and Italy in 1941, but American Catholic anticommunism harmonized with the post-1945 Cold War spirit. Catholic leaders reminded the nation that they had long warned against a Moscow-engineered international communist conspiracy to destroy capitalism and democracy, suggesting that members of their religious faith were the truest American patriots.

Anticommunist excesses were as dangerous to liberal democracy as the targeted enemy. A majority of Catholics, most notably Francis Cardinal Spellman, New York's archbishop, defended Senator Joseph McCarthy's search for alleged subversives in government and the armed forces.[49] Catholic influence on American foreign policy was a factor in its inability to distinguish between the forces of nationalism and communism in the Third World struggle against imperialism and colonialism. The interrelationship between Catholicism and American foreign policy is the main theme of James Carroll's 1984 novel, *Prince of Peace*. It argues that Cardinal Spellman and President Kennedy, though differing on domestic issues, shared the illusion that God commissioned the United States to purge the world of communism. This blasphemy led to the Vietnam quagmire.

Behind the bravado of Irish-American anticommunism lurked a continuing sense of alienation. But the Irish were not the only ones to join the anticommunist frenzy. Many Protestant Americans also thought Joe McCarthy was a hero and subscribed to a single-theme anticommunist foreign policy.[50] Despite a lingering defensiveness, Irish Americans had advanced far beyond the mental and physical ghettos they inhabited in the nineteenth and early twentieth centuries. In the post–World War II years they increased their social mobility, expanded their intellectual horizons, and enlarged the measure of their political and social liberalism. Kennedy's presidency reflected as well as inspired Irish-American idealism. Young people flocked to the Peace Corps, and the Irish added their voice to a growing demand for civil rights and social justice.

Kennedy's presidency coincided with the reign of Pope John XXIII. In the epoch of the two Johns, Irish-led American Catholicism brimmed with confidence, energy, and enthusiasm. New parishes and schools multiplied rapidly in cities and suburbs. Young people became priests, nuns, and brothers in droves, jamming convents, seminaries, and monasteries. Religious vocations had the same appeal for idealists as did service in the Peace Corps. A large majority of Irish-American Catholics enthusiastically supported John XXIII's effort to bring the church up-to-date (*aggiornamento*), and they expected the Vatican Council that convened in 1962 to accomplish that task.

Before Vatican II, American Catholicism offered mostly enthusiasm, funds, and loyalty to the universal church but had never made a unique contribution to its policies or values. But in 1962, when American bishops arrived in Rome for Vatican II, they were determined to express an American point of view. Divided and moderate in opinion, they played a relatively insignificant role in liturgical and theological discussions, but they did change the church's position on its relationship with the state and attitudes toward other religions. On the advice of John Courtney Murray, S.J., American bishops persuaded the council to adopt American principles on separation of church and state, freedom of religious expression and conscience, and friendly relations with Protestants and Jews. Because of the American ecumenical thrust, the Catholic church began to eliminate negative references to Jews from the liturgy and to discuss common beliefs and interests with Protestant churches.

When Vatican II ended in 1965, prosperous, respectable, and politically powerful American Catholics had made their church the most glittering jewel in the Roman crown. In 150 years the Irish had led American Catholicism from deferential insignificance, to ghetto defensiveness, and, finally, to confident national and international prominence and glory. But, as the old cliché says, perhaps a candle burns brightest just before it goes out.

Hints of a restless undercore in the American church surfaced in reactions to liturgical changes and to Pope Paul VI's encyclical, *Hu-*

manae Vitae. After Vatican II, the church introduced vernacular languages into Catholic services, turned the altar around so that the priest faced the people, permitted and encouraged popular forms of music to replace Gregorian chants, and emphasized sermons. Although liberals welcomed modernization in dogma and theology and conservatives opposed adjustments to modern situations, many of both persuasions lamented the loss of liturgical history and mystery. To most Catholics, the traditional liturgy was more important than theology. It provided security, a conviction that the church never changes. The English language, guitar music, and even Protestant hymns in the mass undermined confidence in the historical continuity of Roman Catholicism.[51]

Even more startling than liturgical innovations was the contents of *Humanae Vitae.* The liberal spirit of Vatican II and John XXIII's emphasis on reconciling the church to modern realities encouraged expectations that Rome would revise its position on contraception. Catholics in the United States and western Europe believed that the church would finally come to realize that sex in marriage is even more important as a bond of love than as an act of procreation. They also expected religious authority to understand that having children in a modern setting necessitated giving them opportunities in life through education, health care, and a decent standard of living. The financial burdens of responsible and loving parenting demanded limitations on the size of families. Realizations that the world population was exceeding its resources also supported lay demands for birth control.

The only concession that the church has made to family planning is to advocate self-denial during a woman's fertile period. Through experience, most Catholic's have little confidence in the rhythm system or "Roman Roulette." It often has failed and is more unnatural than contraception, placing restraints on the free flow of affection between husbands and wives. In 1967, a year before the encyclical, a papal commission recommended that the number of children in a family should be determined by the discretion and consciences of parents. On the basis of the sexual puritanism of Roman Catholicism, reinforced by the attitudes and frustrations of a celibate clergy, particularly those in positions of authority, and fearing that older Catholics who had suffered because of the church's position on birth control would resent a more liberated and happier sexual life and more joyful parenting by a newer generation, Paul VI rejected the recommendation of his own commission. Instead, in *Humanae Vitae*, he took a hard line. In response, the American Catholic majority, for the first time, openly rejected a papal directive on an issue of faith and morals.[52] Dissent on *Humanae Vitae* opened a Pandora's box of defiance among American Catholics. Many have gone on to disagree with the church on divorce, clerical celibacy, and an exclusively male priesthood. Although most oppose abortion on demand, a majority have decided that such extenuating circumstances as rape, incest, and the physical or psychological ill health of an expectant mother justify the termination of a pregnancy. Polls taken before Pope John Paul II's 1979 and 1987 visits to the United States indicated that although a majority of Catholics continued to proclaim their faith and their respect for the papal monarchy as a force uniting the church, their sexual attitudes and conduct do not diverge much from the American norm and that they are reluctant to accept Rome as an infallible guide to faith and morals.[53]

The defiance of American Catholics involves much more than negative reactions to traditional Catholic views on marriage, sexuality, Roman authority, and the nature and role of women. Economic affluence, social mobility, education, and suburbanization have altered the texture of American Catholicism. The vast majority of upper working- and middle-class Catholics are no longer culturally, intellectually, and socially isolated, and as they blend into the general community, sharing social, educational, and recreational situations and activities with Protestants, Jews, and nonbelievers, they are less reliant on the parish. In prosperous sections of the city and in the suburbs, Catholics often send their children to public schools, then to prestigious state or non-Catholic private colleges and universities.[54] Social and educational mixing has increased the number of interfaith marriages.

In contrast to their slavish adherence to Roman authority and doctrine, the progressive majority of the Irish-American Catholic hierarchy has tried to be innovative in liturgical matters and flexible on social and political questions. It has encouraged lay participation in the management of parish affairs, including finances. It also has issued liberal statements concerning interracial and social justice, disarmament, and foreign policy. Progressive American Catholic bishops have interpreted the right to life as meaning more than just opposing abortion. They believe that it necessitates an agenda on such matters as the alleviation of poverty, the elimination of war, and the end of capital punishment. In November 1988, just a week after the national election, Archbishop John May of St. Louis, president of the National Conference of Catholic Bishops, in a congratulatory message to President-elect George Bush, said that the hierarchy would continue to speak out on political, social, and economic matters: "Our people need to hear that the work we have begun on 'social issues'—whether on nuclear policy, human rights or advocacy of the unborn, the poor and the homeless—will continue."[55]

Recently, progressive Catholic forces in the United States have faced counterattacks from Rome and from within the American hierarchy. Determined to roll back post–Vatican II reforms, John Paul II has emphasized traditional Catholic sexual morality and prohibitions on contraception, a married priesthood, and the ordination of women. He also has made it clear that Roman Catholicism is authoritarian and not democratic. On June 26, 1990, the Congregation on Christian Doctrine, headed by Joseph Cardinal Ratzinger, made public a document sent out on May 24 instructing theologians that they must conform to the church's teaching magisterium and not express public dissent.[56] The instruction pointed particularly to the birth control question. This Vatican directive seriously jeopardizes the academic standing of Catholic theology in colleges and universities. To promote his "counterrevolution," John Paul II has filled open positions in the American and European hierarchies with conservatives and reactionaries.

In the United States, the conservative cause focuses on abortion. Starting in 1989 and continuing into 1990, some members of the American hierarchy, including such Irish Americans as John Cardinal O'Connor, archbishop of New York, his suffragan, Bishop Austin Vaughan, and Thomas Daily, bishop of Brooklyn, have put tremendous pressure on Catholic politicians who support choice in the abortion debate. In January 1990, Vaughan said that Mario Cuomo, New York's governor and potential presidential candidate, was in "serious risk of going to hell" because of his pro-choice views.

In June 1990, Archbishop O'Connor said that Catholic politicians who approve of abortion hazard excommunication. Bishop Daily endorsed this position.[57] Catholics and non-Catholics alike have to recognize the rights of bishops to speak out on issues that touch them and their church, but in their antiabortion crusade, prelates such as O'Connor have been crude and imprudent and narrow in their focus. For a believing Catholic, excommunication cuts off the sacramental instruments of saving grace and is a public disgrace in the eyes of the Catholic community. The victory of Lucy Killea in the November 1989 California senate election, after the bishop of San Diego told her that because of her pro-abortion stand she should no longer receive communion, indicates that the hostility of prelates might not seriously damage Catholic politicians and, in fact, could help them at the polls. But the techniques of the clergy in the abortion debate trouble many Americans and resurrect the issues of whether the Catholic church can properly function in a liberal-democratic American environment and whether Catholics in political office can properly represent constituents who are not members of their church.[58]

Another disturbing aspect of Catholic antiabortion fanaticism is its exclusiveness. Seldom do militant pro-life advocates verbally chastise or threaten to punish politicians who vote for the unrestricted sale of guns or for capital punishment and who vote against educational, health, or social welfare benefits for the poor. Evidently, for many so-called right-to-lifers, life in its full meaning ceases with birth.

Although liberal members of the laity remain critical of many church positions concerning sex and marriage and the role of women in Catholicism, they view kindly the progressive statements of bishops on social, economic, and foreign policy. By contrast, conservatives want the hierarchy and clergy to confine their attentions to religious matters. They refuse to accept the idea that the implications of Christian charity extend beyond the church and parish.

Many people from all segments of Catholic opinion find the tortured English, simple-minded hymns, and atrocious sermons in the post–Vatican II liturgy ugly, boring, or both. They miss the mystery, the tradition, the links with the past that Catholicism once provided. Consequently, there has been a large drop in the number of people attending mass and other religious services and in the use of the Sacrament of Penance. Catholics also express their disapproval of or indifference to the contemporary church by a significant decline in financial contributions. In most parts of the United States, bishops and priests are finding it difficult to meet diocesan and parish religious, educational, and social obligations with a rapidly diminishing income. Consequently, in many cities, such as Chicago and Detroit, the church has thought it necessary to close down parochial schools and to consolidate parishes. Some bishops are attempting to convince the laity to contribute a certain proportion of their income to the church, describing this program as stewardship.

Even more critical for the American church than the money problem is the personnel shortage. From 1966 to 1969, an estimated 3,413 priests resigned. In 1964, 44,500 future priests were preparing for ordination. Twenty years later, the number had dropped to around 12,000 and 241 seminaries had closed. In the 1960s, the church also began to experience a decline in the number of women religious. From 1965, a peak year, to 1980, the number of nuns declined from 181,421 to 126,517. In 1965, 12,539 brothers taught high school or college or worked in hospitals. In 1980, their numbers had dropped to 8,563. With so many leaving and so few entering religious life, the average age of priests, nuns, and brothers has increased. Older people in any profession tend to become less dynamic and more inflexible.[59] The shortage of priests portends a future when many Catholics will experience substitute services for Sunday mass. Declining numbers of nuns and brothers seriously threaten the continued existence of a significant and vital Catholic educational system. Parish elementary schools and Catholic high schools cannot afford the salaries demanded and needed by competent lay teachers.

Clerical quality as well as quantity has suffered in recent years. Because Irish and other ethnic families no longer offer their best and brightest to the church, the intelligence and dedication of seminarians have declined. "Air heads" and pseudo-intellectuals who substitute pop sociology and culture for theology, philosophy, and a sense of history, such as Porter in J. F. Powers's *Wheat That Springeth Green*, appear frequently on altars and in pulpits. Their silly sermons complement vacuous folk masses. In addition to the shortage of priests and the decline in their quality, many Catholics are disturbed by an increasing trend toward homosexuality. Estimates indicate that from 20 to 40 percent of priests are gay. Another problem faced by church authorities and an embarrassed laity is the numerous scandals and lawsuits involving pedophile priests.[60]

Celibacy is largely blamed for the shortage of priests and the declining quality and homosexuality so prominent in religious life. Normal sexual urges and the need for love and companionship from members of the opposite sex have deterred some people from entering religious life and prompted others to abandon their vocations. But celibacy does not adequately explain the church's personnel difficulties. The Anglican church does not preclude a married clergy and has a higher percentage of gay priests than Catholicism.[61] Perhaps the large number of homosexual or intellectually mediocre priests in Anglicanism and Catholicism and ministers in other Christian churches says more about the status, image, contents, relevance, and message of Christianity in contemporary America than it does about sexual frustration.

In American Catholicism, the falling numbers of priests, nuns, and brothers and their intellectual and other deficiencies indicate that the religious life has lost influence and status. Because of celibacy, the church always attracted some people with homosexual tendencies or minimal sexual appetites, but the power, dignity, and respect once attached to the priesthood, sisterhood, and brotherhood aided its members in sublimating sexual urges and in directing their energies to the service of God. The glory and importance of their callings compensated for sexual denial and the loneliness of the rectory, convent, or monastery.

In contemporary America, priests and nuns no longer have much standing in the Irish-American community. Bright young Catholic men and women now have alternative routes to prestige and success. Because of opportunities in business and the professions, parents have ceased to pressure their children to enter the church. They are as proud of their professor, doctor, lawyer, and company executive daughters and sons as they once were of nuns and priests. With prospects for women improving so rapidly, they no longer have to choose between marriage and the convent.

In several 1960s and 1970s novels about the Jersey City Irish, especially *The God of Love, Romans, Countrymen, and Lovers, The Sandbox Tree, The Good Shepherd,* and *Promises to Keep,* Thomas Fleming discussed existing and anticipated reasons for dissension and revolt in post–World War II Irish-American Catholicism. Conceding that their religion once sheltered the Irish cast adrift in urban industrial America, Fleming argued that this function had become redundant and negative. After the retreat of nativism and a national adjustment to and accommodation of diversity, the Catholic mental ghetto and its authoritarian incompatibility with the American liberal spirit prevented the Irish from taking advantage of many opportunities.

According to Fleming, Catholic colleges and universities were irrelevant medieval intellectual detours from modern American realities. Their suburbanite graduates smugly criticized the materialism and secularism of other Americans while congratulating themselves on their superior virtue. But Catholic business and professional men were as unscrupulous money-grubbers as non-Catholics. The middle-class Catholic marriages in Fleming's books feature strife and indifference. The Roman ban on contraception made women into baby-making machines and entrapped them and their husbands in loveless, contentious unions. Compelled to sublimate the natural physical impulses and desires of love, they copulated by the thermometer and the calendar, and the church called it natural.[62]

During his 1979 and 1987 travels in the United States, Pope John Paul II had other explanations for American Catholic rebelliousness. He lectured his audiences, blaming their secularism, hedonism, and materialism for the crisis in their church. No doubt, material comforts and the abandonment of Catholic puritanism have contributed to the decline in American Catholics' submissiveness to church authority. But present-day American Catholic attitudes express more than self-interest and pleasure seeking. They also represent a new Catholic Americanism. The old Gibbons-Ireland brand was superficial, never really facing up to the incompatibility between Roman authoritarianism and American liberalism. Contemporary Irish Americans, successful and integrated into the mainstream, are abandoning their contradictory loyalties to Western civilization's most open political and most closed religious systems. They are decompartmentalizing their minds. No longer does the separation of church and state create a gulf between religion and politics. Irish Americans and other Catholics in the United States are insisting that their church show the same respect for individual rights and dignity, for the integrity of private conscience, and for the inquiring mind as their country does. Although not as devout or obedient as before, they still consider themselves Catholic, at least in a cultural sense. While their bishops are reluctant to quarrel with papal authority, in the choice between Roman authoritarian and American liberal values, they have chosen the latter.[63] Many are thinking and some are saying "no popery here."

1. Members of a large 1880s Irish family gather outside their thatched roof cottage. A majority of the children from such families would be living in American cities by the time they became adults. Courtesy of the National Library of Dublin.

2. Irish shanty town on New York's Fifth Avenue, between 116th and 117th
Streets (home of the High Rock Gang). Courtesy of the New-York Historical
Society.

3. Pictured at their farm near Wexford, Iowa, the family of Patrick Ryan from County Limerick after the funeral of his wife, Margaret Guider Ryan from Tipperary. Courtesy of Anne Siewers Coyne.

4. Cartoon portraying both Jews and Irish as ugly people, reflecting American anti-Catholic nativism. From the collection of John and Selma Appel, East Lansing, Mich.

5. St. Patrick's Church, Chicago's first West Side Irish parish church. Such churches functioned as peasant villages in an urban setting, providing social community, educational opportunities, and religious comfort. Courtesy of the *New World*, Chicago.

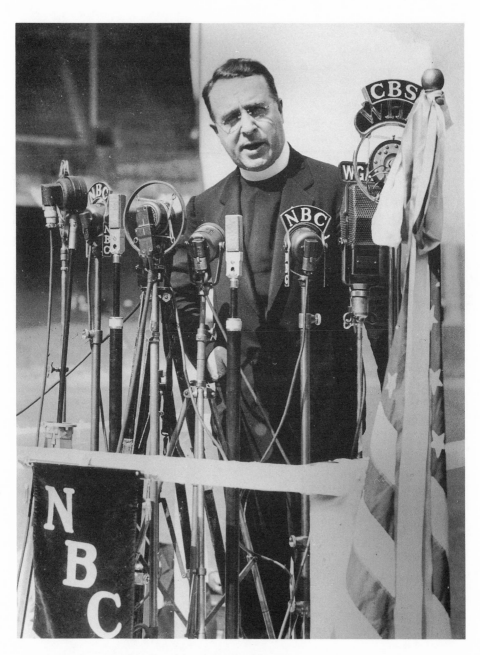

6. Father Charles Coughlin, populist demagogue of the 1930s. Reprinted with permission from the *Chicago Sun-Times*.

7. Irish America sent its best talent into religion and politics, represented here by Chicago's auxiliary bishop, Bernard J. Sheil, with prominent Irish Catholic layman G. Howland Shaw, and Mayor Edward J. Kelly. Courtesy of the *New World*, Chicago.

8. Mayor Richard J. Daley and John F. Kennedy in a Chicago torchlight parade two days before the 1960 election. Courtesy of Daniel P. Lydon.

9. Congressman Thomas P. (Tip) O'Neill of Massachusetts, one of several
Irish Americans who have served as Speaker of the House of Representatives.
Reprinted with permission from the *Chicago Sun-Times*.

10. Supreme Court Justice William J. Brennan, Jr., champion of civil liberties and social welfare. Courtesy of the Supreme Court of the United States.

11. George Meany, President of the AFL-CIO, 1955 to late 1980s, one of many Irish Americans who have played an important role in the development of the American labor movement. Courtesy of Daniel P. Lydon.

12. John O'Mahony, founder of the Fenian Brotherhood. Courtesy of R. V. Comerford.

4

Power with or Without Purpose?

Catholicism has been the cohesive force, the cultural essence of Irish America; politics has used its talent and given it power. In 1894, a nativist enemy John Paul Bocock, lamented the Irish "genius for municipal government or at least for getting political office."[1] Still, he had to concede that they played the American political game with skill and dexterity. Twenty-two years later, Sir Cecil Spring Rice, Britain's ambassador to the United States, described Irish Americans as "the best politicians in the country . . . with unequaled power of political organization."[2] In 1976, a scholar, James P. Walsh, entitled a book *The Irish: America's Political Class.*[3]

Accusations of Irish-American graft and corruption have balanced tributes to their political skills. Critics have complained that once in office they have abused power or failed to manage it constructively. Nineteenth-century nativists interpreted Irish-American politics, like Catholicism, as an assault on Anglo-Protestant institutions and values. Bocock wondered, "How has it come about that the system of government so admirably conceived by the fathers has worked out so perfectly in national affairs and so poorly in municipal affairs . . . since from the turbulence of municipal politics the Irish-American has plucked both wealth and power?"[4]

Many Anglo-American Protestants took offense at the intense Irish Catholic political influence in rapidly expanding industrial America. Their concept of the American ideal had both religious and sectarian foundations. The largely Calvinist component of seventeenth-century Protestant immigration came to North America to establish a pure Christian commonwealth, free from Roman corruption. During the eighteenth century, Enlightenment thought gave a more secular dimension to Americanism. A belief in and emphasis

89

on progress through the use of reason, leading to the eventual perfection of mankind, found expression in Thomas Jefferson's portrait of the ideal American as a virtuous, self-sufficient, and independent small farmer. American nativism blended religious and Enlightenment secular thought into an image of the United States as a Protestant, rural nation. These native Protestants reacted in anger and fear when millions of Irish Catholics entered their country, settled in cities and swelled the urban population, generated American industrialism with their unskilled labor, and gradually seized the reins of city governments.

Complaints about Hibernian politics have come from within as well as without the Irish-American community. In 1963, scholar-politician Senator Daniel Patrick Moynihan, in his capacity as a sociology professor, argued that though the Irish have been remarkably gifted in the acquisition of political power, they have been inadequate in its application. He said that their Catholic peasant provincialism made them guardians of the status quo. According to Moynihan, Irish political management has prevented cities from responding to new challenges of urban decay and the problems of its recent African- and Hispanic-American settlers: "The Irish were immensely successful in politics. They ran the city. But the very parochialism and bureaucracy that enabled them to succeed in politics prevented them from doing much with government. . . . They never thought of politics as an instrument of social change."[5]

Anticipating Moynihan, Thomas J. Fleming's 1961 novel, *All Good Men*, charges Irish politicians in New Jersey with "ineptitude and rotten morals" as well as provincialism. Disgusted with boss rule, Larry Donahue, a reform crusader, complains: "I'm serious. Thirty years of absolute power. What would a Jew have done with it? Or a New England Yankee? We'd be living in a dream city with equal housing and equal opportunity and equal justice for everybody."[6]

Another Irish-American writer, Edward R. F. Sheehan, accuses his people of practicing the politics of revenge as well as corruption, ineptitude, and peasant Catholic conservatism. In his 1970 novel, *The Governor*, he describes many Irish politicians in Boston as incarnations of Irish historical memories. Attempting to avenge Anglo-Protestant oppressions on both sides of the Atlantic, they conquered and pillaged the leading urban citadel of Yankee power. Francis Xavier Cassidy, commissioner of public works, is such an Irish agent of retribution: "There, in those deep and misty bogs of his mind, he inexorably relived all the nightmares of his race, even the nightmares he never dreamed. There in the most wretched hovels of his soul, he felt the pangs of potato hunger and the British lash against his back, only to take flight across a hostile sea to meaner hovels still and horrid mills whose owners paid him pennies and then posted notices at their gates NO IRISH NEED APPLY."[7]

Sheehan's James Michael Curley, the often elected and highly popular Boston mayor, is another "tribal hero who squandered his remarkable talents and devoted a lifetime to settling old scores, a crippled warrior egging on an amused mob of shanty Irish in the sacking of the Yankee Troy."[8] James Carroll, in his 1976 novel, *Mortal Friends*, presents a more polished literary portrait of Curley than Sheehan's. Carroll's Curley is charismatic and possesses considerable political genius but is flawed by paranoia, narrow vision, and power lust. Instead of leading his people into a cooperative effort with Anglo-Protestants for the common good and toward an appreciation for the cultural and historical heritage of a great city, Curley manipulated their defensive ghetto mentality into a Kulturkampf with the Yankees, paralyzing Irish social mobility and hampering the progress of Boston.[9]

William V. Shannon's scholarly judgment of Curley reinforces the interpretations of Sheehan and Carroll. According to Shannon, Boston's Irish champion

> exploited the sufferings and the inexperience, the warm sentiment, the fears, and the prejudices of his own people to perpetuate his personal power. He solved nothing; he moved toward no larger understanding; he opened no new lines of communication. . . . For more than thirty years, Curley kept the greater part of the Boston populace half drunk with fantasies, invective, and showmanship . . . but he nevertheless committed two mortal sins against the public good; his bad example debased the moral tone of political life in a city for a generation, and his words distorted the people's understanding of reality . . . and to the end of his days he remained a self-crippled giant on a provincial stage.[10]

During the 1960s and 1970s a number of historians and social scientists rejected nativist attacks on Irish political graft and corruption and the complaints of novelists and scholars that the Irish impact on American urban government was exclusive and provincial. They argued that machine politics elevated the Irish from poverty to affluence, moved American liberalism from individualism to communalism, and included the formerly excluded in the American democratic process. They credited Irish urban politicians with offering services to people ignored by Anglo-Protestant politicians and with incorporating Jews and other Catholic ethnics into Democratic political organizations.[11]

In his recent analysis of Irish-American politics, *Rainbow's End: Irish-Americans and the Dilemmas of Urban Machine Politics, 1840–1985*, Steven P. Erie debates the revisionists, repeating charges of parochialism and exclusiveness, insisting that Irish political machines reserved jobs and power for their own people and tried to satisfy other Catholics and Jews with tokens: symbolic recognition, services (vendor licenses), and benefits (labor legislation). Only when other ethnics became restless did Irish politicians in such cities as New York and Jersey City reluctantly spread jobs and patronage around. In Pittsburgh and Chicago, however, where the Democrats had to compete with Republicans for the general ethnic vote, Irish politicians did show some concern for the interests of other groups. Erie also rejects the notion that politics provided the Irish with a route to economic and social mobility. He says that the jobs offered by politics froze them in blue-collar working- and bureaucratic lower-middle-class occupations.[12]

THE MARCH TO POWER

Technologically unskilled Irish immigrants entered nineteenth-century America with political talents learned at home. Daniel O'Connell's mass agitation for Catholic emancipation in the 1820s and his effort to repeal the Union in the 1840s had mobilized the Irish Catholic masses and instructed them in the tactics of public opinion pressure politics. This experience and their familiarity with the English language and Anglo-Protestant constitutionalism aided them in the acquisition of political power in the United States. To a certain extent, political skills compensated for economic deficiencies and yielded job opportunities.

Lacking the agricultural expertise to cultivate vast farms and put off by the loneliness of spacious rural America, the Irish settled in the United States as pioneers of the urban ghetto. Their transition from peasant Ireland to the cities of the United States created social and psychological tensions that often resulted in failure and the virulence of American nativism. But Irish concentrations in metropolitan centers had political advantages. They grew up with urban industrial America, taking charge of its political destiny.

By tightening the bonds between Irish and Catholic identities, American nativism also aided the advance of Irish political power. Defensively, Irish-American Catholicism created an institutional alternative featuring schools that preserved its subculture and guarded against Protestant proselytism and a parish community that served both as a fortress and a sanctuary against nativist enemies. The institutional alternative, plus the insularity of Irish parish life, seemed to confirm nativist charges that Catholicism was indeed an alien creed and culture. Nevertheless, the Irish Catholic ghetto and its subculture encouraged the solidarity and self-sufficiency essential to effective political organization.

Attitudinal contrasts with Anglo-Protestants concerning the importance of politics was another factor assisting the emergence of Irish political power. The individualistic liberal Enlightenment ethos encouraged Anglo-Americans to believe that government that governed least governed best. Because politics seemed to be of minor significance, they sent their best talent into business. Despite Steven P. Erie's thesis that politics directed the Irish into vocational dead ends, they had no choice but to accept "power and security" over "money and status."[13] A paucity of economic skills and the intensity of Anglo-Protestant nativist prejudice barred the Irish from the higher echelons of trade and commerce so they selected politics as the avenue to fame, fortune, and influence. They invested their most promising young people in the Catholic church and in politics. In fact, successful clerical and political personalities were similar. Irish bishops and priests who commanded a growing Catholic church in the United States and nurtured it into becoming the largest, most powerful, and wealthiest

religious body in the country accomplished that feat more with political acumen than spiritual fervor. The American branch of Roman
Catholicism exemplifies the Irish political genius and style.

An overwhelming majority of the American Irish attached
themselves to the Democratic party. Afflicted by Protestant ascendancy and landlordism in Ireland, they appreciated egalitarian Jeffersonian and Jacksonian democracy. Still, their affiliation with the
Democrats was more functional than idealistic. Other parties were
more nativist and less hospitable to immigrants. Democratic politicians speeded the naturalization of Irish newcomers and provided
them with jobs in exchange for their votes.

Irish politics is pragmatic, however, and in certain areas, such as
Ohio and Pennsylvania, where Democrats were weak, they sometimes
joined the Republican party. Two interesting fictional politicians wear
Republican labels: Mary Deasy's Aloyisius O'Shaughnessy of Caroli,
Ohio, and John O'Hara's Mike Slattery of Gibbsville, Pennsylvania.[14]
In style and performance they are carbon copies of Democratic poli-
ticians in other novels.

Irish Americans formed political battalions of voters, fighting
Whigs and later Republicans with fists as well as ballots. Sometimes in
the guise of volunteer fire companies, Irish street gangs protected
Democrats on the way to and at the polls and tried to prevent members of other parties from voting. Violent American urban politics was
associated with prizefighting. Each faction had its champion. John
Morrissey, who in 1853 became American heavyweight champion,
was a muscle enforcer for Tammany Hall. Later, he became a congressman and, surprisingly, a reformer. Maguire in Ramona Stewart's
1968 novel, *Casey*, is a fictionalized version of Morrissey.[15]

Serving in the Democratic ranks was a short-term expedient.
Slowly but surely the Irish took charge of their own neighborhoods,
building mini-organizations within the general party structure, and
rose from precinct or ward captains to aldermen without surrendering
direction of local units. In their drive for power, Irish politicians exploited Catholic solidarity and used saloons as political clubs and police and fire department appointments and city jobs as patronage
sources to recruit campaign workers and voters.

Much to the consternation of nativists, by the 1890s the Irish
were in command of the urban wing of the Democratic party. In "The

Irish Conquest of the Cities," Bocock discusses an "Irish oligarchy" controlling such American cities as New York, Brooklyn, Jersey City, Hoboken, Chicago, Buffalo, Albany, Troy, Pittsburgh, St. Louis, Kansas City, Omaha, New Orleans, and San Francisco and exercising considerable influence in many others.[16]

In 1880, shipping magnate William Grace became New York's first Irish Catholic mayor. Boston's Hugh O'Brien won the same honor in 1886 and Chicago's John Patrick Hopkins in 1893. Having one of their own in the mayor's office was an ego lift for Irish voters, but their politicians had higher priorities. They worked for and got control of city councils and obtained a voice in the selection of Democratic candidates for local, state, and national office.

Irish political machines have captivated the imagination of novelists, historians, and social scientists. New York's Tammany Hall was the most fascinating of the early machines. Founded in 1789, the Society of St. Tammany, bearing the name of a famous seventeenth-century Delaware Indian tribal chief, was started in several cities as a fraternal and charitable organization. During the 1790s, Aaron Burr converted the New York branch into a political club to oppose Alexander Hamilton and advance his own ambitions. It quickly gained control of the local Democratic party. At the start, Tammany was strongly nativist, banning Irish Catholics from membership. By the 1850s, however, increased immigration had made the Irish most important Democratic voting bloc in New York, forcing a policy change in Tammany. In the 1860s, Irish politicians were prominent lieutenants of Tammany's Scots-Irish grand sachem, William Marcy Tweed. Attentive to their needs, Tweed was a hero to the Irish. He had their affection even after his disgrace and fall. Although they offered bread and circuses to their voting supporters, Tweed and his Irish politician comrades were more interested in accumulating private fortunes than in achieving constructive social change.

After Tweed went to prison in 1871 for political corruption, "Honest" John Kelly took the Tammany helm. He did not inject any idealism into Tammany's operation, but he reduced its blatant thievery and gave it a tightly knit organizational structure. As a devout practicing Catholic (John Cardinal McCloskey was his second wife's uncle), Kelly decided that the church offered a model for restructuring Tammany into a centralized monarchy with a pyramid chain of command.[17] In contrast to Tammany's efficiency, Irish politics in Boston, especially after 1900, resembled feudal chaos with chiefs controlling pockets of power all over the city and jealously guarding their bits of turf. And until the Kelly-Nash machine of the 1930s, perfected by Richard J. Daley in the 1950s, Chicago's Irish politics resembled Boston's disorder more than the smooth effectiveness of New York.[18]

Whether operating as the Tammany monolith or as mini-ward machines in Boston or Chicago, Irish-American politics featured corruption. Politicians awarded construction or transportation contracts for payoffs. They often authorized the construction of roads or public service buildings on property they owned, turning a nice profit. In collusion with police officials, many permitted illegal gambling, prostitution, and sale of alcoholic beverages in exchange for bribes from gangsters and vice lords. They also loaded city payrolls with political supporters, depending on an army of patronage workers to strengthen their power and hold on to their offices.

Chicago exhibited the worst aspects of Irish-American political graft. From the 1880s through the 1920s, especially when Carter Harrison I and II were mayor and the Irish dominated the city council, gambling and prostitution flourished. Politicians and policemen prospered from vice payoffs. Aldermen padded their wallets by selling city franchises to businessmen, a practice known as boodling. Johnny Powers, "Bathhouse" John Coughlin, and "Hinky Dink" Kenna were among the most notorious boodlers As Brian De Palma's 1987 film *The Untouchables* accurately and graphically describes, during the prohibition era Chicago's Irish politicians and police officials were pawns of Al Capone and other mobsters.[19]

Tammany's Richard Croker exemplified corrupt Irish urban politics. Croker, the son of a Protestant veterinarian, left Cork at age three with his family and emigrated to New York. Because his education was limited to elementary school and he was not self-educated, Croker was an ignorant man. Nevertheless, starting as a Tammany muscle man, he climbed its leadership ladder. By age twenty-five, Croker was an alderman. Crude but shrewd, he grasped the connections between Irish religious and ethnic identities and turned Catholic. His prospects dimmed in 1874, when he spent some time in jail accused, probably wrongly, of killing in a political brawl a worker for

"Famous" Jimmy O'Brien, a Kelly foe, and once Croker's patron. After his acquittal, Croker earned the gratitude and became the protégé of the Tammany leader. When Kelly died in 1886, the younger man succeeded him as boss. Croker's reign was a record of ruthless dictatorial power and massive corruption. When scandal finally forced his resignation in 1903, he settled as a multimillionaire in Ireland to breed and race horses.[20]

The Irish hibernicized American political graft, but they did not invent it. Corruption in American politics existed before the Irish arrived and continued in places where they had little impact. Jacksonian democracy established the American political principle "to the victor belongs the spoils." And when the Irish won they took the awards that went with power. The so-called politics of revenge is every bit as American as Irish. Scots-Irish boss Tweed was far more corrupt than his successors, Kelly and Croker. Huey P. Long in Louisiana and Memphis boss, Edward H. Crump offer twentieth-century evidence that Anglo-Americans in both rural and urban politics have operated machines loaded with graft and corruption.[21] Finley Peter Dunne's Martin Dooley, fictionalized saloon keeper and social historian of the turn-of-the-century Chicago Irish, observed that Irish lads, making their political way in the United States, adopted Anglo-Protestant business ethics. He suggested that in the rough and tumble of urban America, the Irish were more victims than culprits.[22]

Irish-American politicians often justified graft as payment for beneficial personal and community services. In Joseph F. Dinneen's novel *Ward Eight*, set in the late nineteenth- and early twentieth-centuries, Hughie Donnelly, boss of Boston's North End at a time when it was in transition from Irish to Italian, told his young assistant, Tim O'Flaherty, that grafters operated a more prosperous, contented city than Anglo reformers intent on business-oriented government. Although grafters spent tax dollars recklessly, they took only 10 percent off the top, far less than bankers' fees, and they put the rest in public works projects that provided employment for the poor and at least temporarily beautified the city. In contrast, cautious reformers restricted urban economic growth.[23] Sociologist Terry N. Clark gives support to Donnelly's statement. His analysis of fifty-one cities between 1880 and 1968 indicates that the larger the percentage of

Irish citizens, the lesser the amount of political reform but the greater the increase in government expenditures benefiting lower socio-economic groups.[24]

Moynihan's contention that Irish Catholic peasant conservatism obstructed city government's response to new economic, social, and demographic challenges distorts the intent and nature of early American reformism and the personality of Irish-American politics. Many proponents of good government were more determined to abolish such social evils as drunkenness, gambling, and prostitution than they were to use political power to attain social justice. Others who were intent on improving the lot of the destitute did not understand or empathize with the religion or the values of non-Anglos in urban America. They resembled British government officials during the Great Famine in Ireland who believed that Irish poverty and hunger were products of a faulty national character, induced by a superstitious and authoritarian Roman Catholicism that encouraged ignorance, laziness, and sloth.[25] So much of Anglo-Protestant philanthrophy was offered with such condescending haughtiness that it violated the dignity and alienated the goodwill of its recipients.

Although Moynihan exaggerated the political conservatism of Irish Catholics and, like Larry Donahue in *All Good Men*, the selfless benevolence of Anglo-Protestant reformers, he accurately caught the cautious bent of Irish minds. Their Catholic skepticism questioned the Enlightenment tenets of the natural goodness and perfectibility of man and the inevitability of progress that are fundamental American values. Philosophically, the Irish view of man and the world is far more Burkeian than Jeffersonian, accepting a dark side of human nature, the existence of objective evil, and the impact of irrational forces on the human personality and the historical process.

Late nineteenth- and early twentieth-century Anglo-Saxon and Anglo-Protestant laissez-faire individualism added a Social Darwinist, survival-of-the-fittest racial apologia for unrestrained capitalism.[26] Consequently, the socially conservative, often cynical Irish have been more productive as practical reformers than ideological liberals. They have tried to improve rather than perfect society, always conscious of blending change with traditional values, without intellectual or emotional antipathy to government taking responsibility for trying to bring some equipoise to the social order.[27] Balancing the Anglicized and Romanized aspects of their ethnic personality, the Irish have created a unique political style that blends a commitment to liberal democracy with a Catholic communitarian rather than an individualistic view of society.

In his revisionist look at Irish-American politics, Steven P. Erie points out that it was not until the twentieth century that machine bosses became generous benefactors to the poor. Hesitant to alienate the Anglo-Protestant upper and middle classes, they were conservative taxers and spenders. Without much bread to offer, they tried, with limited success, to please voters with circuses. Dissatisfied with the poor return for their votes, many Irish and German workers in New York gave Tammany a scare by supporting Henry George, the socialist proponent of the single tax, and his United Labor party in the municipal elections of 1886 and 1887. Cooperation between city, state, and federal governments in the pre-Depression twentieth century, the movement of many tax-hostile middle-class people to the suburbs, and the willingness of those who remained in the city to contribute to civic improvements increased the financial resources of machines. They were able to award a considerable number of jobs directly and indirectly related to politics but were reluctant to give the non-Irish anything but symbolic recognition, public services, and beneficial economic and social legislation.[28]

No doubt, the affability and generosity of Irish politicians have been romanticized in fiction and even in scholarship. Nevertheless, Erie underestimates the importance of the symbolic recognition, services, and benefits that the Irish extended to others. Catholics and Jews could not expect such perquisites from an indifferent Anglo-Protestant establishment. Irish politicians changed relationships between government and the citizenry. Dispensing buckets of coal on cold, wintry days, distributing food baskets to the hungry, and finding jobs for the unemployed were done more to gain votes than as a manifestation of Christian charity or an ideologically liberal concern for the needy, but the services of Irish politicians did contain an element of Catholic communalism. They developed an inefficient, graft-ridden social justice system, but it, rather than Anglo individualistic liberalism, was the precursor of the American welfare state.

Novels offer some of the best perceptions of the Irish political style. Dinneen's *Hughie Donnelly* is modeled on Michael Lomasney, boss of Boston's West End. Donnelly looks after the comprehensive needs of his constituents, finding them jobs and housing, making sure that they have food on the table. In addition, he solves personal and family problems. When there are legal difficulties, he provides bail and a lawyer. When there is sickness, he sends a physician. If there is a death in the family, he manages a wake and a funeral. He supervises considerable graft but little reaches his own pocket, and what does is justified as small payment for large services. He needs and wants loyalty more than money. His politics evolve from tribalism to accommodation. When Italians begin to replace the Irish in ward eight, he assimilates them into the Democratic organization, forging a multi-ethnic coalition.

A similar fictional figure is Galway-born John Gorman in Edwin O'Connor's 1956 novel, *The Last Hurrah*. Gorman, "a tall, superlatively erect old man," had come from Ireland to the United States as a young boy. Although he never held public office, politics was his profession. For fifty years he was a ward boss. He never married, and, like a celibate parish priest, he was preoccupied with the people of his district.

> It was he who found jobs and homes for the recently arrived, who supplied funds in time of distress, who arranged for hospitalization and the payment of medical bills, who gave the son of the family his start in life and the subsequent necessary pushes up the ladder, who built the playgrounds for the children of his populous district, and who, in these days when the aged, the helpless, and the indigent had come to depend increasingly upon government beneficence, saw to it that the baffling complexity of preliminary paper work was solved and that funds were ultimately secured. He had won for his efforts the devotion and the obedience of most who lived within the ward, and this in turn, as it was the largest ward in the city, had given him an extraordinary political significance.[29]

Gorman is the lieutenant of Frank Skeffington, a more polished, kinder version of James Michael Curley. His many years as mayor of a New England city are blemished by corruption, but, like Hugh Donnelly, he has given away most of the money that came his way. His public works projects are expensive and often unnecessary, but they provide employment and recreational and health care facilities for the needy. Handsome, witty, articulate, and charismatic, a conscientious attender of wakes, weddings, church socials, and public functions, Skeffington has meshed Irish, Italian, and Jewish voters into a powerful political force.

Although fiction often smoothed the rough edges and brightened the dark corners of Irish-American politics, real-life counterparts of Donnelly, Gorman, and Skeffington lived in and worked the precincts and wards of urban America. Between 2:00 A.M. and midnight on one day, Tammany's George Washington Plunkitt bailed a bartender out of jail; visited the scene of a fire to console its victims and to find them a new place to live; visited a police court and persuaded the judge to release six drunken constituents and paid the fine of a seventh; recruited a lawyer to aid a widow threatened by a landlord with eviction; found employment for four people in his district; "sat conspicuously up front" at an Italian funeral; met with district captains to discuss political strategy; went to a church fair and bought ice cream for little girls and liquor for their fathers; listened to the grievances of a dozen pushcart operators; and attended a Jewish wedding after sending an expensive gift to the bride.[30]

Johnny Powers, saloon keeper and alderman of the nineteenth ward from 1888 to 1927, was a Chicago version of Boston's Michael Lomasney and New York's George Washington Plunkitt. Powers provided bail for jailed constituents and fixed their court cases; paid rents for hard-pressed tenants; placed thousands on the public payroll; attended weddings and funerals, bringing presents to the former and flowers to the latter, paying the undertaker for impoverished bereaved families and even providing carriages to the cemetery; supplied railroad passes for people who had to visit far-off sick relatives; purchased tickets for benefits and church bazaars; and, during the 1897 Christmas season, personally distributed six tons of turkeys and four tons of ducks and geese to people in the neighborhood. Another resident of his multiethnic ward was Hull House's Jane Addams. Although she had to admit that he and other Irish politicians demonstrated more concern for the poor than did Anglo reformers, Addams frequently joined good government advocates in efforts to unseat the alderman.

But Powers always prevailed, boasting that his many saloons sent more voters to the polls than all of the exhortations of clergymen, reformers, and social workers.[31]

Other ethnics often resented Irish power and influence in the American Catholic church, urban politics, and the labor movement and, as Erie argues, their reluctance to share the spoils of political power. Yet the careers of Powers, Plunkitt, and Lomasney provide strong evidence that Irish politicians were effective in dealing with Germans, Italians, Poles, and Jews as well as the Irish. They protected their constituents from the indifference and hostility of the Anglo-Protestant establishment. Many ignored the graft taken by Irish politicians, viewing them as modern Robin Hoods robbing the rich to help the poor.

It was natural and understandable that Irish politicians took better care of their own than other people, but they were gifted power brokers, melding groups that hated each other—Poles and Lithuanians, Serbs and Croats, Germans and Slavs, Jews and gentiles—into one Democratic voting bloc. Irish politicians could even resolve problems between diverse factions within ethnic groups. In John Ford's 1958 film version of *The Last Hurrah*, conservative Italian members of the Knights of Columbus want a statue of Christopher Columbus in their neighborhood. A more radical element demands one of Garibaldi. Skeffington pleases both by providing a monument to Mother Cabrini, America's first saint.[32]

Perhaps the greatest service that the Irish provided other Catholic ethnics was teaching them to adjust to American politics. Unlike most other European Catholics, the Irish came to the United States committed to the principles of liberal democracy and familiar with their operation in an Anglo-Protestant context. Through their religious, political, and labor leadership they were able to prevent the complete isolation of Catholic America by integrating it into the national political consensus.

FROM POWER TO PRAGMATIC IDEALISM

Economic and social mobility broadened the scope of Irish-American politics, encouraging it to become more attentive to matters of principle and less to the acquisition of power for its own sake.[33] As times changed, Irish politicians were more likely to emerge from the legal profession than from the ranks of saloon keepers or morticians (not necessarily a moral improvement). They also became increasingly prominent on the state and national political scenes.

Al Smith's rise from Tammany Hall to the governorship of New York and his accomplishments in Albany represented new dimensions of Irish-American politics. Though conservatively skeptical about political remedies for social and economic ills, Smith pioneered legislation protecting women and children in the workplace. He also introduced a large measure of efficiency and competency into the state bureaucracy. His governorship established precedents that guided Franklin D. Roosevelt's New Deal policies. Smith's achievements earned him the Democratic party's 1928 presidential nomination. His harsh urban accent, ever-present cigar, brown derby hat, opposition to prohibition, and scorn for rural and small-town America established him in many Protestant minds as the quintessential urban Irish Catholic politician. This perception rekindled nativist fanaticism, recruiting new members for the Ku Klux Klan. During the election campaign, fiery crosses burned on Catholic lawns. Even without the religious issue, Herbert Hoover, the Republican candidate, representing the party in power during an economic boom, would have easily defeated Smith.[34] But many Catholics interpreted the election returns as clear evidence that they were still not welcome in the United States. In the 1930s, Roosevelt eased this anxiety by appointing Catholics, mostly Irish, to a fair share of federal positions. During the New Deal years, Irish-American politicians, bureaucrats, Supreme Court justices, and civil servants aided in the liberalization and modernization of the American economic and social systems and the internationalization of American foreign policy.[35]

During the 1930s, Father Charles Coughlin tarnished the Irish political image. In 1926, as the young pastor of the Shrine of the Little Flower in Royal Oak, Michigan, Coughlin began a series of radio talks on Detroit's station WJR. At the beginning, they were addressed mainly to children and contained few comments on economic, social, and political matters. Coughlin's melodious and powerful oratory was so popular with the radio audience that his program was picked up in 1929 by WMAQ Chicago and WLW Cincinnati and the next year by the Columbia Broadcasting System. As his following grew, the radio priest switched his emphasis from spiritual subjects to the evils of communism. He insisted that the best way to combat and defeat communism was by promoting social justice. He recommended Leo XIII's encyclical, *Rerum Novarum,* as the formula for a properly balanced society. Coughlin attacked the ineptitude of the Republican administration in dealing with the Depression, calling it a puppet of international banking. People from all over the United States, representing all shades of religious opinion, made Father Coughlin's radio hour a listening must. On summer and early autumn Sunday afternoons his voice flowed out the windows and through the fields and streets of rural, small-town, and urban America.

Coughlin gave strong support to Roosevelt in the 1932 presidential race. FDR welcomed the priest's backing during the election and the early days of the New Deal. Coughlin, however, lacked the personality of a loyal and patient follower. Roosevelt grew tired of his insistence that the administration become more radical in its economic policies. Coughlin, like many populists before him, demanded that silver have equal status with gold as a currency support. When he became convinced that the New Deal was more of the same old thing, his slogan "Roosevelt or Bust" was changed to "Roosevelt and Bust." In 1936, the Detroit priest created the Union party and backed populist Republican congressman William Lemke for president. The North Dakotan gathered the allegiance of other fringe groups such as Reverend Gerald L. K. Smith's Share the Wealth followers, Dr. Francis E. Townsend's proponents of old age pensions, and those loyal to the memory of Louisiana's recently assassinated senator, Huey Long.

Lemke got less than a million popular votes and none in the electoral college. After this defeat, Coughlin's opinions became more extreme and his voice more shrill. In 1938, he formed the League of Social Justice based on the antibanking, pro–cheap money appeals of his previous agitations. His ideas of social justice resembled the corporate state theories of Benito Mussolini, Italy's fascist dictator. Coughlin's attacks on bankers always contained anti-Semitic nuances. Late in the 1930s, he exploded into virulent condemnations of Jews as the core components of both international banking and bolshevism.

Although Coughlin never explicitly recommended that the United States adopt fascism, he considered it a force against and a better choice than communism. Consequently, Coughlin strongly urged American neutrality before and after the start of World War II. From the late 1930s into the 1940s, a Coughlinite group, the Christian Front, physically attacked Jews in New York and Boston. When the United States entered the war, Coughlin was such an embarrassment to American Catholicism that in 1942 his religious superior, Detroit's Archbishop Edward Mooney, silenced the radio priest. He obediently returned to his duties as a parish priest.

As the 1936 election results demonstrated, once Coughlin began to criticize Roosevelt, he lost most of his support, even among Catholics. Of the many Catholic diocesan newspapers, he was left with the support of just two, the *Michigan Catholic* and the *Brooklyn Tablet*. Only a small number of discontented, Depression-haunted German and Irish working-class Catholics continued to believe in him. Within the hierarchy, just two, Archbishop Francis Beckman of Dubuque and Bishop Michael J. Gallagher of Detroit, his old friend and sponsor, praised Coughlin. Most prelates disliked his intrusion into politics. Bishop Bernard Sheil of Chicago and Monsignor John Ryan of the National Catholic Welfare Conference openly attacked Coughlin's anti-Semitism and his sympathy for fascism.[36]

Coughlin was a colorful but nasty Irish-American political aberration. The overwhelming majority of Irish Americans remained true to the Democratic party, and they were very visible in its leadership. James J. Farley of New York, postmaster general, was party chairman. Roosevelt appointed Senator Thomas Walsh of Montana to his first cabinet as attorney general, but Walsh died two days before the inauguration. In 1938, the president selected Frank Murphy for that position. Like Walsh, Murphy was a strong social justice Catholic. He had been mayor of Detroit, governor-general of the Philippines, and governor of Michigan. After two years as attorney general, Murphy accepted a Supreme Court appointment. Thomas Gardiner Corcoran ("Tommy the Cork") was a close personal adviser to and wrote speeches for FDR. He also recruited talent for government agencies and lobbied New Deal policies with members of the House and Senate. Two bright young congressmen from Massachusetts, John W. McCormack and Joseph Casey, helped guide Roosevelt's domestic and foreign policies through the House of Representatives. This took political courage because internationalism was highly unpopular among their anti-British Irish constituents. Roosevelt appointed Joseph Kennedy to chair the Securities and Exchange Commission, the Wall Street watchdog, and then to chair the Maritime Commission. After his fine performance in those positions, the president named Kennedy United States ambassador to Great Britain.[37]

If Coughlinism was the shadow, McCarthyism was the substance of a serious danger to American liberal democracy. Coughlin functioned in the midst of an American public hostile to his views. Joseph McCarthy exploited a confused American mind that doubted the patriotism of its own government. Post–World War II Soviet expansionism in eastern Europe, communist victory in China, Cold War tensions, frustrations with the Korean War stalemate, the Alger Hiss case, and other examples of subversion had made many Americans, notably Catholics, who tended to believe that they were the only people in the country who fully understood the dangers of Marxist-Leninism, worry about the security of their country.

Joe McCarthy took advantage of and manipulated American insecurities to become for five years a major factor in the domestic and foreign affairs of the United States. In 1949, McCarthy had been in the Senate for three years with no visible accomplishments. To overcome his reputation as a "good-time Charlie" political lightweight, he frantically cast about for an issue to give him the visibility and significance to retain his seat from Wisconsin. After Father Edmund Walsh, S.J., founder and regent of Georgetown University's School of Foreign Service, suggested to McCarthy that he might profit by searching out communist subversives in government, the senator was off and running. In a February 1950 speech in Wheeling, West Virginia, he charged that there were 205 "card-carrying" communists in the State Department. McCarthy was not deterred when the Truman administration challenged this charge and the Senate's Foreign Relations Committee investigated it. He kept repeating his accusation of disloyalty in the highest levels of government, changing only the numbers involved, and he branded the Democrats "the party of treason."

Because he was an enemy of the communist Antichrist and one of their own, McCarthy became popular in Catholic America. Much of his Irish-American support expressed remnants of alienation, a desire to get even with Anglo-Protestants high in the upper ranks of

American society, people such as Alger Hiss, who had belittled and exploited the Irish but never loved the United States as deeply as they did. Maureen Howard, the Irish-American novelist, saw this attitude in her father's support for "tail gunner Joe," the fake World War II marine hero. She realized that his attitude had no tinges of fascism or fear of communism: "I have tried to justify his allegiance on the grounds that my father wanted revenge, along with the Senator from Wisconsin, on a society that had treated the Irish like guttersnipes and cartoon drunks when he was a kid."[38]

Priests were great fans of McCarthy. New York's Archbishop Francis Cardinal Spellman was particularly fond of him. Such prestigious and high-quality Catholic periodicals as *Commonweal* and *America* and the distinguished diocesan paper the *Davenport Messenger*, edited by Donald McDonald, deplored McCarthy's anti–civil liberties witch-hunting, but most of the Catholic press joined the right-wing *Brooklyn Tablet* in praising his patriotism. Joseph Kennedy, before 1936 a friend of Father Coughlin, found a new comrade in McCarthy. Some of his enthusiasm passed to his son Robert, who served as assistant counsel of McCarthy's Senate Investigating Subcommittee. Robert's older brother John, congressman and then senator from Massachusetts, liked McCarthy but found his tactics crude and uncouth. JFK, however, did not want to offend Catholic voters by criticizing him.

McCarthy's attacks on the Truman administration and the Democratic party did not produce the 1952 Eisenhower landslide, but they did have an influence on Catholic voters, and many Republican leaders, such as Senator Robert A. Taft of Ohio, endorsed McCarthyism for political advantage. Not even Dwight D. Eisenhower had the courage to defend his old patron in the military, General George C. Marshall, from McCarthy's charge that as Truman's secretary of state he was "soft on communism."

Once the Republicans had gained the White House, the maverick McCarthy became a nuisance and an embarrassment to the administration, particularly when he began to investigate alleged subversion in the military. Edward R. Murrow's "See It Now" television program exposed McCarthy's career and methods, and the widely viewed army-McCarthy hearings in 1954 revealed the senator from Wisconsin to be a boor and a bully. In December 1954, the Senate extinguished what was left of his political significance by a sixty-seven to twenty-two vote of condemnation.

In labeling him an advanced guard of fascism, some of McCarthy's liberal critics were as paranoid as his followers. In reality, he was an adventurer without principles or programs, an outsider who could neither lead nor follow, a searcher for personal fame and glory rather than America's security or welfare. Although he attracted leftover Jew-haters from the Coughlin era, McCarthy's anticommunist crusade was not anti-Semitic. Roy Cohn, chief counsel of the Senate Investigating Subcommittee, was the senator's close friend and adviser. He recruited his college chum David Schine to the McCarthy staff. In fact, it was Cohn's resentment at the army for drafting Schine that triggered the 1954 showdown with the military.

McCarthy was a totally negative force. He and his associates did not uncover communists in government, but they tarnished reputations, cost people jobs, and created an atmosphere of fear and suspicion that continued to trouble the United States long after McCarthyism was a spent force. Fortunately for the country, McCarthy was a lone-wolf, alcoholic, rudderless buccaneer. If he had combined ideological conviction, passion, and determination with his ability to capitalize on the fears and anxieties of a troubled, insecure people, he could have caused deeper and more permanent damage.

Although McCarthyism expressed a lingering alienation among many members of the American Catholic working and lower middle classes, many of their suburban, well-educated, upper-middle-class coreligionists found the senator an embarrassment. Although opposition to the Wisconsin senator cost Millard Tydings of Maryland his Senate seat, a number of Irish-American politicians, including Senators Brien McMahon of Connecticut and Joseph O'Mahoney of Wyoming and Congressman Eugene McCarthy of Minnesota, did not hesitate to condemn Joe McCarthy and his methods. In 1954, six of the eight Catholic senators present voted to censure their Wisconsin colleague (John Kennedy was in a hospital undergoing back surgery, but he did not pair his vote with an absent McCarthy backer). At the same time that Spellman was bestowing blessings on McCarthy, Chicago's auxiliary Archbishop Bernard Sheil denounced him and the national neurosis that he represented. Sheil called the senator a false crusader and said the best way to fight communism in the United

States was to address the problems of poverty and prejudice, not to curtail American freedoms. He reminded Catholics that their religion did not condone lying or bearing false witness.[39]

Despite the strong support that Irish Americans gave Joe McCarthy, the vast majority remained New Deal and Fair Deal Democrats on social issues. In 1953, while warning other Americans that Irish Catholicism endangered their culture and institutions, Paul Blanshard had to admit that "on the whole, Irish Catholicism in the United States tends to be left of center, and the voting record of its congressmen in Washington is generally progressive on every issue concerning which contrary orders have not come from Rome. Its racial policy is magnificently humane and liberal, partly because the papal policy on racial segregation is broadly equalitarian."[40]

The novels of Thomas J. Fleming ably portray Irish America's political evolution from obsession with power to pragmatic idealism. In *All Good Men*, Dave Shea, thirty-year mayor and machine boss of a New Jersey city, is matched in a 1951 election against party renegade Matty Blair. A coalition of Anglo-Protestant reformers and Italians, Poles, and blacks, resentful of long Irish dominance, supports Blair. Overconfidence and isolation from the changing currents of public opinion doom Shea. Even his most talented and realistic lieutenant, Ben O'Connor, county commissioner, is barely able to carry his own thirteenth ward. Like other such fictional urban politicians as Skeffington, Donnelly, Slattery, and O'Shaughnessey, Ben entered politics because, except for the church, it was the only opportunity inside the law for bright Irish lads in anti-Catholic America. Disabled by a gangrenous leg, Ben enlists the campaign assistance of his cynical, purposeless son Jake, a World War II navy officer veteran and law school graduate under the G.I. Bill of Rights. Once he becomes involved in the election, Jake's Irish political instincts and talents surface. Although he inherits his father's vocation, Jake is determined to apply its potential to something more important than perpetuating machine politics.

In *King of the Hill*, Jake, financed by Paula Stapleton, member of one of the city's most distinguished Anglo-Protestant families, leads the opposition of reform Democrats to a Blair administration more corrupt and less competent and serviceable than its Shea predecessor. In *Rulers of the City*, Jake now married to Paula, an uncomfortable

Catholic convert, is in his fourteenth year as the city's progressive mayor. His liberalism, like John F. Kennedy's, is pragmatically Irish Catholic, seeking to improve rather than to perfect society, to effect the possible over the impossible. Paula, however, is rigidly ideological, certain that there are solutions to all social conflicts and problems. Their marriage is endangered when Paula insists that Jake obey her uncle, a federal judge, who orders that African-American children must be admitted to public schools in a Catholic ethnic neighborhood. The mayor does not share the prejudices of his Irish, Italian, and Polish constituents, but he understands their fears, and he needs their votes to achieve his goal, the United States Senate. He therefore seeks alternatives to the court order. But a personal encounter with violence during a busing incident and reflections on the Irish experience in the United States finally persuade Jake to comply with Judge Stapleton's decision. At a St. Patrick's Day banquet, he reminds listeners that their ancestors, like present-day African Americans, were unwelcome in the city, and he urges them to be in the vanguard of the civil rights effort. At the novel's conclusion, Jake is certain that the future of the United States demands a merger of Anglo-Protestant optimism and idealism with Irish caring and political genius, a combination symbolized in his marriage to Paula.[41]

PENNSYLVANIA AVENUE

All Good Men is based on politics in Jersey City. Dave Shea bears a striking resemblance to Frank Hague, the longtime boss of that city. In 1949, John V. Kenney created a coalition, recruited many disgruntled Italians and Poles, and split the Irish vote to defeat Hague's nephew and "designated heir apparent," Frank Hague Eggers, in a contest for mayor. Hague's Jersey City opponents followed the pattern set by Fiorello H. La Guardia, who in 1933 organized Jews and Italians, angry at the Irish monopoly of power, and some reform-minded Irish into a Fusion ticket that toppled Tammany in the New York mayoral election.[42] The La Guardia and Kenney victories were serious blows at Irish machine politics already endangered by Depression-induced state and federal spending cuts. Roosevelt's New Deal appropriated many funds for social programs, but the novelist Edwin

O'Connor argued that the result was to scuttle rather than salvage Irish machine politics.

In *The Last Hurrah*, Skeffington has powerful enemies. Wealthy Anglo-Protestants, Amos Force, newspaper publisher, and Norman Cass, banker, are determined to end the reign of an Irish chieftain who has irritated them for a very long time. Skeffington also has foes in the Irish Catholic community. His successful contemporaries, the cardinal and Harvard-educated Roger Sugrue, blame him for exemplifying the public stereotype of the corrupt Irish politician and for not providing a better example to his people. Young college-educated liberal organizer Jack Mangan acknowledges Skeffington's intelligence and charm and even the good that he has done but regards him as a political fossil surviving beyond his time. Skeffington's enemies join forces behind Kevin McCluskey, a dimwit with attributes attractive to new television-prompted voters: a Jesuit education, military service in World War II, a photogenic face and family, and a rented dog. The coalition is sure that McCluskey will be its puppet. Much to his surprise, Skeffington badly loses the election. Mangan interprets the returns as less a victory for the McCluskey crowd and more a triumph for New Deal welfarism, which has made the Irish political machines superfluous. He tells the mayor's nephew, newspaper cartoonist Adam Caulfield:

> All over the country the bosses have been dying for the last twenty years, thanks to Roosevelt . . . the old boss was strong simply because he held all the cards. If anybody wanted anything—jobs, favors, cash—he could only go to the boss, the local leader. What Roosevelt did was to take the handouts out of local hands. A few little things like Social Security, Unemployment Insurance and the like—that's what shifted the gears, sport. No need now to depend on the boss for anything; the Federal Government was getting into the act. Otherwise known as the social revolution.[43]

In *Rainbow's End*, Steven B. Erie agrees in part with O'Connor's thesis. New Deal social programs, along with benefits won by labor unions and the competing paternalism of big corporations, did intrude on the welfare functions of Irish political machines. But as Erie points out, in some instances the New Deal sustained and even resurrected the fortunes of the machine. It bypassed Tammany in New York and mini-organizations in Boston but energized those in Chicago, Pittsburgh, and Albany. Because these machines were permitted access to federal patronage while others were excluded, they were able to place many constituents on the public payroll through the Works Progress Administration. After World War II, when African Americans were moving from the South into northern cities, whites were moving to the suburbs, and the federal government and the labor unions were playing Santa Claus, machine politics again faced hard times. Under Richard J. Daley, Chicago's Democratic organization remained effective because it persuaded Washington to channel federal funds through the machine to the people and pleased white homeowners with low taxes and excellent services, middle-class African Americans with employment in government agencies, and the poor of their race with welfare.[44]

Elected in 1955, one year before the publication of *The Last Hurrah*, Daley was Chicago's mayor for twenty-two years. In this office and as chairman of the Cook County Democratic Central Committee, he created the most efficient and powerful organization in the history of American urban politics. Its powers came not only from control of federal funds but from its monopoly of local patronage. Although frequently insensitive to the problems of African and Hispanic Americans (giving weight to one aspect of Moynihan's critique of Irish urban politics), intolerant of opposition, and indifferent to the mutual problems of city and suburbs, Daley made Chicago the best administered, most dynamic, and progressive of America's large metropolises. Under his management, it continued as the architectural gem of the United States. The downtown and North Shore building booms might have masked poverty neighborhoods to the south and west, but they represented energy and confidence, lured investment, and provided employment.[45]

Downstate contempt for Chicago, particularly its Catholics and Jews, nourished a provincialism in the city's Irish. Their politicians have had little interest in Springfield or Washington. Only one, Edward F. Dunne, has been governor of the state (from 1912 to 1916), and none have served in the United States Senate. In the House of Representatives, those from Chicago have not had the same leadership role as other urban Irish politicians, even from places where the Irish are not as numerous or have not achieved the same degree of social mobility.[46] Daley was an exception to Chicago Irish political provincialism. Although the city was his first love and concern, he was involved in national affairs. The efficient Cook County Democratic machine offered access to badly needed Illinois electoral votes in presidential election contests, and Daley played kingmaker. In 1960, he decided that it was time for the first Catholic president of the United States and that John Fitzgerald Kennedy was best suited for the position.

Kennedy first captured national attention at the 1956 Democratic convention in Chicago. Illinois Governor Adlai Stevenson, the party's presidential nominee, decided to let the delegates select his running mate. Kennedy made a run for the vice-presidency and gave Senator Estes Kefauver of Tennessee a close contest before finally losing. Before the convention, few Americans in the television audience knew anything about the junior senator from Massachusetts, but they liked what they saw and heard from Chicago. Losing the nomination was actually a blessing for Kennedy. If he had been on the ticket, his Catholicism might have targeted him for the blame when Eisenhower won a landslide victory in November. But his convention exposure put him in a favorable position to pick up the Democratic pieces after the election humiliation.

As soon as the 1956 presidential contest concluded, Kennedy began constructing a national organization in preparation for 1960. In Wisconsin's 1960 primary he defeated Senator Hubert Humphrey from neighboring Minnesota. He repeated the victory in West Virginia, a state not known to be friendly toward Catholics. Despite the growing grass-roots movement for Kennedy, the spread of his efficient machine, and his impressive primary triumphs, many Irish Catholic political leaders hesitated to jump on his bandwagon. They feared that if Kennedy won and the country then plunged into an economic depression or a foreign policy debacle, Catholics would become scapegoats for presidential failures or the vagaries of history. And they worried that if Kennedy became the Democratic candidate and then lost the November election, the mood of depression and insecurity that had afflicted Catholics after the 1928 election would reappear. Some also thought that a Catholic presidential candidate would seriously damage the chances of those lower down on the Democratic ticket. Richard J. Daley, however, was convinced that Irish Catholics had labored long in the Democratic vineyard without sufficient return and that their time for glory had come. He persuaded such other important Catholic politicians as William Green and Jim Finnegan of Philadelphia, David Lawrence of Pittsburgh, Robert Wagner of New York, Governor Mike Di Salle of Ohio, and Governor Steve McNichols of Colorado, men who could command convention and popular votes, that he was right.[47]

As Kennedy's candidacy advanced, he had to overcome the hostility of powerful forces in the Democratic party. Lyndon Johnson, Senate majority leaders from Texas, also wanted the nomination, as did Adlai Stevenson, the twice defeated former candidate. Johnson's power in the Senate gave him considerable political clout, and Stevenson was the darling of the party's liberals. Many of them, afflicted with intellectual elitism and snobbery, would rather have lost with Stevenson than win with anyone else. Former president Harry Truman, a strong foe of Kennedy's father, argued that the forty-three-year-old senator from Massachusetts was too young and inexperienced to be the leader of the free world. And when the Los Angeles convention delegates gathered in July, Eleanor Roosevelt, the popular and articulate widow of FDR and a fervent Stevenson supporter, called a press conference to announce that the United States was not yet ready for a Catholic president. Family connections were a handicap to Kennedy. Many liberal Democrats despised Joseph Kennedy for his isolationism before American entry into World War II and for his support of Senator Joseph McCarthy. In fact, all of the Kennedys were tainted by their association with McCarthy.

Kennedy's head start and the power of his organization overcame the opposition. After he handily won the nomination, Kennedy, in a bid to win southern votes and to ensure party harmony, offered the vice-presidential spot to Lyndon Johnson. Kennedy also worked hard to convince Jewish and other liberals that he was something more than his father's son. Eleanor Roosevelt finally endorsed his candidacy and participated actively in the campaign, but many sulking Stevenson fans sat out the election. Kennedy's candidacy unleashed a flood of anti-Catholic propaganda, some of it dating back to the "Protestant crusade" of the early nineteenth century. Voices from Protestant pulpits claimed that Kennedy was an agent of a foreign despot, the pope. Norman Vincent Peale, the "power of positive thinking" minister, led a group of Protestant clergymen called the National Conference of Citizens for Religious Freedom, which issued a statement that said Roman Catholicism was irreconcilable with American values. In response to these attacks on his religious affiliation, Kennedy argued that Catholics had fought and died for the United States in many wars and on many battlefields and on the sea and in the air and thus were entitled to the opportunities of full citizenship, including the right to be president of their country. In September, he told an assemblage of Protestant ministers in Houston, Texas, that he was "not the Catholic candidate for President" but the Democratic party's choice for that office, "who happens also to be a Catholic." He went on to say that "if this election is decided on the basis that 40,000,000 Amercians lost their chance of being President on the day they were baptized, then it is the whole nation that will be the loser in the eyes of history, and in the eyes of our own people." He promised the audience and listeners and watchers on radio and television that if as president he ever faced a conflict between his Catholic and American consciences he would resign from office. Kennedy's words left his listeners with a favorable impression. The ministers in Houston gave him a standing ovation, but anti-Catholicism continued to be a significant factor during the campaign.[48]

Hostility to Kennedy's religion did not necessarily win him the enthusiasm of Catholic priests. During the Roosevelt years, the overwhelming majority of the hierarchy and clergy shared the laity's Democratic loyalty.[49] After World War II, the flag-waving, anticommunist paranoia of the time and the increasing middle-class and suburban character of American Catholicism produced more conservative and Republican bishops and priests. Cardinal Archbishops Spellman and James McIntyre of Los Angeles were openly supportive of Vice-President Richard Nixon, the Republican standard-bearer. Some priests felt that as president, Catholic Kennedy would be too sensitive to the issue of separation of church and state to recommend federal funds for Catholic education. The large number of Republicans among the Catholic clergy led Kennedy to joke that he could understand why Henry VIII established his own church and how pleased he was that the nuns were for him even though so many priests were on the other side. When the November election results were in, they again demonstrated that Irish voters pay attention to the political opinions of priests only when they coincide with their own. Some priests' opposition to Kennedy and the lukewarm attitude of others probably helped persuade wavering non-Catholic voters that Kennedy indeed was independent of clerical influence.

In his 1960 run for the presidency, Kennedy faced some of the same obstacles that Massachusetts Governor Michael Dukakis would encounter in his 1988 effort. Both battled vice-presidents of extraordinarily popular presidents in what the public perceived as good times. But unlike Dukakis, Kennedy seized the initiative and set the agenda and mood of the campaign. He effectively told voters that for eight Eisenhower years the United States had been a slumbering giant. He convinced most of them that it was now time for Americans to wake up and get their country on the move and the best way to do that was by passing the leadership on to a younger generation who would establish a "New Frontier" of national progress. In television debates with Nixon, Kennedy was articulate, confident, and poised, persuading many voters, previously skeptical about his credentials, that he had the maturity and the manner to lead the country.

It is difficult to evaluate the religious quotient in the narrow Kennedy victory. Although his candidacy alienated millions of Protestant voters, it brought many Catholics who had voted for Eisenhower back to the Democratic fold. Kennedy focused his campaign in densely Catholic areas, where there also were heavy concentrations of African-American and Jewish voters. He revived the Democratic ethnic, religious, and racial coalition that had voted for Roosevelt in 1932, 1936, 1940, and 1944 and for Harry Truman in 1948.[50] Most white Protestants have had a long tradition of voting Republican, but Catholics, Jews, and African Americans cannot select a president by themselves. Kennedy did get many if not a majority of Protestant votes. Johnson's presence on the ticket certainly helped attract southern Protestant support.

Irish and other American Catholics rejoiced at President Kennedy's popularity at home and abroad. His glow reflected on them. But what Kennedy represented was far more important than his personal or political qualities. His presidency was the climax of the long, difficult Irish-American journey to acceptance and respectability. As John Ford expressed it, now they felt like first-class citizens. Kennedy rescued Irish America from lingering remnants of defensiveness and paranoia and redeemed it from the sin of McCarthyism.

President Kennedy shared political power and prominence with other Irish Americans. Mike Mansfield of Montana was Senate majority leader; John W. McCormack of Massachusetts was Speaker of the House of Representatives; and John Bailey of Connecticut chaired the Democratic National Committee. They did not ride presidential coattails. Their importance preceded and survived Kennedy's brief period in the national spotlight.

Late in the 1960s, America's role in Vietnam, much of it a Kennedy legacy, became a divisive element in the nation's politics. In the 1950s, when he was a Democratic congressman from St. Paul, Minnesota, Eugene McCarthy had the courage to denounce and debate Senator Joseph McCarthy. In 1968, as a member of the Senate, he challenged President Lyndon Johnson's Vietnam policy. The considerable support McCarthy received in the New Hampshire primary and his impending victory in Wisconsin contributed to Johnson's decision not to seek reelection. Except for an assassin's bullet, another Johnson foe, Senator Robert F. Kennedy of New York, Jack's brother, might have been elected president in 1968. In 1980, Senator Edward M. Kennedy of Massachusetts and a fellow Irish American, Governor Jerry Brown of California, tried to oust fellow Democrat Jimmy Carter from the presidency. In the spring of 1979, the *U.S. News and World Report* poll of 1,439 prominent Americans rated three Irish Americans, Kennedy, Thomas "Tip" O'Neill, Speaker of the House of Representatives, and George Meany, president of the AFL-CIO, as the second, third, and fourth most powerful figures in the United States.[51]

In the 1980s, some of these politicians faded in importance. After deciding not to run for reelection to the Senate, Eugene McCarthy attempted an independent 1976 challenge to Carter and President Gerald Ford. Following his failure, Minnesota voters rejected him as a carpetbagger from New York when he tried to recapture his old Senate seat. Edward M. Kennedy, one of the most consistent and undaunted champions of the liberal tradition, remains an important and respected member of the Senate, but his messy private life has dimmed his presidential hopes. A widely shared belief that Jerry Brown coped inadequately with a medfly scourge in California contributed to his loss of the governorship. In 1989, however, he enjoyed a political comeback as chair of his state Democratic party organization. In 1986 "Tip" O'Neill retired from Congress into private life.

The Irish are still well represented in congressional leadership roles by George J. Mitchell of Maine, Senate majority leader, and Thomas S. Foley, Speaker of the House of Representatives. Both are intelligent and articulate, and the Democrats' need to recapture the Catholic ethnic vote may result in their future candidacy for the presidency or vice-presidency. For a while, another talented Irish American, Congresswoman Patricia Schroeder of Colorado, was a contestant in the 1988 Democratic race for the presidential nomination. Although she dropped out of contention, her intelligence, sense of humor, and verbal skills won her a great deal of respect. Today there are a bevy of talented Irish politicians in Congress who have the potential to lead the House and the Senate and perhaps the country.

The most important liberal Irish-American Catholic voice has come from the Supreme Court, not from the White House or Capitol Hill. In October 1956, Dwight Eisenhower appointed William J. Brennan, Jr., to the United States Supreme Court. In July 1990, he retired from that position, having served longer than all but four previous justices. A native of Newark, New Jersey, Brennan was born in 1906. Both his parents were immigrants from County Roscommon, Ireland. William J. Brennan, Sr., was a labor union leader and a prominent politician in Newark. William, Jr., was educated in a parochial grammar school and a public high school. After earning his B.A. cum laude in 1928 from the University of Pennsylvania's Wharton School, Brennan entered Harvard Law School. In 1931, he graduated in the upper 10 percent of his class. Brennan went from Harvard to a Newark law firm and then in 1942 into the army as a major. He was discharged in 1945 as a colonel, having been awarded the Legion of Merit. Following military service, Brennan rejoined his old law firm as a senior partner. In 1949, the governor appointed him to the Superior Court of New Jersey and three years later to the state supreme court.

No doubt, Eisenhower selected Brennan to woo Catholic Democratic votes. But he also evidently thought that Brennan was of a moderate disposition. In 1961, Eisenhower confessed that he had made a mistake in two appointments in his administration, both to the Supreme Court—Earl Warren and William J. Brennan, Jr. No Supreme Court justice in the twentieth century has had a greater impact on American life and institutions than Brennan. Burt Neuborne, a member of New York University's law faculty, rates Brennan as the most important Supreme Court justice since John Marshall.[52] Because of his liberal opinions and his ability to convert them into Supreme Court majorities, conservatives consider Brennan a menace, the force behind excessive criminal rights, abortion, oppressive federal government power, and racial quotas that have resulted in reverse discrimination. They also blame Brennan for disturbing the balance of power in American politics, usurping the role of Congress and the presidency, and converting the Supreme Court into a legislative body. Catholics on the right cannot understand how a practicing member of their faith, the son of hardworking immigrant parents, and a devoted father of three children could extend privacy rights to legalize abortion, encourage obscenity and pornography under the guise of freedom of speech, interpret separation of church and state to keep religion out of public schools and community Christmas celebrations, and extend sympathy for the poor into advocacy of the welfare state.

The *National Review,* perhaps the most articulate and intelligent conservative periodical, while criticizing Brennan for his influence on the United States, has had to admit his significant talents: "It was Brennan who provided the leadership and intellect during the early period of the Warren Court, and Brennan who was the major force in institutionalizing the Warren Court's opinions long after it had given way to a new era." According to the writers, Stephen J. Markman and Alfred S. Regnery, "an examination of Brennan's opinions, and his influence upon the opinions of his colleagues, suggests that there is no individual in this country on or off the Court, who has had a more profound and sustained impact on public policy in the United States for the past 27 years." Their article concludes: "That the Brennan social agenda has become America's social agenda is all the more remarkable because it was and still is an agenda almost entirely at variance with that of the citizens of the country and their elected representatives. Justice Brennan, more than virtually anybody else in public life today, has made a difference."[53]

Courtly and gentle Brennan, sometimes described as a kindly "Irish uncle" or "Irish grandfather," and his supporters defend his record as indicating concern for preserving the Bill of Rights. They argue that he has defended minority rights against majority prejudices, prevented the state from interfering with the private activities and concerns of citizens, protected the rights of free speech and other kinds of expression against passions of the time, and guaranteed the equality of women. Interpreters of Brennan's influence as positive rather than negative argue that Supreme Court justices must defend the stated and implied rights guaranteed in the Constitution from majority fads and society's passing emotions. If what they do infringes on the responsibilities of the legislative branch, it is because members of the House and Senate have been irresponsible. In this day of politics by public opinion polls and pressure groups, presidents, congressmen, and senators are afraid to tackle the tough issues, leaving a decision vacuum in Washington that the Supreme Court has filled. Although Brennan's liberalism has stirred the ire of some Irish Catholics, he may have remembered the Irish historical experience of poverty and oppression here and in Ireland that they have forgotten and applied it to the misfortunes and problems of others.[54]

With some exceptions, Irish politicians on the national level remain in the Democratic party, and, like Senators Kennedy and Mitchell, Congressman Foley, and former Justice Brennan, they speak for its liberal social welfare, civil rights, peace-seeking wing. In contrast, Irish and other American Catholic voters in increasing numbers are moving toward the Republican fold. According to Theodore H. White, the National Broadcasting Company's exit poll showed that Ronald Reagan in 1980 "carried the Irish vote in every major state but the results are astounding (California 64/28, New York 53/35, Texas 65/31)."[55] The American Broadcasting Company–*Washington Post* 1980 exit poll recorded that Irish Americans voted 52 percent for Reagan, 39 percent for Jimmy Carter, and 7 percent for Congressman John Anderson of Illinois (an independent candidate).[56] The 1984 ABC-*Post* exit poll tabulated a 59 percent Irish-American vote for President Reagan and a 40 percent vote for former Vice-President

Walter Mondale. According to ABC, the total Catholic vote for Reagan in 1980 was 46 percent. Four years later, it jumped to 56 percent. Still, this was considerably lower than the 66 percent Protestant vote listed for the president. And though the Irish vote for Reagan exceeded the Catholic average, it was far less than the German-Austrian 67 percent, the English-Scottish-Welsh 70 percent, or the Scandinavian 62 percent.[57] According to a *New York Times*–Columbia Broadcasting System exit poll, Catholics in 1980 gave 49 percent of their vote to Reagan, 42 percent to Carter, and 7 percent to Anderson. In 1984, they selected Reagan over Mondale 55 to 44 percent. White Protestants gave Reagan 73 percent of their support, an increase of 10 percent over 1980. The Gallup Poll, however, indicated that in 1984 both Catholics and Protestants voted 61 percent for Reagan and 39 percent for Mondale.[58] This was a considerable shift in the Catholic vote since Gallup began its postelection analyses in 1952. In eight elections before 1984, Catholics averaged a 20 percent Democratic majority.[59] In a *Chicago Sun Times*–Gallup Poll, published the day before the 1988 presidential election, 64 percent of Protestants and 50 percent of Catholics intended to vote for Vice-President George Bush, the Republican candidate. The Democratic nominee, Michael Dukakis, had 32 percent of the Protestant and 46 percent of the intended Catholic vote.[60] Exit polls conflicted in interpreting the various shares of the 1988 results. There was agreement that George Bush received about two-thirds of the white Protestant vote, but the *New York Times*–CBS results gave Bush 52 percent of the Catholic vote while the *Wall Street Journal*–NBC estimate gave Dukakis the same percentage. According to early *Washington Post*–ABC exit polling, Irish, Polish, and other Slavic Catholics all gave a slight edge to Dukakis while the Italian vote split evenly between the Democratic and Republican candidates.[61]

Why has the Democratic party lost so much of the Irish and other Catholic ethnic electorate? Reasons include class interests as well as values. For some middle-class Catholics whose parents were Kennedy enthusiasts and whose grandparents believed in FDR and the New Deal, the Republican party represents their ambitions, interests, or needs. Even working-class Catholic ethnics complain that Democratic politicians seem overly solicitous in responding to African-American complaints while ignoring the problems of urban whites.

They resent the ubiquitous presence of the Reverend Jesse Jackson at Democratic party conventions and forums. Many Catholics from all classes believe that since Senator George McGovern's 1972 presidential candidacy, a radical yet snobbish group of intellectuals, described by Peggy Noonan as a "contemptuous elite" agitating for an offensive social agenda, constantly disparaging the United States and its citizens, has determined the direction of the national Democratic party.[62] Like most Americans, they are unwilling to grant that homosexuality is an acceptable life-style, are wary of extreme feminism, and cannot consent to abortion on demand. Catholics share a common national concern that massive drug use and violent crime indicate a collapsing society. In pushing a civil libertarian program, the national Democratic party often seems indifferent to public anxieties. Taking advantage of this, Republicans in the 1988 presidential election were able to ignore the deficit, a multitude of scandals involving members of the Reagan administration, the attempt to trade guns for hostages with Iran, an unfavorable trade balance, a polluted environment, insufficient health care and maintenance, the faltering savings and loan industry, and one of the worst educational systems in the advanced industrial world to win a presidential election by concentrating on crime, patriotism, and family values.

Events and policies in Washington have done much to limit the effectiveness of Irish politics on the local level. President Reagan's cutbacks in social programs, endorsed by his successor, President Bush, have seriously damaged the Daley formula for preserving the machine. Without funds from Washington, city governments can no longer pacify middle-class African Americans with jobs in government agencies or underclass African Americans with generous welfare programs. Money shortages have forced them to raise taxes and cut back on services, alienating upper-working- and middle-class white property owners. Recent experiences in Chicago have demonstrated Steven P. Erie's thesis that African-American leaders will face a perplexing challenge when they attempt to achieve and retain power by imitating the example of Irish political machines. African Americans lack the alliances with state and federal governments that generated Irish urban patronage possibilities, and it is difficult for them to coalesce with Hispanics and Asians in common cause.[63]

Irish political power remained more significant and lasted longer in Chicago than in New York, Philadelphia, Jersey City, or San Francisco. But after Mayor Richard J. Daley succumbed to a heart attack in December 1976, the Democatic machine that he perfected split into rival factions. Edward Bilandic, a Croatian Catholic ethnic, became mayor. In 1979, he was toppled by Jane Byrne, like Bilandic a Daley protégé, running as an antimachine Democrat. Four years later, she and Richard M. Daley, son of the former mayor, split the white vote, opening the way for Congressman Harold Washington, an African American, to win the Democratic primary. Later that year, he defeated the Jewish Republican candidate, Bernard Epton, who attracted a massive portion of the white ethnic vote. In 1987, Washington won his second term as mayor but then died of a heart attack. The city council chose Alderman Eugene Sawyer, another African American, to serve as acting mayor. In the spring of 1989, he lost the Democratic primary to States Attorney Richard M. Daley, who went on to defeat Alderman Timothy Evans, also an African American, running on the Harold Washington party ticket. In both the primary and mayoral elections, Hispanics and lakefront liberals, many Jewish, who had voted for Washington, supported Daley. These liberals were offended by the anti-Semitism prevalent in the African-American community, particularly among key supporters of Evans. Most Hispanics decided that black politicians were not really interested in their concerns, and so they transferred their affection for Richard J. Daley to his son. But as mayor, Richard M. Daley seems determined to prove that although he respects the old school, he realizes that his father's approach to urban politics needs to be modified to respond to the needs of a rapidly changing city, increasingly African and Hispanic American, containing discontented white ethnic home owners, and cut off from the federal funds that once preserved the machine.[64]

Chicago is also an example of another important change in urban affairs: the shift of Catholic ethnic politicians from the Democratic to the Republican party. James O'Grady is one notable defector. Once the Chicago police superintendent under a Democratic administration, O'Grady became Republican sheriff of Cook County. Former tenth-ward alderman and chairman of the Cook County Democratic Central Committee Edward Vrodolyak ran and lost twice as a Republican candidate for mayor and for the patronage-rich post of clerk of the circuit court. Terrance W. Gainer, member of the Illinois state police force and a lawyer, ran and lost as a Republican against Richard M. Daley in the race for states attorney. Jack O'Malley is Republican States Attorney in Cook County.

Some politicians moving from the Democratic to the Republican party believe that they are reflecting the values of white ethnic voters. They are also aware that because African Americans are becoming more effective as political organizers and vote mobilizers, the future for white politicians in urban government is limited. They are now courting the votes of whites who have fled the city for the suburbs and turned Republican in the transition. It is no accident that some of the prominent new Republican politicians are former or present policemen. They represent the emphasis on law and order that has become so important in the minds of voters.

Despite the lingering presence of a significant Irish force in local and national politics, it is diminishing, and the quality, especially on the lower levels, is declining. Once politics, like the church, was a route to power and influence denied talented Irish in other areas. Now opportunities in business and the professions are abundant and attract Irish ambition and ability. Too many contemporary Irish politicians, like others in the country, are second-rate lawyers. The have the power lust of the old ward bosses without their intelligence, shrewdness, and concern for constituents. Today, the best and brightest Irish Americans are neither in the church nor in politics. Many are applying their political instincts and skills in corporate boardrooms.

13. James T. Farrell, Irish-American author who focused on Irish social mobility and lingering insecurities. Reprinted with permission from the *Chicago Sun-Times*.

14. Elizabeth Cullinan. Courtesy of Elizabeth Cullinan.

15. Thomas Flanagan. Courtesy of Thomas Flanagan.

16. Cornelius McGillicuddy (Connie Mack), owner and manager of the Philadelphia Athletics, and Charles Comiskey, owner of the Chicago White Sox, 1917. Reprinted with permission from the *Chicago Sun-Times*.

17. St. John's University basketball coach, Frank McGuire, and two of his early 1950s stars, brothers Dick and Al McGuire, who himself later coached a national champion team at Marquette University. Courtesy of Marquette University.

18. George M. Cohan, who epitomized the show business Irish, with his family. Reprinted with permission of the *Chicago Sun-Times*.

19. James Cagney as George M. Cohan in a scene from the 1942 film, *Yankee Doodle Dandy*. Courtesy of the Museum of Modern Art.

20. Jackie Gleason and Art Carney, two exemplars of the Irish comedy tradition, in a scene from "The Honeymooners." Courtesy of MGM.

21. Helen Hayes, actress, receiving the Sword of Loyola at the annual
awards dinner of Loyola University of Chicago's Stritch School of Medicine.
Courtesy of Loyola University of Chicago Archives.

22. Bing Crosby and Barry Fitzgerald in a scene from the 1944 film, *Going My Way*. Courtesy of the Museum of Modern Art.

23. Grace Kelly, actress, in a scene from *High Society*, personifying the transformation of the Irish-American image from despised pioneers of the urban ghetto to middle-class respectability. Courtesy of the Museum of Modern Art.

5

"From a Land Across the Sea"

Religion, politics, and nationalism combined to define Irish America. Catholicism comforted, sheltered, coalesced, disciplined, and educated the Irish in the United States. Politics provided them with an avenue to power and, through power, to economic security and, eventually, social mobility. Nationalism expressed their rage, frustration, and quest for respectability. To the overwhelming majority of Irish Catholics in Ireland and in the United States, their religion and nationality have been synonymous. In the ideology of both political and cultural nationalism, however, there is no religious litmus test for Irishness. From the time of Daniel O'Connell to the present, nationalist leaders in word, if not always in deed, have branded sectarianism as divisive. Ever since the Young Ireland rebellion, tensions have existed between the Catholic church and physical force Irish nationalism, triggering occasional outbursts of anticlericalism. Irish and Irish Americans trying to improve the intellectual quality of their communities or to raise the economic and social living standards of their peoples have protested the puritanism, intellectual oppressiveness, and conservatism of a Catholic church they believe has had a negative impact on Irish life and culture. In the United States, a few Irish liberals, radicals, and socialists, rejecting Catholicism as an agent for constructive change, have turned to the Irish nationalist tradition to preserve their ethnic identity and to inspire their struggles against social injustices.[1]

THE ORIGINS OF IRISH NATIONALISM

Irish nationalism evolved over many centuries. When the Norman English invaded Ireland in 1169, they entered a country united in a

125

common Gaelic culture but divided by clan and territorial conflicts. Taking advantage of this political chaos and their superior military equipment and tactics, the invaders swept through Ireland, making it England's first colony. In the fourteenth century, however, English influence in Ireland began to decline. Irish clan chiefs learned Norman military tactics and acquired Norman weapons and thus were able to restore and maintain their local power. Many Norman feudal lords in remote parts of the country went native, marrying local women and adapting to the Gaelic culture and life-style. Others, tired of cold, damp, primitive conditions, returned to the relative comfort of England, turning over the management of their estates to agents. In time, effective English authority was restricted to the eastern province of Leinster, known as the Pale. Its inhabitants developed a set of political and legal institutions, including a parliament, based on English models. But even in the Pale, the descendants of Norman conquerors developed local allegiances. Although remaining loyal to the Plantagenet monarchy and to English culture and institutions, they formed a pride in Ireland as their country, insisting that it was a separate political entity. Therefore, the Norman English, not the Gaelic Irish, developed the concept of an Irish political nation and then created its institutions.

When Henry VIII became king of England in 1509, his possessions in Ireland were divided into the Anglo-Irish Pale, a little England with Irish nuances; Gaelic Ireland, most strongly represented by the province of Ulster, where the inhabitants rejected the authority of the Leinster Parliament; and a mixed Gaelic and English cultural Ireland in the provinces of Munster and Connacht. Henry's effort to create a unified, English-controlled Ireland through the spread of feudal institutions failed. His daughter Elizabeth, determined to prevent Ireland from becoming a welcome mat for Spanish invaders, achieved her purpose through a military conquest that took on the emotional proportions of a Protestant crusade. Elizabeth's successor, James I, intent on weakening Gaelic culture in its heartland, planted Ulster with lowland Scots Presbyterians and English Anglicans, making it the only part of Ireland with a large non-Catholic population.

In two seventeenth-century wars of liberation, Old English Catholic descendants of the Normans and Gaelic Catholics joined to reverse the Tudor conquest and the Stuart plantations, but with different ends in mind. Clan chiefs hoped to restore the Gaelic cultural order as well as recover lost property and authority. The Old English also wanted to reacquire confiscated land, but they had another ambition—to resume leadership over the Irish political nation. The rebellions failed, and the victories of Oliver Cromwell and William III, followed by land confiscation and anti-Catholic penal laws, melded Old English and Gael into the defeated, underground, Irish Catholic religious and cultural nation. Throughout the eighteenth century, the oppressed, impoverished, largely illiterate rural Irish focused their attention on survival. Most of the people spoke Irish, but their language did not express national self-consciousness. Irish culture and identity wore the religious badge of Catholicism. Unfortunately, exile and forced religious conversion deprived Catholic Ireland of most of its cultural and political leadership.[2]

While poverty and oppression were enervating the Catholic majority, the English colony in Ireland was cultivating a local patriotism. As the penal laws demoralized, depressed, humiliated, and psychologically terrorized Catholics into a state of passivity, Anglo-Irish Protestants and Scots-Irish Presbyterians began to shed their siege mentalities. No longer fearing a Catholic uprising, they did not feel dependent on Britain for survival. Because of this new sense of self-reliance, they resented British mercantilist restrictions on the Irish economy, limitations on the sovereignty of the Irish Parliament, and insistence on the right to legislate for Ireland. Anglo-Ireland shared with Anglo-America opposition to British imperialism and colonialism. Both communities fostered local patriotisms based on the political theories of John Locke, the intellectual hero of England's Glorious Revolution.

When Anglo-American patriotism led to rebellion, the Anglo-Irish took advantage of British preoccupation with the New World. With so many troops overseas, the French and Spanish governments committed to the Americans, and the Bourbon navies in temporary control of the seas, the British could not guarantee the security of Ireland. In response to this emergency, Irish Protestants raised a Volunteer force to defend their island from possible invasion. But once they were mobilized and armed, the Volunteers demanded and won free trade and parliamentary sovereignty from a harassed British government. Although Irish independence was limited by a royal veto, exercised on the advice of English ministers, on bills passed by the Irish Parliament, from 1782 until 1801, Ireland, for the first time, had the contours of a political nation. But it was strictly Protestant, excluding Catholics from representation or influence.

A few Protestants knew that ostracizing 75 percent of the population jeopardized their nation. Henry Grattan, the leading hero of the patriot movement, argued that Protestants could not really be free as long as Catholics were slaves. Theobald Wolfe Tone and other leaders of the Society of United Irishmen wanted to expand Irish sovereignty beyond the limits imposed in 1782 by establishing a democratic republic that would embrace Catholics and Nonconformists as well as members of the Church of Ireland. But during the uprisings of 1798, there was little evidence of religious cooperation. Catholic peasants in Wexford killed Protestant landlords and in turn were brutally slaughtered by Presbyterian and Anglican yeomen from Ulster. In Antrim and Down, an army including Catholic militiamen crushed Presbyterian and Anglican rebels. When the French general Jean Humbert arrived in Mayo with nearly a thousand troops, local peasants joined him to fight for the pope and the Blessed Virgin, not for the "Liberty, Equality, and Fraternity" slogan of both the Jacobins and the United Irishmen. General Charles Cornwallis's army that eventually forced Humbert's surrender included many Catholics.[3]

The Irish Protestant nation was finished in 1798. William Pitt the Younger, the British prime minister, decided that the rebellions revealed Ireland as a fertile field of discontent, ready for French cultivation. And he doubted the ability of Anglo-Irish Protestants to prevent their country from becoming the Achilles' heel of British security. He concluded that the only way to guarantee Ireland's reliability during the conflict with Bonaparte was by totally integrating it into a United Kingdom. Many Irish Catholic religious and lay leaders supported the proposed Act of Union because Pitt promised that it would be accompanied by their emancipation. He pointed out that because Catholics would be a small minority in the United Kingdom, the British Parliament would be fairer to them than the defensive Anglo-Irish Protestant legislature. Protestants loyal to the patriot tradition opposed the Union, but others, fearing they had lost control of Catholic Ireland, supported the British connection to reinforce their ascendancy and property.

Despite Pitt's sincerely meant pledge, the British crown, House of Lords, and general public rejected political equality for Catholics. Therefore, on January 1, 1801, Ireland entered the United Kingdom with its large Catholic majority as second-class citizens. Some could vote, but none could sit in Parliament or hold political office. Sectarian discrimination doomed the Union. Catholic discontent became the seed bed of modern Irish nationalism, which Daniel O'Connell fashioned in the campaign for Catholic civil rights. In agitating for Catholic equality, he transformed the religious dimension of majority culture into nationality by inviting tenant farmers and artisans to become associate members of the Catholic Association, an organization previously restricted by fees to the gentry and middle class. For only a shilling a year, or a penny a month, or a farthing a week, ordinary people could participate in their own liberation. To guarantee the success of his mass movement, O'Connell recruited Catholic priests as his lieutenants.

Most people in rural Ireland could not afford even a shilling to join the Catholic Association, but at least two hundred thousand tenant farmers were able to make the sacrifice. Poor tenants and agricultural laborers became moral supporters of the agitation. Large gatherings at O'Connell rallies gave notice to British and Irish Protestants that he had raised millions of impoverished and oppressed Catholics from their knees and given them hope and expectations. By grafting a nationality onto a religion, he had mobilized their loyalty and enthusiasm, disciplined their emotions, arranged them into a powerful force of public opinion, and educated them in the techniques of political action.

During the general election of 1826, priests countered the pressures of landlord agents by leading tenant farmers to the polls to vote for Protestants prepared to support Catholic emancipation in the British House of Commons. The emergence of politically organized Catholicism and the defeat of landlord power persuaded the Duke of Wellington, the British prime minister, that prudence demanded some concession to Catholic claims. When in 1828, O'Connell ran and won a Clare by-election, again featuring a showdown between priest and landlord power, and then refused to take the anti-Catholic oaths that would admit him to the House of Commons, the government faced a crisis.

During the Catholic emancipation agitation, O'Connell insisted that his followers operate peacefully within the law, promising that they would triumph through the democratic power of organized public opinion. At the same time, he made it clear that if British politicians denied Catholics a legally won victory, they would prove that the British constitution applied only to Protestants and that Ireland was not an integral part of the United Kingdom. O'Connell also warned Britain that Irish Catholics had shrugged off the apathy and depression that had held them in bondage and would never again think like serfs. If Britain refused them civil rights, there was a good chance that they would abandon moderate, reasonable constitutional leaders like him and turn to proponents of physical rather than moral force. O'Connell admitted that the British army could put down an Irish Catholic rebellion, but the costs in life and property would be immense. In addition, the mask of the United Kingdom would be torn off, exposing a tyrannized Irish colony held down by a British army of occupation. Wellington and Sir Robert Peel, Tory leader in the House of Commons, personally preferred maintaining the exclusion of Catholics from public life, but to preserve the Union they chose reform to prevent revolution. In 1829, a relief act admitted Catholics to Parliament, most political offices, and professional honors.

Emancipation had little effect on the lives of most Irish Catholics. Farmers and agricultural laborers continued to till rocky fields, hoping that they would be able to pay the rent and have a roof over their heads and enough potatoes in the pot and on the table. Few middle-class professionals or businessmen would have the income to enjoy the luxury of politics. It was not until Charles Stewart Parnell led the Home Rule movement of the 1880s that most Irish members of Parliament were Catholics. Still, with all its limitations, the Catholic emancipation agitation of the 1820s had a major impact on the course of Irish history and Anglo-Irish relations. Its success increased expectations that change could be effected through politics. The Catholic Association provided a model for a multitude of British as well as Irish reform movements during the nineteenth century. And Irish nationalism emerged out of the contest for Catholic civil rights.

Some consequences of Catholic emancipation were more negative than positive. Because they were convinced that Irish nationalism contained the ambitions for power of a Catholic peasant democracy, O'Connell's methods and his victory strengthened loyalty to Britain among Irish Protestants. Some nationalists would join friends of the Union in criticizing O'Connell for assimilating nationalism and Catholicism and for bringing priests into politics.[4] But O'Connell emphasized rather than invented the historical associations between religion and nationality in Ireland, and with Protestant Irishness turning into Britishness, Catholics were the available nationalist constituency. O'Connell had to enlist priests in the Catholic emancipation agitation. They were the only leaders in rural Ireland capable of balancing the power of Protestant landlords.

O'Connell's campaign for Catholic emancipation had almost as much impact on Irish America as on Ireland. He politically civilized Irish Catholicism by attaching it to liberal-democratic Irish nationalism, making it different from conservative, Old Regime Continental Catholicism. Irish-American religious, political, and labor leaders, formed by the values of Irish Catholicism and Irish nationalism, were able to adjust Catholicism in the United States to the American political consensus.[5]

When in the 1840s O'Connell launched an effort to repeal the Union and restore the Irish Parliament, he found valuable lieutenants in Thomas Osborne Davis, Charles Gavan Duffy, and John Blake Dillon. In October 1842, these three young men founded a well-written, intelligent, and influential weekly newspaper, the *Nation*. They and their comrades at the *Nation* had the collective identity of Young Ireland. Inspired by the European romantic movement, they defined their mission as the creation of an Irish cultural nationalism to liberate the Irish mind and soul from the oppressive effects of an urban, industrial, materialistic British culture. Young Irelanders insisted that cultural, intellectual, and psychological freedom was more important than political independence. What good would it be, they asked, if Ireland had its own parliament but the Irish people remained enslaved by English values? *Nation* essays tried to make readers conscious of the noble Irish historical and cultural heritage featuring the Gaelic past. Articles and editorials encouraged new literature and art inspired by the past genius of the Irish race. According to Young Ireland, one of the best ways to foster a unique and creative Irish culture and to isolate Ireland from detrimental English materialism was to resurrect the Irish language where it had died and to preserve it where it still lived.

Writers in the *Nation* believed that language formed and expressed the national mind. If the Irish people continued to speak English, they would think and act like the English, but if they expressed themselves in their native tongue, they would be spiritually and culturally Irish.

Young Ireland expected that a common pride in Irish history and culture would reconcile Catholics and Protestants, Anglo-Irish and Celts, in an inclusive nationalism. Some Protestant unionist intellectuals, such as Sir Samuel Ferguson and Standish O'Grady, did encourage members of their community to develop an interest in the Gaelic tradition and the history of their country. Ferguson and O'Grady intended cultural nationalism as an alternative to political nationalism. It could be a bridge of communication between the Protestant upper classes and the Catholic masses, preserving both the status of the former and the Union. The vast majority of Protestants, however, had no empathy with or interest in the Gaelic past, which they associated with the Catholic, not their own, tradition. Rejecting both the cultural nationalisms of Young Ireland and the Ferguson-O'Grady Tory version, they reaffirmed their position as the British colony in Ireland.

Although Young Ireland failed to indoctrinate Protestant Ireland, it did strike a chord with members of the Catholic middle class suffering from an inferiority complex and needing to be told that they were as significant a people as their British and Anglo-Irish oppressors. In 1846, Young Irelanders split with O'Connell over a number of issues, including the validity of physical force reactions to British oppression and the ties between Irish and Catholic. In 1847, they formed the Irish Confederation as a rival to the Repeal Association, but most of the people followed the priests in their allegiance to "the Liberator" and "Old Ireland." Consequently, when Young Irelanders, caught up in the general European revolutionary fervor of 1848, attempted a rebellion against British colonialism, their effort collapsed because it was poorly organized (idealistic intellectuals often make incompetent revolutionaries) and lacked popular support. Yet, when the Famine was over and most of the Catholic population became literate through the national school system, Young Ireland's ideas and values became the ideology of Irish cultural nationalism.[6]

The Famine institutionalized emigration as an economic and social safety valve to preserve a reasonable Irish standard of living. Economic conditions forced parents to raise most of their children for export, but nationalism insisted that emigration was exile from British oppression. At the same time, nationalists pointed to Irish-American successes as evidence that the Irish were a talented people who flourished in freedom. They considered the Irish-American experience a prophecy of the future of an Ireland emancipated from British tyranny.

THE EMERGENCE OF IRISH-AMERICAN NATIONALISM

Notwithstanding nationalist propaganda, Irish-American progress was slow. Early Irish failures in the United States nurtured grievances that evolved into nationalism. Lacking economic skills, forced into backbreaking, low-paying jobs, besieged by anti-Catholic nativism, locked into ghettos of mind and place, the Irish found consolation in Catholicism, but they voiced their anger and frustrations in nationalism. To survive in an alien, competitive, urban industrial society, Irish Catholics were forced to band together, to place common ethnicity over the importance of their townland, village, or county origins in Ireland. Because of the fragility of their situation, they became more passionately and aggressively Irish than those who remained in the Old Country. As Thomas N. Brown has said, "In the alembic of America the parochial peasant was transformed into a passionate Irish nationalist."[7]

During the agitation for Catholic emancipation, O'Connell became an Irish American as well as an Irish hero. In 1843, when he unsuccessfully attempted to repeal the Union, a large portion of Irish America sent him verbal and financial support. Repeal clubs started in New York, Boston, Philadelphia, Baltimore, Charleston, Savannah, New Orleans, Natchez, St. Louis, Cincinnati, and Pittsburgh. Even small Irish communities in the East, Midwest, and South had organizations that collected pennies, nickels, dimes, and dollars for repeal.

O'Connell thanked Irish Americans for their assistance, and he warned Britain that its tyranny had manufactured an Irish nation in exile, determined to aid in the liberation of its mother country. He informed Irish Americans, however, that he did not want the money of those who supported or favored slavery because it would be wrong to free Irish slaves with funds acquired from the exploitation of

African-American slaves. He also said that he would rather abandon repeal than countenance a disreputable, anti-Christian social and economic system. When people in Ireland and the United States complained to O'Connell that his denunciation of slavery hampered the growth of Irish-American nationalism, he replied that he would not compromise Christian morality and that the right of all people to be free was the basic principle of Irish nationalism.

In the autumn of 1843, Cincinnati repealers wrote to O'Connell to say that he had no right to criticize an institution legal in the United States. They argued that slavery was a natural condition for morally, intellectually, and physically inferior African Americans, and they reminded O'Connell that many members of the American Catholic hierarchy and clergy defended slavery. O'Connell responded that no man should be the property of another and that no law or constitution could make a wrong into a right or deprive a person of human rights and dignity. He also rejected religious or racial justifications for slavery by insisting that God created all men equal and that the apparent inferiority of African Americans was the result of a brutal social and economic system rather than their lower nature. O'Connell said that any Catholic clergyman who did not condemn slavery contradicted the teachings of his religion and the stated position of Rome.

O'Connell chided Irish Americans for being among the most notorious defenders of servitude in the United States. He asked them to look into their hearts and to realize how far they had strayed from the tolerant and humane spirit of the Irish people and the principles of Jefferson's Declaration of Independence. He then reminded Irish Americans of their own history, and told them that they, of all people, should identify with African Americans. They should join in efforts to end bondage in their adopted country and to extend full citizenship to former slaves.[8]

Irish-American nationalism, diminished and divided by the O'Connell-slavery controversy, was rekindled, unified, and impassioned by reactions to the Great Famine. Catholic and Gaelic traditions led the Irish in Ireland to accept the hunger, death, and massive exodus of the 1840s with a large degree of fatalism. Passively, they considered their suffering a test of faith or Divine punishment for transgressions. On the American side of the Atlantic, memories of the

Famine crystallized and focused Irish hatred of the British as the source of their miseries in Ireland and the cause of their exile in a strange and alien land, where again they suffered from economic hardships and social and religious intolerance.

A popular folk ballad "Skibbereen" expresses the bitterness of Famine refugees. In the lyric, a father explains to his son why they had to leave their farm near the town of Skibbereen, one of the most Famine-ravaged areas in West Cork, for urban America. The potato crop failed, and they could no longer pay the rent. When the landlord and his bailiff evicted them, the farmer's wife fainted on the snowy ground and later died. After listening to his father's sad tale, the young man rose and said:

> Oh, father dear, the day may come
> when in answer to the call
> Each Irishman, with feeling stern,
> will rally one and all
> I'll be the man to lead the van beneath
> the flag of green,
> When loud and high we'll raise the cry—
> "Remember Skibbereen."

Fury also motivates Neddy Shea in Charles Kickham's 1869 novel *Sally Cavanagh*. As a one-armed Union veteran of the American Civil War, he returns to Ireland to place a marker on the grave of his mother, who had died following eviction from her small cottage and farm. Standing next to her final resting place, Neddy promises that although he has lost one arm for American unity, he would happily give the other to rescue Ireland from British tyranny.[9]

Because of the poverty and the political, social, and religious oppression they experienced in Ireland, a large number of Irish Americans were left psychologically scarred, full of "great hatred," carrying from their "mother's womb a fanatic heart."[10] As a result, much of Irish-American nationalism contained far more hatred of Britain than love of Ireland. John Mitchel, the most bitter and unforgiving of the Young Irelanders, communicated this rage and Anglophobia:

> I have found that there was perhaps less of love in it [nationalism]
> than of hate—less of filial affection to my country than of scorn-

ful impatience at the thought that I had the misfortune, I and my
children, to be born in a country which suffered itself to be oppressed and humiliated by another. . . . And hatred being the
thing I chiefly cherished and cultivated, the thing which I especially hated was the British system . . . wishing always that I
could strike it between wind and water, and shiver its timbers.[11]

Fanatic immigrant hearts were not pacified in an American urban environment featuring unemployment or backbreaking work, res-
idence in squalid attics and basements, and the intense anti-Catholic
hatred of American nativists. Many of the Irish who entered the
United States ready to forget the ugly past and begin anew in a promised land turned bitter when they confronted the realities of America.
They channeled their frustrations into nationalism. Patrick Ford left
Galway when he was only four, a few years before the Famine. Growing up in Boston, he knew little of Irish history, but when he began to
look for work and saw signs that said "no Irish need apply," young Ford
began to ponder the misfortunes of his people. He concluded that
Anglo-Protestant prejudice originating in England and spreading to
America was the ultimate source of Irish privations on both sides of
the Atlantic. Thus was born one of the most passionate, articulate,
and effective voices of Irish-American nationalism.[12]

Irish-American zealots differed with most nationalists in Ireland
on the virtue and efficacy of physical force. O'Connell opposed revolution. He told Irish Catholics that they could win their national
freedom within the ground rules of the British constitutional system
by mobilizing for political action and by applying the moral force of
public opinion. He argued that Irish peasants armed with pikes could
never overcome well-armed and trained British soldiers. Reminding
his audiences that 1798 begot the Act of Union, he said that revolution in Ireland had led to the loss of lives and property and diminished
personal and national liberty.

Irish-American nationalists often spoke more belligerently than
did repealers in Ireland. They recommended the example of the
American colonies that ended British rule with musket and shell.
O'Connell was not pleased with American tactical advice, fearing
that it might encourage hotheads in Ireland to pursue violence, giving
the British government an excuse to smash the repeal movement.

Conceding that the United States was a positive result of revolution, O'Connell described the difference between the American and Irish situations. Because of the geographic distance and the ocean that separated the New from the Old World, revolution in America had a better chance of success than one in Ireland. He also said that times had changed since 1776. Catholic emancipation's success was evidence that political action could improve the Irish situation.

Unpersuaded by O'Connell, Irish Americans continued to gravitate toward physical force nationalism. No doubt, the quarrel with O'Connell over slavery was a factor, but Famine-induced rage and the teachings of Young Ireland were more important ingredients in this momentum. Even more insecure than those in Ireland, Irish Catholics in the United States needed assurances that they were indeed a noble people with a significant past and the potential for an even greater future. Before it became a consensus in Ireland, the ideology of Young Ireland swept through Irish America. After the 1848 rebellion aborted in Widow McCormick's Tipperary cabbage patch, Irish America welcomed its refugees. Young Irelanders provided a leadership cadre for the Irish nation in American exile.

Following the Civil War, when the United States needed industrial labor and the quality of Irish immigrants improved considerably, many Irish Americans began to experience economic mobility. But the doors of respectability remained closed to them. This was frustrating to a people who wanted to participate fully in American life. Never fully comprehending that their political, religious, and labor leadership over an expanding Catholicism, centered in cities, was offensive to an American nativism that insisted that the United States was essentially Protestant and rural, the Irish found it difficult to understand why they were not socially acceptable. They decided that their condition reflected Ireland's colonial status. Consequently, the resentment of early Irish-American nationalism shifted to a search for respectability. Both dimensions expressed alienation.

Many economically successful Irish Americans wanted to assimilate into the mainstream, but they were rejected by middle-class Anglo-America. Forced back into their own communities, they tried to instill in them a pride of nationality and to demonstrate to the general American public that they were making a productive and honorable contribution to the United States.[13] In addition to elevating the image of Irish America, its nationalist leaders were determined to eliminate the British presence from Ireland. They insisted that once Ireland was an independent nation, its sons and daughters at home and abroad would become acceptable and respectable. Associations between Irish freedom and the progress of Irish America were the theme of an 1880 speech in the United States by Michael Davitt, a hero of the land war in Ireland. "You want to be honored among the elements that constitute this nation. . . . You want to be regarded with the respect due you; that you may thus be looked on, aid us in Ireland to remove the stain of degradation from your birth . . . and (you) will get the respect you deserve."[14]

Irish America's search for respectability through the liberation of the mother country established a precedent and a pattern followed by other ethnic groups in the United States. The concerns of American Jews, Poles, Greeks, Lithuanians, and others for their homelands have had as much to do with their American condition as with the freedom and the welfare of their native lands.[15]

EXPRESSIONS AND STRATEGIES
OF IRISH-AMERICAN NATIONALISM

Emigration internationalized the Irish question. Before millions of Catholics from Ireland arrived in the United States, Irish nationalism posed a time-consuming, irritating, but manageable nuisance for British governments. But the combination of Irish-American anger and political influence produced a threat to British rule in Ireland beyond the easy containment of police and military power.

Because "England's difficulty was Ireland's opportunity" was a basic premise of Irish nationalism, Irish-American nationalists often attempted to promote wars between Britain and its French and Russian hereditary enemies. From the Crimean War in the 1850s to the diplomatic crises between Britain and Russia in the 1870s, Irish Americans promised czarist regimes their support. And they offered aid to Spain if it should try to recover Gibraltar. Determined on humiliating the proud British navy, Irish-American nationalists in the 1870s gave John Holland $60,000 for his submarine research. Neither the Russian nor the Spanish governments took Irish Americans seriously, and eventually the United States Navy reaped the benefits of Holland's work.

The priorities of Irish-American nationalism were the encouragement and sustenance of freedom movements in Ireland and the promotion of conflict between the United States and Britain. Aware of increasing Irish-American political influence and power, some holders and seekers of office in American local, state, and national governments have called for an independent Ireland. As early as 1843, William Seward, Whig governor of New York, said he favored repeal of the Union. That same year, Robert Tyler, son of the Whig president of the United States, often spoke at repeal rallies. In July, his father, John, said: "I am the decided friend of Repeal of the legislative Union between Great Britain and Ireland. I ardently and anxiously hope that it may take place and I have the utmost confidence that Ireland will have her own Parliament, in her own capital, in a very short time. On this great question I am no half-way man."[16]

In asking for American commitments to Ireland, Irish Americans emphasized that the United States had found it necessary to declare independence from Britain and to fight for it. Events such as the War of 1812, the Oregon boundary dispute of the 1840s ("fifty-four forty or fight"), British sympathy for the South during the Civil War, and the building and outfitting of Confederate blockade runners in British ports, leading to the *Alabama* claims, all encouraged Irish nationalist hopes that a military engagement between the United States and Britain might occur that would lead to an independent Irish nation-state. But as Irish immigration nourished American nativism, intensifying its Anglo-Saxonism, Anglo-Americans felt an increasing affection for Britain as their cultural homeland. Nativism neutralized Irish political power and preserved an Anglophile bias in American foreign policy.

Irish America had a more powerful impact on Anglo-Irish than Anglo-American affairs. Without Irish-American passion, enthusiasm, determination, and dollars, efforts to liberate Ireland from British control might have faltered and ultimately failed. The Irish in the United States not only fueled Irish nationalism, they also shaped its personality. Since the Society of United Irishmen, there had been a republican tradition in Irish nationalism deriving from the ideologies of both the American and French revolutions, mainly the former.[17] Republicanism had shallow roots in the Irish Catholic population, but emigration and contacts between the Irish in Ireland and those in the United States and the image of America as the land of freedom and opportunity strengthened the democratic contents of Irish nationalism and gave credence to the republican position. In general, emigration added to the political sophistication of the Irish. In 1887, one British politician, Lord Spencer, in making a case for Irish self-government, wrote that

> the Irish peasantry still live in poor hovels, often in the same room with animals; they have few modern comforts; and yet they are in close communication with those who live at ease in the cities and farms of the United States. They are also imbued with the advanced political notions of the American republic and are sufficiently educated to read the latest political doctrines in the press that circulates among them. Their social condition at home is a hundred years behind their state of mental and political culture.[18]

The "advanced political notions of the American republic" bothered Anglo-Irish Protestant landlords and many Catholic bishops and priests. Members of the aristocracy and gentry and the clergy observed that post-Famine Irish Catholics were increasingly assertive and less deferential to the upper classes and to religious and secular authority. They attributed this impudence to American influences, particularly as manifested in Fenianism.[19]

Fenianism

Fenianism was originated by James Stephens, John O'Mahony, Michael Doheny, and Jeremiah O'Donovan Rossa. The first three were veterans of the ill-fated Young Ireland insurrection. Doheny escaped arrest and made his way to the United States; Stephens and O'Mahoney escaped to France. Paris became their school for revolution. Learning insurrection tactics from 1848 refugees from many European countries, they began to plan a revolutionary effort that would result in an Irish republic. Although O'Mahony and Stephens were impressed with and inspired by European socialism, they decided to exclude a solution to Ireland's most pressing economic issue, land, from their republican program. Like so many others coming out of the Young Ireland movement, they believed in the possibility of Protestant involvement in Irish nationalism, and they feared that any threat to property ownership would end such a hope.[20]

While Stephens and O'Mahony were planning Irish revolutionary republicanism in Paris, Doheny was creating the Emmet Monument Association in New York, dedicated to Robert Emmet, the young patriot executed after the defeat of his poorly planned 1803 rebellion. In his speech from the dock, just before he received the death sentence, Emmet asked his countrymen to delay monuments to his memory until "my country takes her place among the nations of the earth, then, and not until then, let my epitaph be written." Among the Irish in Ireland and in the United States Emmet's speech made him the most popular of all Irish heroes. Many learned it by heart. Determined on building the monument to Irish liberty that Emmet requested, Doheny wrote to O'Mahony and Stephens soliciting their help. O'Mahony sailed for New York to assist Doheny, while Stephens traveled through Ireland and Britain recruiting young men for the republican cause. In 1858, Stephens founded the Irish Republican Brotherhood (IRB), absorbing Jeremiah O'Donovan Rossa's Phoenix Society, a revolutionary republican organization in Cork.

The same year that Stephens initiated the IRB, O'Mahony converted the Emmet Monument Association into the Fenian Brotherhood. A Gaelic scholar of considerable ability, he named the American branch of republicanism after the Fianna of Irish legend. Stephens assumed the title of head centre in Ireland and Britain; O'Mahony did the same for the United States. Although Stephens claimed leadership over the entire republican movement, this assertion was not always acknowledged in Irish America. Fenianism became the popular designation for republicanism in the United States, Britain, and Ireland. In Northern Ireland today, unionists still refer to nationalists as Fenians. To achieve secrecy, Irish republicans borrowed tactics from the Italian Carbonari, dividing their organizations into cells or circles with members of each knowing only their local comrades. IRB members also took a secrecy oath when joining. So as not to offend the American Catholic hierarchy, Fenians took a pledge rather than an oath. Despite security precautions, British spies and Irish and Irish-American informers infiltrated the republican movement.

Republicanism in Ireland appealed to shop assistants, artisans, publicans, members of the building trades, shoemakers, and tailors in towns and cities. It also attracted relatively well-educated young men from the lower middle classes, frequently journalists blocked in their ambitions by people from two nationalist establishments: O'Connellites and Young Irelanders. Republicanism gained them notice and recruited a constituency. Many young men joined the IRB because it provided recreational opportunities in a country where social life was restricted by a rigid class structure, poverty, and puritan Catholic mores. Young republicans socialized at picnics and on walking excursions, they competed at and as spectators enjoyed athletic contests, and their circles featured discussion groups.[21]

Republican organizations enlisted about the same number of members in both Ireland and the United States, about fifty thousand in each country. As it did in Ireland, republican nationalism offered urban Irish Americans fun and games. Picnics and clambakes with patriotic orations and dancing were so important in Irish-American life that Finley Peter Dunne, humorist and social historian of the late nineteenth-century Chicago Irish, remarked that "if Ireland cud be freed be a picnic, it'd not on'y be free to-day, but an impire, begorra."[22]

Nonmembers as well as members contributed money to the Fenian Brotherhood. In 1865, it collected about $228,000; the next year over $500,000. This money was intended to finance a rebellion in Ireland.

Despite its impact on Irish America, in Ireland republicanism never represented majority nationalist opinion. With few exceptions, Young Ireland leaders rejected Fenianism. In 1868, a Fenian, incensed by his criticism of the organization, assassinated Thomas D'Arcy McGee on the steps of the Canadian parliament building in Ottawa. McGee, once a contributor to the *Nation* and a journalist in Irish America, was an architect of Canadian federalism. The Catholic hierarchy in Ireland also condemned the IRB, complaining of its secrecy and American radicalism and violence. Convinced that William

Ewart Gladstone, leader of the British Liberal party, was about to make major concessions to Irish Catholic interests, bishops feared that Fenianism would have such an adverse effect on British public opinion that he would have to retreat from plans to render justice to Ireland. Distrusting activities outside their control or supervision, the hierarchy and clergy also frowned on the social dimensions of republicanism. Cardinal Cullen was an outspoken critic of Fenianism, and Kerry's bishop, David Moriarity, said that hell wasn't hot enough or eternity long enough to punish them. Bishops ordered priests to refuse members of the IRB the sacraments.

The hostility of bishops and priests to the IRB introduced a note of anticlericalism into Irish republicanism. Charles Kickham, a devout Catholic and the author of the 1879 novel popular at home and among the diaspora, *Knocknagow or the Homes of Tipperary,* wrote in the IRB newspaper, the *Irish People,* that the laity should heed priests when they discussed morality and religion, but that clerical authority and expertise ended on the borders of politics.

In 1861, American Fenians mounted a challenge to Cullen by transporting the body of Terence Bellew MacManus, an 1848 veteran, from San Francisco to Ireland for burial. Before the body left New York, Archbishop John Hughes, like MacManus a native of Ulster, officiated at a funeral mass in St. Patrick's Cathedral. While the corpse was crossing the Atlantic, Cullen made it clear that though he was not opposed to a Catholic funeral service in Dublin, it could not be an occasion to celebrate revolutionary republicanism. Therefore, the IRB used the Mechanic's Institute (later the Abbey Theatre) to wake the body, and fifty thousand people participated in the funeral procession to Glasnevin cemetery, while an even larger throng lined the way.

MacManus's funeral was the emotional high point of Fenianism. The American Civil War slowed republican momentum. Numerous Irish Americans joined the Union and Confederate armies to acquire military experience and training for later use against Britain, but the conflict between North and South delayed the prospect of revolution in Ireland.[23] Following the Confederate surrender at Appomattox, Fenians restructured their organization on the American political model. O'Mahony was demoted from head centre to president and made responsible to a legislature divided into a Senate and House of

Delegates. Led by Colonel William D. Roberts, the Senate decided to fight Britain in Canada and to let the Irish in Ireland take the main responsibility for their own revolution. Controversy over this tactical switch and conflicts between O'Mahony and the Senate delayed arms supplies to the IRB, causing Stephens to cancel plans for an Irish rebellion in 1866.

While Irish republicanism was divided over the proper strategy, British authorities moved against the IRB. On the evidence of a spy in the offices of the *Irish People*, they closed down the newspaper and arrested its staff and James Stephens. To offset British intelligence, the IRB had infiltrated the British military and the police in Ireland. Prison guards with republican connections assisted Stephen's escape from Dublin's Richmond prison. He left for New York by way of Paris to end the split in American Fenianism. But his abrasive personality and egotism widened the rift.

On May 31, 1866, after deposing O'Mahony as president, the Fenian Senate sent eight hundred men across the Niagara River into Canada. After occupying Fort Erie and winning a brief encounter with a group of Canadian student volunteers, they retreated south of the border before advancing British troops. In late 1866, when activities on the Canadian border again made Stephens decide to postpone revolution, Irish Americans deposed him of his assumed title of head centre of the Fenian Brotherhood. They let him remain as civilian head of the IRB but gave control over its military operations to Colonel Thomas J. Kelly, soon to be known as chief executive of the Irish Republic. A deflated and humiliated Stephens departed New York for another Paris exile.

Anticipating insurrection, in early 1867 the British government transferred Irish soldiers garrisoned in Ireland to other parts of the United Kingdom and the empire, replacing them with English, Welsh, and Scottish troops. It also suspended habeas corpus in Ireland and arrested a number of IRB leaders. Nevertheless, in the snowy late winter, Fenian companies in counties Kerry, Cork, Tipperary, Limerick, Clare, and Dublin attacked Royal Irish Constabulary barracks. Aided by the army, the police quickly defeated and captured the underarmed and undermanned rebels.[24]

Republican violence spread from Ireland to Britain. In February 1867, when Fenians in Manchester rescued Colonel Kelly and his associate, Colonel Thomas Deasy, another Irish American, from a police van, someone shot and killed a policeman. Although there was no convincing evidence that any of the accused fired the fatal bullet, in the midst of anti-Irish hysteria a jury convicted and a judge sentenced W. P. Allen, Michael Larkin, Edward O'Meagher Condon, and Michael O'Brien to death. At the last moment, the government reprieved Condon, an American citizen. Toward the close of 1867, another Fenian project ended in violence, further antagonizing anti-Irish British opinion. An unsuccessful dynamite attempt to free Richard O'Sullivan Burke from Clerkenwell prison killed 12 and wounded 120 Britons living or strolling nearby.

Defeated and no longer considered dangerous, Fenians became nationalist martyrs. Prayers for the "Manchester Martyrs" rose from Catholic altars. Many bishops and priests joined with business and professional men in an Amnesty Association petitioning for the release of republican prisoners. Condon concluded his speech from the dock with the words "God Save Ireland." He was echoed by the other three Manchester defendants and inspired T. D. Sullivan of the *Nation,* a strong foe of the IRB, to write a patriotic ballad to the American Civil War Union army tune "Tramp, Tramp, Tramp, the Boys Are Marching." Until the "Soldier's Song" (1907) was made popular by the Irish volunteers in 1916, "God Save Ireland" was the anthem of Irish nationalism in Ireland and the United States.

> God Save Ireland said the heroes
> God save Ireland, say we all
> Whether on the scaffold high
> Or on the battlefield we die,
> What matters where for Erin dear we fall.

While patriotic ballads and folklore were enshrining Fenians in the pantheon of martyr heroes, republicanism was fading in Ireland. Federalism or Home Rule replaced it as the major expression of nationalism. Dissensions, two more failed Canadian invasions, and the hostility of the American government reduced the Fenians' significance in the United States. For a short while the Republican administration in Washington flirted with Fenianism to force Westminster to negotiate on the bill the United States submitted for the damages done by a British-built Confederate blockade runner, the *Alabama*, and for the acceptance of American naturalization of former British citizens. During this brief period, the United States sold Fenians surplus Civil War weapons at low cost, ignored their mobilizations on the Canadian border, and provided them with railroad tickets home after their retreat from Ontario. After Britain conceded to American demands in 1870, President Ulysses S. Grant said that he would no longer tolerate a self-designated Irish republican government operating freely in the United States or violations of the frontier of a friendly neighboring nation.[25]

In the years before he died in 1877, John O'Mahony, in a lonely exile in New York, longing for the day he could be buried in Irish soil, fairly well depicted the condition of American Fenianism. In *The Tenants of Time*, Thomas Flanagan describes O'Mahony's situation:

> A strong-farmer's son from the old Catholic gentry, the chiefs of the Comeraghs; he had thrown it away to ride into Ballingeary with revolver and rifle. A scholar, in New York in the first confident years he had translated Keating's old history out of the Gaelic; learned men had praised it. It was his scholarship which had found for them their famous name, from the warrior brothers in the ancient saga: the Fenian brotherhood. Now he had this, these rooms, a bottle brought as a gift. He was banished from the Council, like Stephens. But power had been stripped from him so long ago that he had been forgiven. They brought him out on ceremonial occasions.[26]

The Clan Na Gael and the New Departure

The Fenian Brotherhood survived in name and with a small membership until 1886, but by the mid-1870s it had lost out to the Clan na Gael as the main representative of Irish-American republicanism. Jerome Collins, science editor of James Gordon Bennett's *New York Herald*, founded the clan in 1867, but John Devoy became its dominant figure. A native of County Kildare, Devoy joined the IRB as a youth and in 1861 enlisted in the French Foreign Legion to gain military experience to employ against Britain. After serving a year in Algeria, Devoy deserted the Legion, returned to Ireland, and resumed his activities in the IRB. He concentrated on recruiting Irish soldiers in the British army. In 1866, he arranged Stephens's escape from Richmond prison. That same year, the British arrested Devoy, and a court sentenced him to fifteen years of penal servitude. On the condition that he reside outside the United Kingdom, the British government paroled Devoy in 1871. He arrived in the United States determined to mobilize Irish-American resources to abolish British rule in Ireland. Like John O'Mahoney and the fictional Ned Nolan in *The Tenants of Time*, Devoy was a rebel exile until his death in 1929. As Sean O'Faolain in *Come Back to Erin* described Frankie Hogan, another Irish revolutionary on the run in the United States, Devoy was in but not of America.[27]

Devoy was a journalist in New York and Chicago before settling in on the staff of the *New York Herald*. Eventually he published and edited two Irish-American newspapers, the *Irish Nation* and the *Gaelic-American*. In choosing an organizational affiliation, Devoy decided that the Clan na Gael was more united and vital than the faction-ridden Fenian Brotherhood. At the peak of its strength, the clan enrolled only about ten thousand members, but it received the financial support and the affection of a large portion of Irish America. More than the Fenians, the clan spoke for economically mobile Irish Americans searching for respectability. Such prominent people as Terence V. Powderly, grand master workman of the Knights of Labor; S. D. Conover, United States senator from Florida; and John W. Goff, New York Supreme Court justice, were proud members of the clan.

Under the guidance of Devoy and Dr. William Carroll, a Philadelphia Irish Protestant, in 1871 the clan formed an alliance with the IRB. Two years later, they established a joint seven-member Revolutionary Directory. Because of its American position and financial resources, the clan was the senior partner. It forced the IRB to dismiss members involved in the Home Rule movement.

Isaac Butt initiated Home Rule in 1870 to achieve a federal contract between Britain and Ireland. He believed that such an arrangement would satisfy the aspirations for sovereignty of Irish nationalism without provoking British fears that a self-governed Ireland would lead to complete political separation of the two islands, thus

jeopardizing Britain's security. He also thought the conservative nature of Home Rule would encourage Anglo-Irish Protestants and
Scots-Irish Presbyterians to join Catholics in an effort to create a society in which each would make a contribution and none would have
reason to fear the loss of status, property, or identity.

Butt was deservedly popular among republicans in Britain and
Ireland for defending Fenian rebels in court without charging a fee and
for heading the Amnesty Association's drive for their parole. Charles
Kickham, the IRB leader, thought it permissible for republicans to
participate in other Irish freedom efforts. But the clan insisted that
Home Rule was a dangerous deviation because its constitutional approach to self-government opened nationalism to the corrupting influences of parliamentarianism. American pressure forced Kickham
and his Irish colleagues to expel Home Rulers from the IRB Supreme
Council.[28]

The Clan na Gael's narrow republicanism shared the Irish-
American nationalist stage with the multidimensional interests of
Patrick Ford. As proprietor and editor of the *Irish World,* the most influential newspaper voice of Irish America, Ford insisted that Irish nationalism should direct its attention to economic and social issues as
well as political freedom. He believed that the clan's concentration on
revolutionary conspiracy caused it to lose touch with the basic concerns of the Irish at home and abroad. Ford argued that not only did
Ireland need to be liberated from British imperialism but the Irish in
Ireland had to be emancipated from manorial capitalism and the Irish
in the United States from industrial capitalism.[29]

Ford's radicalism appealed to Irish Americans shaken by the
tremors of a boom-and-bust industrial economy. And in the late
1870s, his attacks on landlordism became increasingly relevant to
Irish tenant farmers suffering from depression in the agrarian economy. A series of wet summers followed by bad harvests and vast
amounts of American and Canadian grain entering a free trade
United Kingdom market combined to spell disaster for Irish agriculture. From 1877 and into the 1880s, Ireland experienced its worst
times since the Great Famine. Conditions were particularly bad in the
overpopulated, underdeveloped west. But all over the country tenants
had a difficult time meeting their rent obligations. Evictions were
common, and emigration again reached panic proportions.

The plight of Ireland added weight to Ford's argument that Irish nationalism should respond to the economic needs of its constituency, and Devoy was persuaded to revise the clan's tactics. The result was a new Departure strategy emphasizing a war on landlordism to mobilize and energize Irish peasants for a revolutionary effort. John Boyle O'Reilly of the *Boston Pilot,* another powerful Irish-American newspaper, endorsed the New Departure. O'Reilly, a native of Drogheda, County Louth, was a journalism apprentice in Britain. In 1863, he joined the IRB and then enlisted in the British army to recruit Irish soldiers for Fenianism. In 1866, British authorities discovered his activities, arrested and tried him, and then commuted his execution sentence to life in prison. The next year, O'Reilly escaped from Dartmoor prison. He was recaptured and transported to Australia. In 1869, he fled on a New Bedford whaler to the United States. In addition to editing the *Pilot,* O'Reilly was a popular poet, novelist, essayist, and public speaker. Even Boston Anglo-Protestants liked and respected him. O'Reilly continued to labor in the United States for Ireland's independence, but, like Ford and unlike Devoy, he also was involved deeply in Irish America. His American positions, however, were less radical than Ford's. O'Reilly conscientiously tried to reconcile Boston's Yankee and Irish populations.[30]

To supplement the agrarian dimension of the New Departure, Devoy and his associates attempted an alliance with Charles Stewart Parnell, leader of a small group of activists in the Irish parliamentary party, the voice of Home Rule at Westminster. Parnell, descendant of an old Wicklow Protestant patriot landlord family, dissented from Butt's policy of trying to conciliate British parliamentary opinion with reason and moderation in the House of Commons. He insisted that the only way to gain the attention of British politicians was by exhibiting strength and determination. Working on that premise, in 1877 he and a few other Irish party members of Parliament delayed passage of British and imperial legislation. This tactic of obstruction gained Parnell considerable support from the Irish in English and Scottish cities. Their organization, the Home Rule Confederation of Great Britain, full of ex-Fenians, replaced Butt with Parnell as president. Parnell, however, was not yet ready to take Butt's place as Irish party chair or president of the Home Rule League. He was waiting until the situation in Ireland promised a stronger nationalist organization and a more dedicated and talented body of parliamentary representatives. But Parnell did want to capture the enthusiasm, the passion, and the financial resources of the American Irish as well as those in Britain.

The New Departure set 1882 as the year for revolution as a centennial tribute to Henry Grattan and the Volunteers who had intimidated Britain into conceding Irish parliamentary sovereignty. Events would begin when Parnell, in the House of Commons, demanded immediate Home Rule. When Britain refused, as it surely would, Parnell would lead his little band of obstructionists back to Dublin and establish an Irish government. Peasants, inflamed and disciplined by their war on landlordism and equipped with military equipment furnished by Irish in America, would defend an independent Ireland.[31]

In 1879, the clan sent Michael Davitt, a recent IRB parolee from a British prison who was then lecturing in the United States, back to Ireland to begin the agrarian phase of the New Departure. He organized the Land League of Mayo, which quickly evolved into the National Land League.[32] Parnell, not wanting either to be a pawn of the Clan na Gael or to antagonize the Catholic hierarchy by consorting with Irish-American revolutionary republicans, rejected the alliance. He did, however, become involved in the land struggle and, at Davitt's request, took on the office of Land League president. Insisting that economic issues were divisive, Kickham and the IRB refused to cooperate with the New Departure. Still, there was a Fenian presence and a militant tone to the land war.[33]

Boycotting was one of the most effective tactics of the Land League. The term originated when the league ordered servants and agricultural laborers to refuse to work for Captain Charles Boycott, an estate manager in County Mayo. Sometimes agrarian protest went beyond boycotting and spilled over into violence. From a British perspective, Ireland bordered on insurrection. Agrarian protest in Ireland finally persuaded William E. Gladstone, the Liberal prime minister, to push a land act through Parliament in 1881. The act offered Irish farmers fixed tenures at fairly evaluated rents and the free sale of their contribution to the farm on leaving. Gladstone's legislation resulted in dual ownership of the land rather than the end of landlordism. But it did begin a process that eventually solved the land question—peasant proprietorship.[34]

Instead of setting the stage for a revolution leading to an Irish republic, the land agitation strengthened the Home Rule movement, placing Parnell in charge of activities in Ireland as well as Britain. And it gained him majority Irish-American opinion and funds. American money collected for the land war went to reform and strengthen the Irish parliamentary party. Parnell replaced the Home Rule League with the Irish National League, and the Irish National League of America financed much of constitutional and parliamentary nationalism in Ireland and at Westminster.

Although Parnellism represented majority Irish-American opinion, a powerful faction in the Clan na Gael, dominated in the mid- and late 1880s by Alexander Sullivan of Chicago, used a skirmishing fund to organize and endow terrorism in the United Kingdom.[35] Dynamiters attempted to blow up such places as London Bridge and planned to do the same to the Houses of Parliament. In 1882, a group of assassins, the Invincibles, murdered Lord Frederick Cavendish, the Irish chief secretary and Gladstone's nephew by marriage, and his under secretary, T. H. Burke, as they walked in Dublin's Phoenix Park.[36]

DISILLUSIONMENT, DISUNITY, AND DECLINE

In the late 1880s, factionalism again disrupted Irish-American nationalism. Many of the Irish in the United States thought that some trends within the movement jeopardized Irish respectability. They were displeased with Patrick Ford's attacks on capitalism; his support for Henry George's single tax, anti-property socialism; and his and Davitt's desire to replace landlordism in Ireland with land nationalization rather than peasant proprietorship. Dynamiters and assassins influenced a number of Irish-Americans to agree with John O'Leary, William Butler Yeats's IRB hero, that there were some things that nationalists could not do for their country. They worried that the violence of the Sullivan wing of the clan made the Irish seem barbaric to other Americans. When some of Sullivan's henchmen murdered one of his critics, Dr. Patrick Cronin, and distributed the body throughout the Chicago sewer system, Irish-American nationalism received a bad press and many of its supporters backed away from the discredited clan.[37]

Politics in Ireland also factionalized and disillusioned many Irish Americans. In 1890, Parnell's role in a divorce scandal cost him the leadership of the Irish party and divided Home Rule into majority anti-Parnellite and minority Parnellite wings. Irish Americans were as hurt and confused by the feud that involved Catholic bishops and priests against Parnell as were the Irish in Ireland. Like those in the Dedalus Christmas dinner scene in James Joyce's *Portrait of the Artist as a Young Man,* Irish families in the United States were bitterly divided on whether to remain loyal to the "Chief," as did John Casey, or to denounce him, as did Mrs. Riordan (Dante), as an "adulterer," a "fiend," and a "devil out of hell."[38] In both Ireland and the United States emotional and financial commitments to Home Rule declined. Some energy, confidence, and generosity returned in 1900, when John Redmond, the Parnellite faction leader, became head of a united Irish party and Home Rule movement.

Added to the divisiveness of Ford's radicalism, renegade violence, and the Parnell scandal, the political activities of Clan na Gael leaders split Irish-American nationalism. In 1886, Ford and an activist priest, Father Edward McGlynn, antagonized Tammany Hall and Archbishop Michael Corrigan by recruiting many Irish votes for Henry George in New York's mayoral election. Nationalist scorn for pragmatic Irish-American politics and anger with the Democratic party for taking the Irish vote for granted led John Devoy and others in the Clan na Gael to endorse Republicans in the 1884 and 1888 presidential elections. Devoy insisted that Irish-American politics should concentrate on liberating Ireland and that voters should cast ballots for the candidates and party that would do most to advance that cause. He and his friends believed that Republicans were more trustworthy in that regard than Democrats. Ireland-first nationalists competed unsuccessfully with politicians closer to voters and more aware of their immediate American needs. When nationalism entered the political arena, it shed its romantic idealism for political power, disillusioning much of Irish America.[39]

Although withering since 1890, Irish-American nationalism has continued to affect Ireland's progress toward independence. Moderate Irish Americans contributed funds to Home Rule; fanatics sustained the Irish Republican Brotherhood. During the early years of World War I, Irish Americans joined German Americans in urging neutrality.[40] Devoy and his friends went farther by participating in the planning of the 1916 "Blood Sacrifice" Easter Week rebellion in Dublin. When it was over and the executions of Patrick Pearse, James Connolly, and other rebel leaders converted them into martyr heroes, Britain realized the necessity of appeasing Irish nationalism on both sides of the Atlantic if it was to persuade the United States to enter the war against the Central Powers. John Redmond, however, rejected a Home Rule offer that would have partitioned Ireland permanently into a mostly Protestant North and an overwhelmingly Catholic South. When the United States did enter the war in April 1917 on the British side, Irish Americans patriotically enlisted in the armed forces and enthusiastically supported the Allied cause. But from 1919 to 1921, when Irish republican rebels engaged Britain in a war for independence, many Irish Americans aided their effort and demanded that the United States recognize the Irish Republic and put pressure on Britain to do the same. To many Anglophiles, Irish-American sympathy for the Easter Week rebellion that "stabbed Britain in the back" during its struggle for survival against Germany and their support for the Irish Republican Army during the Anglo-Irish War were offensive. Despite this incitement to nativism, Irish-Amerian opinion played a major role in persuading Britain in 1921 to concede dominion status to a twenty-six-county Irish Free State.[41]

A large number of republicans resented the lingering British connection that dominion status involved. For ten months in 1922 and 1923, the Free State government was busy suppressing republican rebels. During the Treaty debate and the civil war, the British partition of Ireland in 1920 into a Protestant majority North and a Catholic majority South was not a pressing issue. But when in 1925, the Free State government accepted the findings of a boundary commission confirming the border, divided Ireland fueled republicanism. Led by Joseph McGarrity, an immigrant from County Tyrone who settled in Philadelphia and became a prosperous wine and spirits merchant, the Clan na Gael assisted the Irish Republican Army in a steady guerrilla war against the British presence in Northern Ireland. This campaign involved sabotage in Britain before America's entry into World War II.[42]

Partition did not seriously trouble most Irish Americans. They thought that the Free State was a reasonable response to the Irish demand for freedom, and that dominion status promised an evolving sovereignty. The fratricide of the civil war alienated and puzzled Irish Americans; so did the new Irish-Ireland emphasis in Irish nationalism. By insisting that Ireland must be "Gaelic as well as free," post-treaty Irish nationalism became parochial, exclusive, isolationist, and irrelevant to the Irish of the diaspora making their way in the urban industrial centers of the English-speaking world.[43] A shift in the main Irish emigration route from the United States to Britain also had a negative impact on Irish-American nationalism. American immigration restrictions, the Depression, and World War II erected barriers against entry to the United States, lessening cultural and interest ties between Ireland and Irish America.

The socialist dimension of twentieth-century Irish nationalism had a greater impact on Irish America than Irish-Ireland cultural values. Patrick Pearse committed physical force nationalism to a Gaelic Ireland; his 1916 Easter Week partner, James Connolly, was equally determined to create a socialist workers' republic. Socialism could never compete with the Catholic tradition in Irish nationalism, but during the civil war some republicans reacted against more than the oath of allegiance to a British monarch. They interpreted the support of priests, shopkeepers, strong farmers, and Protestant unionists as a sign that the Free State represented conservative special interests, and they wanted an economic and social as well as a political revolution.[44] Socialists remained a significant minority within republicanism, exerting a disproportionate influence on its policies. Connolly's ideas also entered Irish America. According to Joshua B. Freeman, Irish republican immigrants in New York after 1922 were much more radical in their social and political views than those who came to the United States before the Anglo-Irish and civil wars. They cooperated with members of the Communist party in establishing the powerful Transport Workers Union in New York City.[45]

Growing Irish-American indifference to Ireland revealed Americanization as well as a decline in immigration and negative reactions to the civil war and Irish-Ireland nationalism. As the Irish achieved success and respectability in the United States, they became more American and less Irish.

American adaptations did not mean the immediate disappearance of Anglophobia. It remained strong in the minds and hearts of the Irish-American working class that did not experience significant economic or social mobility. This attitude was evident in support for Father Coughlin's and other forms of isolationism in the late 1930s. In December 1941, when the United States entered World War II, however, no group exceeded Irish Americans in devotion to the war effort. Ireland's neutrality in World War II and during the Cold War, while Britain and the United States were locked in alliance against fascism and then communism, augmented Irish-Americans' lack of concern for their ethnic homeland.

THE TROUBLES IN NORTHERN IRELAND

Irish-American apathy toward Ireland disappeared in the late 1960s, when newspapers and especially television reported the Catholic civil rights campaign in Northern Ireland. After the British government partitioned Ireland in 1920 to appease Ulster unionists determined to resist inclusion in an independent, Catholic-majority Ireland, the two-thirds Protestant majority created an apartheid home rule government discriminating against the one-third Catholic minority in political participation, employment, and housing. Most Catholics responded to second-class citizenship by retreating into territorial and psychological ghettos. A few, however, joined the outlawed Irish Republican Army (IRA) seeking to create a united Ireland through physical attacks on such symbols of British and Northern Ireland government authority as constabulary barracks and arms depots. During World War II, the IRA was involved in sabotage throughout the United Kingdom, and the government in Dublin, as well as in Britain and Northern Ireland, interned many republicans.

Beginning in 1947, a British government education act created opportunities for bright Northern Ireland Catholic secondary school graduates to attend universities throughout the United Kingdom. Like most young people, they expected their degrees to open a variety of avenues to middle-class success. But they soon discovered that discrimination in Northern Ireland blocked the mobility of even well-educated Catholics. Refusing to accept limits imposed by sectarianism, they dedicated themselves to leading their community out of the doldrums of Six County apartheid. In their strategy for Catholic progress, new well-educated leaders rejected both ghetto isolation and violence as futile. They decided to concentrate on something more immediate and tangible than the goal of a united Ireland. Inspired by the African-American civil rights movement in the United States, they recommended that Northern Ireland Catholics mobilize and demand equal citizenship in the United Kingdom with a full share in the British welfare state.

A strategy of equal citizenship and justice led in February 1967 to the formation of the Northern Ireland Civil Rights Association, (NICRA). Beginning in Dungannon, County Tyrone, the NICRA quickly spread throughout the province as a coalition of Catholic middle-class moderates, socialists, republicans, and socialist-republicans and the People's Democracy, a radical, nonsectarian student group from Queen's University, Belfast. NICRA members occupied public housing units, insisting that they be allotted to Catholic families on the same basis that they were to Protestants. They marched through the streets of Northern Ireland's cities and towns demanding equal citizenship and opportunities for all people in the provinces, singing the songs of the African-American civil rights movement, particularly "We Shall Overcome." The Royal Ulster Constabulary; B-Specials, a Gestapo-like exclusively Protestant auxilliary police force summoned in emergency situations; and Protestant mobs harassed and sometimes physically assaulted civil rights demonstrators. Television cameras and commentators brought life behind the Orange Curtain into the homes of viewers in Britain, on the Continent, throughout the commonwealth, and in the United States, building a wave of world opinion in sympathy with oppressed Northern Ireland Catholics.

By August 1969, Six County tensions had escalated to the brink of civil war. In Londonderry (Derry to nationalists), the second largest city in Northern Ireland, where a Protestant minority controlled city government, Catholics were battling the constabulary with rocks, pieces of cement and asphalt from the streets, and Molotov cocktails from behind barricades. In Belfast, Catholic enclaves, surrounded by hostile Protestant neighborhoods, had also erected defense barriers. The IRA, moribund since 1962, was revived as a defense force. Responding to pleas from Catholic leaders, the British government sent troops into Northern Ireland to avoid a bloodbath. At first, the Catholic population received the soldiers as saviors—women brought them tea and biscuits—though many Protestants regarded them as meddlers, impediments to their intention of giving the Catholics a violent lesson in subservience.

The British army's popularity in Northern Ireland was of short duration. In constitutional governments soldiers serve civil authority, and the Six County state was Protestant unionist. Enforcing the rules and regulations of the Stormont Castle government, the army soon was at war with an IRA split into Official and Provisional wings. Officials took a Marxist line, projecting a united Ireland workers' republic. Provisionals represented a more traditional, nonideological physical force republicanism. Since 1969, however, many Provisionals have become more radical on economic and social issues. A fundamental difference between the two IRAs involved the use of violence. Before they agreed to a truce with the British army in 1974, and then concentrated on political approaches to meet their objectives, Officials confined their military operations to attacks on soldiers. Provisionals were less discriminatory. Their bombs and bullets have killed many civilians, Catholics and Protestants alike, in efforts to terrorize the British into leaving Northern Ireland. In 1975, a group more savage than the Provisionals, the Irish National Liberation Army, an Official splinter group, came into existence.

Two events increased the unpopularity of the British army among Northern Ireland Catholics. In August 1971, it assisted the Royal Ulster Constabulary in enforcing internment without trial of suspected IRA members and collaborators. On January 30, 1972, soldiers killed thirteen people participating in a civil rights march in Derry. Reactions to "Bloody Sunday" in Northern Ireland, the Irish Republic, Britain, the United States, and throughout the world were so intense that Westminster suspended the Stormont government and imposed direct rule.

At a conference in England at Sunningdale in 1973, Britain and Ireland both accepted the desirability of a united Ireland but agreed that Northern Ireland would remain part of the United Kingdom until a majority of its citizens desired a change. The next year, a Northern Ireland legislature was formed as an experiment in power sharing. Moderate unionists joined members of the Social Democratic and

Labour party, a Catholic nationalist constitutional party, which enjoyed far more support in the minority community than did the IRA, and the nonsectarian, pro-civil-rights but unionist Alliance party to create a government with proportional representation.

As well as a power-sharing government at Stormont, the Sunningdale agreement produced a Council of Ireland in which representatives from North and South would confer on problems of mutual concern and interest. Led by the Reverend Ian Paisley of the Free Presbyterian church, unionist extremists rejected the Council of Ireland as a step toward a united Ireland and power sharing as a contradiction to majority rule. The IRA also opposed Sunningdale as a prop to partition. Paisley forces organized a general strike that coerced the power-sharing government to reject the Council of Ireland and then to dissolve. Britain resumed direct rule but in 1982 created another Northern Ireland Assembly without power sharing but with a Catholic veto over objectionable legislation. John Hume, the Social Democratic and Labour party leader, and his colleagues refused to participate in the deliberations of an assembly that excluded Catholics from direct decision making.[46]

Since the beginning of the Northern Ireland crisis, violence has taken the lives of almost three thousand revolutionary republicans, soldiers, policemen, and innocent civilians. The British and Irish governments agree that Irish-American support for terrorism in the Six Counties is a major cause of death and destruction. Although the accusation is valid, Irish-American involvement in Northern Ireland is complicated and uneven.

In 1969, when Irish Americans learned from newspapers and television that Northern Ireland Catholics sharing their religious and ethnic heritages were victims of prejudice and witnessed Protestant mobs, encouraged or not restrained by the RUC, physically abusing civil rights advocates, they were furious. Stormont's one-sided internment policy, the torture of internees by British soldiers and the constabulary, and the "Bloody Sunday" massacre in the streets of Derry intensified their anger. Many Irish Americans were fuzzy about the historical background of the turmoil in Northern Ireland and could not distinguish between the IRA and NICRA, so that much of the money that they contributed for Northern Ireland equality went into the wrong pockets.

Although a large number of Irish Americans reacted emotionally rather than intellectually to events in Northern Ireland and confused the issues, pro-IRA organizations did emerge in the United States. In 1970, two Provisional IRA leaders, Daithi O'Connell and Joe Cahill, traveled to New York to meet with Michael Flannery, a republican veteran of the Anglo-Irish and civil wars. From their discussions the Northern Ireland Aid Committee (NORAID) was formed. Ostensibly, it exists to assist the families of IRA men killed in combat with the British army or behind prison walls. But the American as well as the British and Irish governments insist that when people drop coins or paper money into NORAID boxes in pubs or attend its various benefits, they are contributing to terrorism and not charity. Although NORAID leaders deny such allegations and hard evidence linking their organization to the purchase and running of guns is sketchy, some of the members have been arrested for such activities.

For a while the Irish National Caucus (INC) also functioned as an IRA support group. Founded by Sean McManus, a Redemptionist priest from County Fermanagh with long family ties to the IRA, the caucus champions a united Ireland and lobbies that cause in Washington. Irish Americans in the House and Senate have shunned INC. Until his recent indictment and conviction on a variety of charges, including mail fraud, extortion, and racketeering, and his subsequent resignation from Congress, Mario Biaggi, an Italian-American House member from the Bronx, was the caucus's leading spokesperson on Capitol Hill. While continuing to advocate the end of partition, the INC has recognized the ever-increasing American antipathy to terrorism and has distanced itself from the IRA.[47]

Among Irish Americans, immigrants, particularly those from the economically bleak Ireland of the 1950s, and their families make up the hard-core membership of NORAID and are the most vociferous defenders of the IRA. In the United States, they express the same nationalist opinions once popular in Ireland. They still believe the simplistic notion that without the British presence, Northern Ireland Protestants and Catholics would negotiate and find common ground in a united Ireland. They refuse to understand Ulster Protestant animosity toward Catholics, their British fanaticism, or their determination to resist a united Ireland.

Frequently, united Ireland commitments communicate bitterness against a country that could not provide emigrants with a decent living. Because NORAID and IRA zealots in the United States hold the Irish government responsible for the economic conditions that compelled emigration and denounce it as a British puppet, they are not impressed when Dublin politicians plead with Americans not to finance violence in Northern Ireland. They seem unconcerned that the tensions and slaughter in the six Counties not only add to the hatreds that divide sectarian communities but that their consequences spill over into the Irish Republic, endangering its liberal democratic traditions.

American responses to Northern Ireland also reveal Irish insecurities in the United States. Immigrants, except for well-educated professionals, are not always comfortable in American cities. They do not share the modernist values, the affluence, or the middle-class respectability of most American-born Irish.

Much of the new Irish-American nationalism resembles the old not only in its expression of frustration and alienation but in its search for respectability. Northern Ireland's troubles have provided immigrants and other insecure Irish Americans with an opportunity to display their ethnicity. Nineteenth-century Irish Americans thought that a liberated Ireland would establish their value in the United States. A minority of twentieth-century Irish Americans, still unsure of their place in society, are attempting to fix their importance by eliminating Protestant oppression in Northern Ireland and, in the process, creating a united Ireland.

Paradoxically, many IRA enthusiasts in the United States come from the least liberal segment of Irish America. They ignore similarities between conditions that pejoratively define African Americans and Northern Ireland Catholics. They also ignore Marxist purposes stated by some IRA leaders. And they refuse to recognize that the Provisionals and the Irish National Liberation Army employ terrorist tactics that they deplore when used by Arab factions in the Mideast.[48]

After their first angry responses to Northern Irish Protestant and British insensitivity to the civil rights issue in the Six Counties, most respectable middle-class Irish Americans have taken a more cautious and prudent approach to the situation. Basically, their priorities are American not Irish. As William V. Shannon put it, they have traveled so far up the road of social mobility and respectability in the United States that they cannot identify emotionally with people who are economically impoverished and psychologically demoralized by generations of oppression. They have either forgotten or ignored the history of their own community, fearful of opening up its wounds to the scrutiny of their own minds and those of their children. For them "to enter into the passions that convulse Northern Ireland would require a journey into the past they are reluctant to make. They are too involved with the American present and future."[49]

Irish-American middle-class opinion has retreated emotionally from the conflict in Northern Ireland while continuing to plead for justice to its Catholic minority. IRA conduct has forced the disengagement. Reacting to terrorism in the Mideast and other places that have resulted in the murder or capture of Americans, most of the Irish in the United States are furious when the IRA ambushes British soldiers or assassinates British politicians. They are angrier when IRA bombs kill women and children. They believe that this barbaric, irresponsible, and futile violence tarnishes the image of the Irish everywhere.

In 1981, when Bobby Sands initiated a hunger strike in Belfast's Maze prison to win the status of political prisoners for incarcerated republicans, his courage and sacrifice won him considerable Irish-American sympathy and respect. At first, contributions to NORAID increased, but when the strike continued, and after nine IRA and INLA prisoners starved themselves to death, American reactions became increasingly negative. From a non-Irish nationalist perspective, the hunger strike became macabre mass suicide, not glorious martyrdom. Like other Americans, the Irish in the United States believe that living for one's country is more constructive than dying for it.[50]

NORAID or INC does not represent majority Irish-American opinion on Northern Ireland. On St. Patrick's Day in 1977, Senators Edward Kennedy and Daniel Patrick Moynihan, Speaker of the House of Representatives Thomas P. "Tip" O'Neill, and Governor Hugh Carey of New York issued an advisory requesting Irish Americans not to contribute to violent forces in Northern Ireland. The "Big Four" worked closely with the Irish ambassador to the United Stated, Sean Donlon, and formed the Friends of Ireland, a bipartisan committee of House and Senate members. This organization enjoys the confidence of the Dublin government and speaks for the Irish-American majority in regard to Northern Ireland. The Friends of Ireland have exerted pressure on the White House to encourage Britain to find a solution to the conflict based on civil liberty and social justice. To encourage such an effort, President Jimmy Carter promised that the United States would respond to progress with financial assistance to the Northern Ireland economy. Carter's successor, Ronald Reagan, reaffirmed the commitment.

Although Irish Americans' involvement in Ireland is considerably less than that of Jewish Americans in Israel, it has had an influence on Britain's policy toward Northern Ireland. Remembering the impact of Irish America on past Anglo-American relations and probably exaggerating its present Irish concerns, British governments have tried to impress the Irish in the United States and to pacify Northern Ireland Catholics with reform. Despite charges by the IRA and NORAID that the Six County situation has remained static, much that is positive has happened there since 1969. In local government the principle of one person one vote and equal electoral districts have replaced gerrymandering and property owning and dual franchises. The result has been Catholic control in places where they are in the majority. Now they also get their share of public housing. Jobs are still a problem but less so in the public than the private sector. Protestant businesses still hesitate to hire Catholics, and British efforts at fair employment have been more the articulation than the enforcement of principle.

The key change in the Northern Ireland situation occurred in November 1985, when the British made a major concession to Irish nationalism. Prime Ministers Margaret Thatcher of Britain and Garret Fitzgerald of Ireland met and signed an Anglo-Irish agreement creating an Intergovernmental Conference through which representatives of both governments would meet frequently to discuss matters of mutual concern regarding Northern Ireland. The Hillsborough accord also granted the Irish Republic an advisory role in governing the province. In return, Dublin accepted the right of the Northern Ireland majority to remain in the United Kingdom as long as they wished to do so. Seven months after the Anglo-Irish agreement, Congress passed a $50 billion aid bill for Northern Ireland. Eventually, a total of $250 billion will go to help revitalize its economy.[51]

Violence and discontent remain in Northern Ireland. Protestant extremists, notably Ian Paisley, complain that the Hillsborough accord was a British sellout to Irish nationalism. Complaining of poverty and unemployment, Catholics say that the Anglo-Irish agreement has done little to improve their economic situation. The IRA, refusing to settle for anything less than the departure of Britain and a united Ireland, continues its violence. Protestant gangs also kill and maim. A variety of incidents have led to tensions between Dublin and Westminster. The British government is annoyed at what it interprets as Irish reluctance to extradite IRA members who have fled to the South after criminal indictment in the United Kingdom. The Irish government accuses Britain of insensitivity to Irish feelings and opinions. To buttress this charge, it points to Westminster's decision not to punish Royal Ulster Constabulary members responsible for killing six unarmed Northern Ireland Catholics in 1982, the 1988 British army slaughter of unarmed IRA members in Gibraltar, the 1988 decision of British courts not to reconsider suspect evidence that jailed six Ulster Catholics for 1974 bombings in Birmingham, and the 1989 revelation that British security forces passed on information concerning IRA suspects to Protestant terrorists.[52]

Despite the slowness of economic and social change in the province and quarrels between Dublin and Westminster, the Anglo-Irish agreement has changed the game in Northern Ireland. Conflict resolution is no longer primarily in the hands of local Catholics and Protestants, or in negotiations between Dublin and Stormont, or Stormont and Westminster. The future of Northern Ireland will be decided by Irish and British politicians, and American economic aid and concern will be components in the outcome.

6

Someplace or No Place?

In the 1820s, Catholics replaced Protestants as the majority of Irish entering the United States. Though less educated, skilled, or sophisticated than English, Scottish, Irish Protestant and Presbyterian, or German immigrants, Irish Catholics had the resources to purchase ship passages and supplies for sea voyages and to begin life in America. They also possessed the courage and determination to leave familiar surroundings, families, and friends and to set out on long and perilous journeys to a land beyond their limited comprehensions. Lacking agricultural and other economic expertise and deterred by their communal backgrounds from settling in lonely rural areas, Irish Catholics became pioneers of the American urban ghetto.

Despite their lack of talents and a hostile environment, early nineteenth-century Irish Catholics managed to build and buy churches and homes. In the 1840s, however, the arrival of the wretched Famine refugees pulled their community back down into destitution. In many cities they huddled in suffocating attics, damp basements, or tar-paper shacks without basic washing or sewage facilities. Still, they made a contribution to their new country. Unskilled Irish labor hastened America's industrial and transportation revolutions. As domestic servants, Irish women increased the comfort and leisure of middle-class Anglo-Protestants by cleaning their houses and minding their children. Irish soldiers died for the United States on Mexican and Civil War battlefields and on the western frontier.

The transition from rural Ireland to urban America was traumatic. Ghetto indigence led to physical and mental disease, alcoholism, crime, brutality, and family disturbances. Irish social disorder and, more significant, Catholicism inflamed American nativism. Struggles for survival and acceptance, frequent failures, and Anglo-

164

American Protestant prejudice added to feelings of defeatism and paranoia carried from Ireland.

Anti-Catholic nativism defined the Irish as a threat to American values and institutions. Hatred of their religion hampered them even when they began to shake off poverty. Despite its burdens, Catholicism comforted the Irish spiritually and psychologically. Attending mass and receiving the sacraments bridged the psychological and spatial distances between rural Ireland and urban America. In both places Catholicism was culture, attitudes, and nationality as well as religion. Irish Catholic parishes in the cities of the United States resembled peasant villages, providing religious inspiration and consolation, education, and community. Catholicism embraced people from various provinces and counties in Ireland and melded them into one ethnic group. Catholic cohesion, identity, and pride enabled the Irish to survive poverty and the assaults of nativism.

Priests, the most important members and leaders of Catholic society in Ireland, retained that status in Irish America. Clerical prestige, plus Anglo-Protestant control of American business, sent the cream of Irish-American ability and ambition into religion or politics. Having a priest in the family brought distinction to all its members. Irish women were the most numerous of their sex to find religious vocations. As nurses and teachers and administrators of schools and hospitals, nuns were role models for young Irish women aspiring to something other than marriage and motherhood.

Catholic solidarity, moral discipline, and education and welfare services (schools, hospitals, orphanages, and asylums) and the example and leadership of priests, nuns, and brothers transformed an impoverished, demoralized Irish rabble into a proud, secure, socially mobile community. In the process, the Catholic church in the United States became an instrument and voice of Irish power.

Politics as well as control of a rapidly expanding American Catholic church strengthened Irish America. In the Irish search for American dignity, political skills compensated for technological incompetence. Daniel O'Connell's work for Catholic civil rights in the 1820s and for repeal of the Union with Britain in the 1840s involved tactics of mass agitation and the pressure of public opinion on government decisions. They prepared the Irish for participation in American liberal democracy. Because emigration involved flight from

Protestant ascendancy, in the United States the Irish naturally appreciated Jeffersonian and Jacksonian democracy. In addition, the Democrats were less nativist than Federalists, Whigs, and Republicans. They welcomed the Irish and sped their naturalization in exchange for their votes.

Demanding a political say, the Irish refused to remain in the lower ranks of the Democratic party. Ambitious, intelligent, and shrewd young men, excluded from business and not inclined toward the church, embarked on political careers. They steadily rose from precinct captains, to ward leaders, to aldermen. By the close of the nineteenth century, the Irish controlled most city governments above and New Orleans below the Mason-Dixon line.

Unlike Anglo-Protestants, who believed that America's main business was business and scorned politics as at best a necessary evil, the Irish treated it as a profession, providing constituents with a variety of services. Although Irish politicians mostly benefited the Irish, they did attend to the needs and concerns of other Catholic ethnics and Jews, people despised and ignored by the Anglo-Protestant establishment. Irish politicians forged the multiethnic urban Democratic coalition that in the twentieth century joined with southern white and urban African-American voters in the North to put Democrats frequently in control of Congress and the White House.

Although tarnished by graft and rascality, Irish-American politics has involved more than greed and power lust. It has combined a pragmatic search for office and common-good idealism. Irish culture blends the Gaelic heritage with Anglicization and Romanization. Although the last two involve contradictory mind-and-soul-tormenting loyalties to the West's most authoritarian religious and most liberal political systems, the mixture has resulted in a unique political style and ethic that tempers individualistic and selfish Anglo-Protestant economics and politics with Catholic and Gaelic communalism. Irish politicians have acted on the premise that government exists to assist the poor, the sick, the very young, and the very old, and not just the affluent.[1]

Politics emerging from Irish urban ghettos originally exhibited more pragmatism than principle, but when Irish Americans moved from the working to the middle class and from cities to suburbs, their politicians became more principled and idealistic. But from the early days, when they distributed coal and food baskets in destitute neighborhoods, to more recent times, when in state legislatures and in the Congress of the United States they have voted for legislation to protect people from the ravages of poverty, disease, and bigotry, Irish politicians have been a major force in making American government sensitive to social needs.

In Ireland, politics and nationalism were inseparable. Efforts at achieving freedom embraced such issues as Catholic emancipation, disestablishment of the Protestant church, secure tenures at fair rents, an expanded suffrage with a secret ballot, and popular control of local government. In the United States, Irish politics and nationalism were separate expressions. Courting voters, office seekers endorsed self-government for Ireland, but many nationalist leaders were reluctant to taint their cause with corrupt and pragmatic Irish-American politics.

British tyranny was the nationalist explanation for Irish troubles in the Old and New Worlds. English invaders and occupiers had deprived Catholics in Ireland of their liberty, property, and dignity, forcing millions into an American exile where they again confronted poverty and prejudice.

There was bitterness, sometimes more hatred of Britain than love for Ireland, in Irish-American nationalism, but it also contained noble sentiments. Patriotic versions of Irish history extolled the glories of Gaelic Ireland and the spirituality and scholarship of early Irish monks who enlightened Europe in the Dark Ages. According to nationalist propaganda, Irish successes in the United States were proof that Ireland would again flourish in freedom. Nationalist heroes who sacrificed their lives for national and individual liberty gave Irish Americans a splendid cause, Ireland's sovereignty, and models of courage and virtue. Irish nationalism's dedication to liberal democracy also helped the Irish in the United States adapt to American political values. The energy, vitality, and expectations of nationalism countered the fatalism and passivity of the Catholic and Gaelic traditions and nourished a historical consciousness necessary to the maintenance and continuity of the Irish-American community. And because of its principles and values and its sense of history, nationalism gave people a way of remaining Irish outside of an allegiance to an intellectually oppressive, religiously exclusive, and socially conservative Catholicism.

When the Irish in the United States began to enjoy the economic opportunities it offered, their nationalism shifted in emphasis from vengeance to the search for respectability. Many economically mobile Irish found it difficult to understand why other Americans continued to snub them in social situations and concluded that they were victims of Ireland's colonial status. They decided that they could free Ireland and improve their American standing at the same time.

Strong cultural ties and filial associations between Anglo-America and Britain frustrated efforts to create a pro-Hibernian American foreign policy, but Irish-American passion and financial resources encouraged and preserved constitutional and physical force nationalisms in Ireland. And Irish-American fanaticism spurred British governments to make concessions to Irish grievances and eventually to concede an Irish nation-state. Although the mythology and the values of Irish nationalism played a significant role in shaping the Irish-American mind, values flowed east as well as west. The American connection fostered egalitarianism and republicanism in Ireland.

The American labor movement also had a strong Irish content. At first, Anglo-Protestant workers loathed the Irish as cheap, scab competitors. But after The Civil War the Irish were prominent as labor organizers. In 1879, Terence V. Powderly, a member of the Irish nationalist Clan na Gael, became grand master workman of the Knights of Labor, the first important effort to mobilize workers on a national scale. Founded in 1886, the American Federation of Labor soon surpassed the membership of the Knights of Labor. By 1910, the Irish controlled more than 45 percent of its presidencies. The labor movement gave the Irish another opportunity to exhibit leadership talents and provided them and others with job security, higher wages and shorter workdays, and better employment conditions. Unfortunately, Irish labor leaders, like Irish politicians, focused attention on the needs of white ethnics to the neglect of African and Hispanic Americans.

Irish America's influence in the Catholic church, urban politics, and the labor movement exceeded its numbers. Late nineteenth-century immigrants from eastern and southern Europe entered an

Irish-controlled Catholic church, gave their votes to Irish political machines, and joined Irish-managed labor unions. Most Americans perceived expanding Catholic America as an extension of Irish America.

Escalating Irish power drew nativist anger. Though moderated by Civil War priorities and a postbellum need for immigrant industrial labor, nativism had a resurgence when economic recessions and depressions stalled the American economy after 1880. Nativists insisted that because the frontier was closed, the United States should reserve limited resources for the native-born. They blamed strikes and labor unrest on foreigners who brought socialism and class conflict to America. Irish labor leaders were seldom ideologically radical. Most advocated collective bargaining within the capitalist system. But that was too extreme for many Americans.

Toward the close of the nineteenth century, racialism, a popular component of European nationalism, infiltrated American nativism. Much of it was directed against Jews, Slavs, and Latins, but the old Anglo-Saxon contempt for Celts found new life in American universities, books, pamphlets, newspapers periodicals, and cartoons.

Racialism had an elitist appeal, but anti-Catholicism continued to fuel the nativism of many intellectuals, while remaining strong in rural areas and small towns. Americans who believed that Catholicism endangered their country's values and institutions were convinced that Irish political, religious, and labor leaders were the agents of Romanism.

Racial and religious nativism perpetuated a defensive American Catholic subculture. Exclusion from the American mainstream and limited economic opportunities led the Irish into entertainment and sports as well as politics, the labor movement, nationalist organizations, and the Catholic church. Irish singers, dancers, comedians, and actors performed on vaudeville and theater stages all over the United States. Show business meant fame and, if not fortune, excitement and higher incomes than the unskilled working class could earn. It also released bottled-up anguish and pain. During the late nineteenth and early twentieth centuries, Americans considered the Irish their country's best athletes. Most champion boxers were Irish, and they excelled at baseball, America's quintessential game. Athletics gave the Irish heroes, and they released ghetto frustrations and anger in competitions with ethnic rivals and the hereditary Anglo-Protestant enemy.

Nativist obstacles did not preclude Irish occupational and residential mobility. Catholic cohesion and moral discipline; political power and patronage; an improved emigration from a better educated and nourished and a more religious post-Famine Ireland; increased opportunities in an economically and geographically expanding America; the benefits of the trade union movement; and the entry of new unskilled European immigrants at the lower levels of the American work force lifted many Irish from the unskilled to the skilled ranks of labor. A few entered the lower middle class. Catholic schools provided enough professionals to serve the educational, medical, and legal needs of Irish and other Catholic communities. Irish occupational mobility encouraged an urge to break out of physical if not mental ghettos. Parish-centered Irish neighborhoods began to appear in new parts of cities and, less frequently, in suburbs.

Local situations determined Irish-American mobility. In the East, particularly New England, their prospects were slow to improve. Social, economic, and geographic borders between Anglo-Protestant and Irish remained impassable. Anglo-Protestants continued to control finance and commerce, and they persisted in loathing Irish invaders and conquerors of their cities. Irish political power brought few economic benefits beyond services and blue-collar or lower-level white-collar employment. The Irish became victims of bitter fatalism and passivity as well as of Anglo-Protestant prejudice.

Most Irish progress took place on the urban frontier, the new cities of the West and Midwest, where economies were dynamic, the class structure fluid, and nativism curbed by economic necessity. These areas attracted high-quality post-Famine immigrants and escapees from the paranoid ghettos of the East. In the Midwest and West, the Irish grew up with the cities they lived in.

In general, late nineteenth-century Irish-American women fared better than men. Following post-Famine Ireland's social patterns, reinforced by Catholic puritanism, young Irish Americans were reluctant to marry unless they were economically secure. Unmarried teachers and nurses, following nun role models, became America's first lay women professionals.

With exceptions in the East, the Irish-American situation continued to improve before World War II. Catholic schools played a key role in this progress by providing a good basic education, but their glorification of a mythical medieval past, combined with a suspicion of the American present and a distrust of lay intellectualism unrestricted by church authority, discouraged excellence. But the values of Catholic education reflected those of Irish families. Unpleasant Old and New World experiences encouraged an obsession with security. Fathers and mothers counseled children to find permanent jobs with good pensions. This advice put many of them in the post office, on the railroad, in police and fire departments, in public school systems, and in political bureaucracies. Perhaps the Irish made a mistake in following the safe course for too long, for not taking more chances in a land of opportunities, for relying too much on politically related employment. But because of their past and the Anglo-American Protestant financial power monopoly, there were few alternatives. The road they took did provide a secure and stable base for their rapid economic and social mobility after World War II.

Although the 1928 presidential candidacy of Irish Catholic Democrat Al Smith produced a massive burst of anti-Catholicism, after 1930 nativist attacks subsided. Because of the Great Depression of the 1930s, World War II, and the Cold War, Americans looked for unifying rather than divisive themes. Their exceptional patriotism during the war against fascism and Japanese imperialism and favorable motion picture portrayals helped make the Irish America's favorite ethnics.

Irish America's anticommunism harmonized with majority opinion in the United States, but its excessiveness convinced many liberals that the Irish had not adjusted to American democratic principles. But the fragment of Irish working-class support given to Father Charles Coughlin after 1936 and the more substantial middle- and working-class support for McCarthyism reflected lingering Irish anxieties concerning their place in the United States rather than any conscious rejection of American political values.

Despite the aberrations of Coughlin and McCarthy, the increasing prosperity of Irish Americans encouraged their religious, political, and labor leaders to be more cosmopolitan and less tribal. Catholic bishops and priests worked to convert American Catholicism from a federation of ethnic enclaves into a national church speaking with one voice, expressing a singular religious culture. Responding to urban working-class social problems, the challenges of communism and socialism, and the message of papal encyclicals, they tried to reform the selfish individualism of American capitalism with a social justice agenda. Irish politicians legislated that agenda on local, state, and national levels. They were major instruments of Franklin D. Roosevelt's New Deal. Irish labor leaders, particularly those in the Congress of Industrial Organizations, mobilized unskilled as well as skilled workers and gave their attention to African and Hispanic as well as white ethnic Americans.

Affluence and assimilation lessened the intensity of Irish-American nationalism. Reduced commitments to Ireland already were obvious in the late nineteenth century. Much of Irish America was disgusted by Alexander Sullivan's terrorist wing of the Clan na Gael, particularly after the 1889 Chicago murder of its leading critic, Dr. Patrick Cronin. Factionalism also damaged the nationalist movement. The Charles Stewart Parnell–Kitty O'Shea scandal in the early 1890s split Home Rulers on both sides of the Atlantic. Nationalist forays into American politics also were divisive. Tammany Hall and Michael Corrigan, the conservative Catholic archbishop of New York, were appalled when Patrick Ford of the *Irish World* endorsed socialist Henry George for mayor, and Irish-American Democrats all over the country did not like it when John Devoy, editor of the *Gaelic American,* and other prominent members of Clan na Gael supported Republican candidates for president.

Nationalism faded further from Irish-American consciousness in the twentieth century. Most of the Irish in the United States accepted the Free State as a satisfactory British concession to Irish demands for sovereignty. And they had little interest in the provincial Gaelic, Irish-Ireland brand of nationalism promoted by Free State and republican governments after 1921. Anglo-American alliances in World Wars I and II and through the Cold War, while Ireland remained neutral, diminished Irish-American Anglophobia and sympathy with Ireland. Decline in Irish immigration since the 1920s has also weakened the cultural ties between Ireland and Irish America.

Irish America's greatest progress came after World War II. In 1944, Congress passed the Servicemen's Readjustment Act that included educational benefits for men and women serving in the armed forces. No other group took more advantage of the G.I. Bill than the Irish. Working-class young men, previously restricted financially from building on secondary school college preparatory courses, entered institutions of higher learning. Many with B.A. and B.S. degrees went on to graduate and professional schools. The G.I. Bill completed the Irish-American economic and social evolution from unskilled working to middle class. An increasing number of the well-educated Irish abandoned urban parish neighborhoods for the suburbs. A mass exodus occurred in the 1960s, when African Americans, fleeing poverty and segregation in the South, crowded into northern cities, frightening whites with prospects of declining property values, rising crime rates, and unfamiliar cultural values.

John F. Kennedy's presidency symbolized the Irish-American success story. Kennedy was less Irish Catholic than his public image, and his administration thrived more on illusion than achievement, but his charm, wit, and energy obscured the meager results of the New Frontier. As the first Catholic president, Kennedy closed the suspicion gap between his coreligionists and other Americans. He inspired people in the United States to feel good about themselves and their country, a euphoria that they have not enjoyed in the same idealistic way since Kennedy was assassinated in November 1963. Kennedy's national and international popularity helped the vast majority of Catholic ethnics to shed lingering doubts about their place in America.

Kennedy's presidency marked Irish America as comfortably middle class, highly respectable, and immensely popular. Irish-American politicians were leading the country, and Irish-American bishops were prominent in the Vatican II reform movement. Seminaries, convents, and monasteries bulged with Irish-American religious vocations. And then suddenly everything began to collapse.

In 1968, majority Irish-American Catholic opinion rejected Pope Paul VI's *Humanae Vitae*. The quarrel with church authority over contraception expanded to include such issues as a celibate clergy, the ordination and role of women in Catholicism, divorce, and even abortion. Confrontations with authority, plus disappointment with the tasteless and boring post–Vatican II liturgy, are reflected in declining mass attendance; smaller financial offerings at Sunday collections; a diminishing quantity and quality of priests, nuns, and brothers; and declining enrollments in and the closing of Catholic schools. In the 1960s, the Catholic subculture began to disappear as Catholics socialized with people of other faiths in suburbia. Country clubs replaced parishes as community centers. Parents registered children and adolescents in public schools, and ambitious young men and women selected prestigious non-Catholic colleges and universities to enhance their career prospects.

Some critics, including Pope John Paul II, blame the spiritual malaise in contemporary American Catholicism on materialism and secularism. There is some truth in this observation because it was easier for Irish and other Catholic ethnics to reject the things of this world when they were ignorant and poor and had no real choice than it is now, when they are relatively affluent. But opposition to church authority, declining religious enthusiasm, and greater involvement in the general American community suggest more than Irish middle-class worldliness. They represent Americanization intellectually as well as materially. Irish Americans have abandoned ghettos of spirit and place, and they no longer divide their minds into religious and political compartments. Most clearly prefer American liberalism to Roman authoritarianism.

Irish politicians are still prominent leaders of the liberal wing of the Democratic party, but since 1968 Irish voters have supported more Republican than Democratic presidential nominees. Their ballots reflect middle-class interests and rejection of a Democratic social agenda that includes racial employment quotas and concessions to homosexual and feminist interests.

Oppressive Protestant and British government responses to the civil rights movement in Northern Ireland reawakened slumbering Irish-American nationalism. But after the civil rights agitation escalated into civil war, Irish Americans' enthusiasm for their Ulster coreligionists subsided. Economically comfortable Irish Americans do not understand the politics of despair, paranoia, and martyrdom that flow from Catholic poverty and powerlessness in Northern Ireland. And the terrorism of the Provisional Irish Republican Army has had a negative impact in the United States. In addition, the Irish, like other Americans, have a short interest span. The crisis in Northern Ireland has lasted too long and its final resolution is too distant to retain their attention.

Film, television, and fiction have created common perceptions of Irish America. With some exceptions, movies and TV have captured its evolving character, if only in superficial glimpses. Lagging behind shifting reality, Irish-American literature has distored as well as illuminated its subject. Much Irish-American fiction is locked in the vision of James T. Farrell and Eugene O'Neill. Mary Gordon's overpraised *Other Side* is a good example of the time warp in Irish-American writing. Her four generations of New York McNamaras have advanced from immigrant working to middle class. But they are a collection of self-hating sexual and religious neurotics, anti-intellectuals, and underachievers, incapable of either happiness or tenderness. Cam, a lawyer, tells her Jewish lover that Phil Donohue and Ted Kennedy represent the only Irish contributions to American culture.[2] After her promising first novel in 1978, *Final Payments*, Gordon has been increasingly pejorative in her fictional interpretations of Irish Americans. Many readers, who once expected much of her, now hope that in the future she will direct her shortsighted, bitter attention to the Italian and Jewish branches of her family tree.

Jimmy Breslin, Pete Hamill, and the late Joe Flaherty also have written about alcoholic and sexually and emotionally repressed working- and lower-middle-class New York Irish-American Catholics. But unlike Gordon, they criticize their people with sympathy and affection rather than hate, some of their characters are men and women of virtue and strength. Although their content is interesting and their writing good, Breslin, Hamill, and Flaherty cover small, unrepresentative pockets of Irish-American failure.

Such writers as James Carroll, Elizabeth Cullinan, Ellen Currie, John Gregory Dunne, Andrew Greeley, Edward Hannibal, William Kennedy, Maureen Howard, and J. F. Powers are aware of variations in class, behavior, and opinion in Irish America. In Hannibal's *Chocolate Days, Popsicle Weeks*, John Fitzpatrick, a native of Somerville, Massachusetts, finances his Jesuit Boston College education by working in an ice cream factory, hence the novel's title. He graduates, marries his longtime girl friend, Janice, a nurse, and fulfills his ROTC obligations in the 1950s as an officer in Germany. Returning to the United States, Fitzie rejects the usual employment choices of college-educated Irish Americans—teaching, law, or insurance. Instead, he tries and succeeds in the competitive world of New York advertising. With their income rising, the Fitzgeralds move from Queens to Brooklyn Heights and finally to Merrimac, a posh suburb. Fitzie's obsession with success, his rapid rise in advertising, and Merrimac's hedonism generate tensions in the marriage. Fitzie remains superficially and negatively Irish in his excessive drinking, sexual guilt, and hostility to Anglo-Protestants, but he dissolves connections with his Somerville past and has little affection for post–Vatican II Catholicism. Increasingly, his commitments are to suburban middle-class values rather than to religion or ethnicity. Fitzie seems to exemplify John Gregory Dunne's brief summary of the Irish-American experience: "immigrant, outcast, assimilated, deracinated."[3]

It has been a long economic, social, and cultural journey from such inner-city neighborhoods as Finley Peter Dunne's Bridgeport of the 1890s and today's suburban Merrimacs, from people who forged steel, slaughtered livestock, laid railway track, carried hods, drove horsecarts, loaded and unloaded ships and barges, extinguished fires, preserved public order, tried to liberate Ireland with picnics and speeches, scrubbed floors, waited tables, minded and taught children, and nursed the sick, to the hucksters of the American consumer economy.

Has the actual as well as the literary Irish-American trek from ghetto to suburbs been a passage from someplace to no place? Thirty years ago it would have been difficult to imagine Irish-American Republican majorities in presidential elections or a large number defecting from or indifferent to Catholicism. Of the two, an unenthusiastic or absent Catholicism says more about the passing of Irish America than does middle-class Republican politics.

Catholicism has been the essence of Irish America. For many years, the church was able to care for the spiritual and psychological needs of immigrants overwhelmed by urban America and to bind generations of Irish Americans into a social and cultural community. Today, with a new liturgy bereft of history or mystery but with an antiquated authoritarian administrative structure and a theology intellectually reactionary and repressive, Catholicism contradicts the values of assimilated Irish Americans.

Because ethnicity is cultural not biological, can Irish Americans continue to survive without an understanding and appreciation of the Irish historical experience or a strong commitment to its hereditary religious culture? Many Americans, including some who are Irish, would say that the question is irrelevant because the integration of all racial, religious, and ethnic strains into a common nationality is the American ideal. But outside of a political consensus, predicated on liberal democracy, is there a cultural America? Except for trivialities revolving around fads in music, dress, and food and consumer desires and tastes, there are no substantial shared values or historical memories that unite Americans. Those who have lost their cultural ethnicity, their sense of historical continuity, have intellectually and psychologically wandered from someplace to no place.

Many Irish Americans who appreciate the liberty and opportunities that the United States provides but abhor its cultural vacuum and believe that ethnic identity is intellectually and psychologically imperative no longer find it in allegiance to authoritarian Roman Catholicism. Some compensate for this loss by cultivating interests in Irish history, literature, and music. The increased popularity of Irish studies in colleges and universities, the success of the American Conference for Irish Studies and the Irish-American Cultural Institute, the readership and quality of such journals as the *Irish Literary Supplement, Eire-Ireland*, and *Irish-America*, all testify to an interest in Irish history and culture. They suggest that although Irish America is diminishing in quantity, it is experiencing a surge in quality and vitality. But Irish America's intellectual interests could be fragile and transitory. Americanization and suburbanization and interethnic marriages challenge its survival.

If Irish advances have provided hope to other ethnic and racial groups, fading Irish identity is not a pleasant portent for American pluralism. The disappearance of any of its parts reduces the brilliance and threatens the permanence of the ethnic mosaic that has made the United States the most interesting and energetic country in the world.

Is Irish America traveling from ambivalence toward extinction or a new creativity? Only time will tell. But whatever their final destination, the Irish have had a major impact on the United States. Their labor was instrumental in the development of American industry. As leaders of the Catholic church, the Irish have provided religious and social services to the immigrant masses; as teachers they have educated children of all races, religions, and nationalities in public and parochial schools; as urban and national politicians they have brought government concern to the needs of the poor, the old, and the afflicted; as writers they have provided audiences and readers with high-quality novels, plays, and short stories; as journalists they have informed the public of local, national, and international events; as doctors and nurses they have cured and nursed the sick; as policemen and firemen they have preserved public order and safety; as soldiers, sailors, and marines they have bravely defended their country; and as entertainers and athletes they have amused, inspired, and thrilled audiences on vaudeville and theater stages, on silver screens, on baseball diamonds, in boxing rings, on basketball courts, and on football fields. Most important, Irish priests, politicians, labor leaders, and educators have led Catholic America to respectability and acceptability.

7

Afterword

Trends evident in post-1960 Irish-America have persisted since 1991 when I put the finishing touches on the original manuscript for *Textures of Irish America*. Irish-American commitments and vocational and financial contributions to Catholicism continue to diminish. At present, 62 percent of priests and 77 percent of nuns are over fifty-one years old, and there are not nearly enough new vocations to replace those who die or retire. For example, in the spring of 1997, Chicago, the second largest archdiocese in the United States, ordained only four priests, none with a distinguishable Irish name.

Pedophile scandals continue to irritate the laity and cost the church vast sums in lawsuits. Discontents with the church's opposition to contraception, women, and married priests, and with aspects of post-Vatican liturgy are reflected in fewer people in the pews at Mass and devotions, and smaller Sunday collections. While urban parochial schools, emphasizing discipline and fundamentals, offer African and Hispanic Americans a valuable alternative to public schools afflicted with drugs and gang violence, in the suburbs many Catholics send their children to public elementary and secondary schools offering broader curricula and better teachers than Catholic counterparts.

Declining Irish-American loyalty to the Catholic base of its ethnic identity involves more than dissatisfaction with the church. Economic, social, and residential mobility have resulted in assimilation, a drift away from a Catholic subculture into the American mainstream. No longer does the parish represent a total experience, social and educational as well as religious. Intelligent sons and daughters of parents who went to Catholic colleges and universities frequently select distinguished non-Catholic institutions of higher learning to prepare them for professional success. And, as emphasized in the main body of this book, as Irish Americans feel more comfortable and secure in the United States, American emphases on individual liberty contradict Roman Catholic authoritarianism.

After majority support for Ronald Reagan and George Bush in 1980, 1984, and 1988, in 1992 and 1996 Catholic ethnics, including the Irish, returned to the Democratic fold. Their votes helped put and keep Bill Clinton in the White House. Although Senator Edward M. Kennedy of Massachusetts and Mayor Richard M. Daley of Chicago are examples of a still important Irish presence in the centers of political power, for a large number of the best and brightest of the American Irish, politics cannot compete with the lure of business and the professions. On the local level, many of those still charmed by the adventure of politics are competing for office as Republicans, especially, but not exclusively, in suburban areas. Neither the Democratic nor Republican parties feature an Irish-American Catholic as a potential presidential candidate, and in 1994 when George Mitchell decided not to run and Thomas Foley lost, Irish Americans were no longer Senate Majority Leader and Speaker of the House of Representatives.

Clinton has demonstrated more concern for Ireland than any of his predecessors, including John F. Kennedy, giving quite a few of the American Irish a reason to vote for him. He urged the prime ministers of Britain and Ireland, John Major and Albert Reynolds, to speed negotiations for a Northern Ireland settlement; granted a visa to Jerry Adams, leader of Sinn Fein, the political arm of the Irish Republican Army, so that he could travel and collect funds in the United States; increased the American contribution to the International Fund for Ireland; and urged American companies to invest in the economies of Northern Ireland and the Irish Republic. Clinton's involvement in Northern Ireland troubles, especially the Adams visa, nettled Major and his Conservative government but it speeded up the peace process in the Six Counties. The president's pressure was certainly a factor in the Downing Street Declaration of 1993 that expressed Britain's and Ireland's common objectives for a Northern Ireland arrangement that would leave its fate up to the will of the majority while respecting the culture and rights of the minority. As a result, in August 1994 the IRA declared a cease fire, followed by a September similar pledge from unionist paramilitaries. Because they believed that Major, indebted to

Ulster Unionist M.P.s who kept his government in office, had stalemated the peace process, the IRA recommenced hostilities in February 1996. Labour's recent victory in the British general election, and the conciliatory attitude of the new Prime Minister, Tony Blair, who in contrast to Major has a warm relationship with Clinton, persuaded the IRA in July 1997 to again agree to a cease fire.

At present, former Senator George Mitchell presides over a peace conference in Belfast attended by Sinn Fein leaders Jerry Adams and Martin McGuiness and representatives from most, but not all, Unionist factions, the Democratic Labour party, and the Alliance party in an effort to find a mutually satisfactory solution to the Ulster conflict. The compromise result will probably be a power-sharing government for the North and the creation of agencies that will facilitate cooperation between the two Irelands on such issues as tourism, industrial development, and energy. Whether the nationalist extremists who demand a united Ireland and the unionist fanatics who resist any ties with the South and insist on majority rule will accept such an arrangement is problematical.

When President Clinton, his wife, Hilary, and daughter, Chelsea, visited Ireland in the early winter of 1995, they received warm receptions in Belfast, Derry, and Dublin. These welcomes were reminiscent of the greeting the Irish gave President Kennedy in 1963. Irish responses to the Clintons and Kennedy have expressed the affection and respect that they feel, North and South, for America and Americans; the country and the people who represent Scots-Irish Presbyterian and Irish Catholic success stories.

Since 1991, it has become clearer that Irish Americans increasingly are seeking their identity in culture rather than religion. Student enrollments in Irish history and literature courses are rising. Boston College has added faculty to an excellent interdisciplinary Irish studies program. Thanks to the generosity of alumni successful in business, after years of exploiting its "fighting Irish" footbal image, Notre Dame has initiated an Irish studies program with considerable promise. New York University is also in the process of putting together a multidiscipline Irish studies program. Large numbers attending "Riverdance" and "Lord of the Dance" performances in many cities in the United States have advertised the quality and popularity of Irish music and dance. Movies and plays with Irish settings and themes have also gathered favorable reviews and audience appreciation. Enthusiastic involvements in many aspects of Irish culture have led me to become more optimistic about the survival of an Irish-American identity. It is certainly stronger and better informed than it was six years ago.

Notes
Recommended Reading
Index

Notes

PREFACE

1. Peggy Noonan, *What I Saw at the Revolution: A Political Life in the Reagan Era* (New York, 1990), p. 346.

1. THE IRISH-AMERICAN EXPERIENCE

1. In "Thanks to the Irish," *America*, May 14, 1966, Philip Gleason effectively argued that it was fortunate that the Irish were the first Catholic ethnic group to enter the United States in large numbers because "they were the best equipped among all the immigrating Catholic groups to assist the church in effecting a positive adjustment to American life." This was so because they understood and practiced the Anglo-Saxon political system and supported their church with their own funds.

2. Edward McSorley, *Our Own Kind* (New York, 1946).

3. Charles Kickham, *Knocknagow or the Homes of Tipperary* (Dublin, 1879).

4. In a 1986 interview with Patrick Farrelly, Jimmy Breslin was irritated with Irish-American insensitivity to the unfortunate, particularly as it related to Northern Ireland: "Oh, they forgot the word 'underdog.' They forgot what the word means, they don't want any part of being with an underdog; the Irish hate the underdog. They want only big winners. They want front runners. They only want to be with winners. No fighting from underneath, none of that. Jesus, do you think that if they put the pressure on, the British would last with their policies in Northern Ireland?" (*Irish-American Magazine*, Dec. 1989, p. 11).

2. FROM GHETTO TO SUBURB

1. For recent general studies of Irish history in the period covered in this book see Karl Bottigheimer, *Ireland and the Irish* (New York, 1982); R. F. Foster, *Modern Ireland, 1600–1972* (New York, 1989); and Thomas E. Hachey, Joseph M. Hernon, Jr., and Lawrence J. McCaffrey, *The Irish Experience* (Englewood Cliffs, N. J., 1989).

2. K. H. Connell, *The Population of Ireland, 1750–1845* (Oxford, 1950), p. 25. Connell warns readers that population estimates before the census of 1821 are unreliable.

3. For discussions of the pre-Famine Irish economic situation see Joel Molkyr, *Why Ireland Starved: A Quantitative and Analytical History of the Irish Economy, 1800–1852* (Boston, 1982), and Connell, *Population of Ireland.*

4. *Poor Inquiry Commission Report, Ireland* (London, 1836).

5. See John Archer Jackson, *The Irish in Britain* (London, 1963); and Lynn Lees, *Exiles of Erin: Irish Migrants in Victorian London* (Ithaca, 1979).

6. For pre-Famine Irish emigration to America see Audrey Lockhart, *Some Aspects of Emigration from Ireland to the North American Colonies Between 1660 and 1775* (New York, 1976); and W. F. Adams, *Ireland and Irish Immigration to the New World from 1815 to the Famine* (New York, 1967).

7. For motives behind Irish emigration and its character since 1800 see Patrick Blessing, "Irish Emigration to the United States, 1800–1920: An Overview," in *The Irish in America*, ed. P. J. Drudy, Irish Studies, vol. 4 (New York, 1985); Kerby A. Miller, *Emigrants and Exiles: Ireland and the Irish Exodus to North America* (New York, 1985); Oliver MacDonagh, "Irish Famine Emigration to the United States," in *Perspectives in American History* 10 (1976): 357–446; Philip Taylor, *The Distant Magnet* (New York, 1971).

8. Among the best studies of the Famine are Cormac O'Grada, *The Great Irish Famine* (Atlantic Highlands, N. J., 1988); Mary E. Daly, *The Famine in Ireland* (Dublin, 1986); R. Dudley Edwards and T. Desmond Williams, eds., *The Great Famine: Studies in Irish History, 1845—1852* (New York, 1956); Cecil Woodham Smith, *The Great Hunger: Ireland, 1845–1849* (New York, 1962); and Thomas Gallagher, *Paddy's Lament: Ireland 1846–47, Prelude to Hatred* (Orlando, Fla., 1987).

9. Janet Ann Nolan, *Ourselves Alone: Female Emigration from Ireland, 1825–1920* (Lexington, Ky., 1989).

10. Terry Coleman, *Going to America* (New York, 1973), and Taylor, *The Distant Magnet,* detail the emigration process. Taylor includes the Irish in a study that encompasses the entire scope of European emigration. Coleman concentrates on the voyage and tribulations of passengers, mostly Irish, sailing from Liverpool.

11. In *The Great Hunger,* Smith estimated that six thousand are buried at Grosse Isle, but a recent study by Padraic Ó Laighin, "Grosse Ile: The Holocaust Revisited," in *The Untold Story: The History of the Irish in Canada,* ed. Robert O'Driscoll and Lorna Reynolds (Toronto, 1988), claims that the British government falsified the number of graves to disguise the extent of the Famine disaster. He says that at least thirty thousand Irish lay buried on the island.

12. Dennis Clark, *Hibernia America: The Irish and Regional Cultures* (New York, 1986).

13. Dennis Clark, *The Irish in Philadelphia* (Philadelphia, 1973), p. 62, says that 84.5 percent of Irish immigrants came from rural backgrounds. Patrick Blessing, "The Irish," in *Harvard Encyclopedia of American Ethnic Groups,* ed. Stephan Thernstrom (Cambridge, Mass., 1980), p. 530, estimates that Irish America in 1920 was 90 percent urban. In *Rainbow's End: Irish-Americans and the Dilemmas of Urban Machine*

Politics, 1840–1985 (Berkeley, 1988), p. 25, Steven P. Erie says that more than 90 percent of the 1.4 million Irish Famine immigrants entering the United States between 1846 and 1855 settled in cities and that by 1870 42 percent of the Irish born in the United States were in its twenty-five cities with populations over fifty thousand. Eire takes his information from MacDonagh, "Irish Famine Emigration to the United States," pp. 430–33. In several works, including *Being Had: Historians, Evidence and the Irish in North America* (Toronto, 1985); *Small Differences: Irish Catholics and Irish Protestants, 1815–1922* (Kingston and Montreal, 1988); and "Data: What Is Known About the Irish in North America," in *The Untold Story: The Irish in Canada,* 1:15–25, Donald Harmon Akenson argues that historians of Irish America have exaggerated its urbanization. He accuses William V. Shannon, Kerby Miller, and me of creating a myth that contradicts historical reality to heap praise on an unskilled Irish community that rose from nothing to significance in urban America. To make his case, he emphasizes the large numbers of rural Irish in Canada and points out that the 1870 United States census showed only 44.5 percent of Irish immigrants living in cities of over twenty-five thousand population. In arguing for the nonurbanization of Irish America, Akenson rejects significant cultural differences between Irish Catholics and Protestants. If one looks at contemporary Northern Ireland, that is a tenuous thesis and never clearly explains when, where, and which Catholics or Protestants settled in rural Canada. But what happened in Canada, where urban industrialism came slower and ethnicity was not as extensive or intensive, has little relevance for the United States. Akenson completely distorts the 1870 census, which shows that the Irish more than any other group settled in cities. In a review of Akenson's *Small Differences* published in a Canadian journal, *Labour/Le Travail*, David W. Miller points out that in 1870 only 15 percent of the total American population lived in cities over twenty-five thousand and only 30.8 percent of non-Irish immigrants compared to 44.5 percent of Irish newcomers to the United States lived in them. Rather than telling us that Irish America was nonurbanized, the 1870 census indicates the opposite. Miller refers to the 1900 census to show that in each decade after the Famine the Irish immigrant percentage in cities over twenty-five thousand increased until in the period from 1891 to 1900 it reached 74.3 percent. During that same period, 19.2 percent settled in towns with less than twenty-five thousand population. Only 6.5 percent went to rural areas. The Irish in towns of less than twenty-five thousand were more likely to be involved in the industrial, transportation, and commercial than the rural economy. It seems that Akenson rather than Shannon, Miller, and McCaffrey is the myth maker. I will not judge his motives.

14. Some members of the American church hierarchy, mainly John Ireland, archbishop of St. Paul, tried to colonize the Irish in rural areas, but Catholicism's corporate and communal character as well as the immigrants' paucity of agricultural skills encouraged them and later European Catholic peasants to settle in American cities. In general, Catholic ethnics tend to be culturally more social and less individualistic and self-sufficient than Protestants, who appear to be religiously and psychologically more adaptable to rural living. James P. Shannon, *Catholic Colonization on the Western Frontier* (New York, 1976), describes the efforts of the Catholic hierarchy and clergy to keep the Irish out of cities.

15. For studies of the early Irish-American urban situation see Oscar Handlin, *Boston's Immigrants* (New York, 1968); Clark, *Irish in Philadelphia* and *Hibernia America;* Lawrence J. McCaffrey, Ellen Skerrett, Michael Funchion, and Charles Fanning, *The Irish in Chicago* (Urbana, 1987); Earl F. Niehaus, *The Irish in New Orleans, 1800–1860,* (New York, 1976); Stephan Thernstrom, *Poverty and Progress* (Cambridge, Mass., 1964); Brian C. Mitchell, *The Paddy Camps: The Irish of Lowell, 1821–61* (Urbana, 1988); Douglas V. Shaw, *The Making of an Immigrant City: Ethnic and Cultural Conflict in Jersey City, 1850–1877* (New York, 1976); R. A. Burchell, *The San Francisco Irish, 1848–1880* (Berkeley, 1980); Jo Ellen McNergney Vinyard, *The Irish on the Urban Frontier: Detroit, 1850–1880* (New York, 1976); David M. Emmons, *The Butte Irish: Class and Ethnicity in an American Mining Town, 1875–1925* (Urbana, 1989); Blessing, "The Irish"; Victor Walsh, " 'Across the Big Wather' ": Irish Community Life in Pittsburgh, 1850–1885" (Ph.D. dissertation, Univ. of Pittsburgh, 1983); and William V. Millett, "The Irish and Mobility Patterns in Northampton, Massachusetts, 1846–1883" (Ph.D. dissertation, Univ. of Iowa, 1980).

16. Hasia Diner, *Erin's Daughters in America: Irish-American Women in the Nineteenth Century* (Baltimore, 1983), argues that Irish women were more successful than Irish men and other women in the United States. In explaining their achievements, she places too much emphasis on gender segregation in Ireland and in Irish America. Other European ethnics and Anglo-Protestants have socially segregated the sexes as much if not more than the Irish. Notwithstanding this criticism, I am much indebted to Diner for my observations on Irish-American women.

17. Handlin, *Boston's Immigrants,* p. 55.

18. On November 5, 1605, Guy Fawkes, a Catholic conspirator, tried to kill James I and members of the English Parliament with a gunpowder explosion. He failed, was arrested and executed. Since then people in Britain have celebrated Guy Fawkes Day by burning him and sometimes the pope in effigy. Now the occasion is one of fun rather than manifest prejudice.

19. The racial connotations in British anti-Irish Catholic prejudices are the themes of L. P. Curtis, Jr., *Anglo-Saxons and Celts: A Study of Anti-Irish Prejudice in Victorian England* (Bridgeport, Conn., 1968), and Richard Ned Lebow, *White Britain and Black Ireland: The Influence of Stereotypes on Colonial Policy* (Philadelphia, 1976). British stereotypes of the "neanderthal, ape-like Irish" were reproduced in American newspaper and periodical cartoons. Anti-Irish caricatures in the United States are described and analyzed in John J. Appel and Selma Appel, "The Distorted Image" (New York, Anti-Defamation League of B'Nai Brith), a slide collection with comment containing examples of negative newspaper and periodical cartoons of the Irish, and Stephan Garrett Bolger, *The Irish Character in American Fiction, 1830–1860* (New York, 1976).

20. George Rogers Taylor, *The Transportation Revolution* (New York, 1964), p. 287, argues that the Irish working class hindered the growth of the American labor movement. His generalizations need modification. David Noel Doyle, *Irish-Americans, Native Rights, and National Empires: The Structure, Divisions, and Attitudes of the Catholic Minority in the Decade of Expansion, 1890–1901* (New York, 1976),

points out that some Irish immigrants did come from towns and cities in Ireland where there were labor unions. T. Desmond Williams, ed., *Secret Societies in Ireland* (New York, 1973), and James S. Donnelly, Jr., and Samuel Clark, eds., *Irish Peasants, Violence, and Political Unrest* (Madison, 1983), demonstrate that in rural Ireland, agricultural laborers and tenant farmers often organized into secret societies or openly agitated to achieve decent wages, fair rents, and security of tenure and employed violent as well as legal forms of coercion in their efforts to dictate a moral economy.

21. Niehaus, *Irish in New Orleans*, pp. 86–87.

22. The most important volumes on anti-Catholic American nativism are Ray Allen Billington, *The Protestant Crusade, 1800–1860* (1938 rpt. Chicago, 1964); and John Higham, *Strangers in the Land: Patterns of American Nativism, 1860—1925* (1955 rpt. New York, 1965).

23. Richard Shaw, *Dagger John: The Unquiet Life and Times of Archbishop John Hughes of New York* (New York, 1977), pp. 193–202.

24. Mitchell, *Paddy Camps*, pp. 135–40.

25. Lawrence J. McCaffrey, *Daniel O'Connell and the Repeal Year* (Lexington, Ky., 1966), pp. 73–75, 205 n. 4, discusses O'Connell's opposition to slavery, his insistence that African Americans deserved full civil rights as well as freedom in the British Empire, and his exhortations to Irish Americans to honor their heritage by joining the abolitionist cause.

26. In *The American Irish* (New York, 1974), p. 55, William V. Shannon designates "obsessive preoccupation with their own problems" as the basic source of Irish hostility to abolitionism. They complained that the northern middle class was insincere in its concern for southern blacks and that it ignored the tribulations of poor whites in the North. He quotes an 1854 comment by Congressman Mike Walsh of New York that "the only difference between the negro slave of the South and the white wage slave of the North is that one has a master without asking for him, and the other has to beg for the privilege of becoming a slave. . . . The one is a slave of an individual; the other is the slave of an inexorable class."

27. The Irish role in the New York draft riot is the subject of chapters 10 through 21 in Joel Tyler Headley, *The Great Riots of New York, 1712–1873*, introduction by Thomas Rose and James Rodgers (Indianapolis, 1970). Shaw, *Dagger John*, pp. 361–69, describes Hughes's reactions to Irish mob activity.

28. Improvements in the condition of post-Famine agrarian Ireland are discussed in Barbara Lewis Solow, *The Land Question and the Irish Economy, 1870–1903* (Cambridge, Mass., 1971); Joseph Lee, *The Modernization of Irish Society, 1848–1918* (Dublin, 1973); James S. Donnelly, Jr., *The Land and the People of Nineteenth-Century Cork* (London, 1975); Samuel Clark, *Social Origins of the Land War* (Princeton, 1979); L. M. Cullen, *The Emergence of Modern Ireland, 1600–1900* (New York, 1981); and Miller, *Emigrants and Exiles*.

29. Fergus O'Ferrall, *Catholic Emancipation: Daniel O'Connell and the Birth of Irish Democracy, 1820–1830* (Dublin, 1985); and Kevin Nowlan, *The Politics of Repeal* (Toronto, 1965).

30. Mary Helen Thuente, "The Folklore of Irish Nationalism," in *Perspectives on Irish Nationalism*, ed. Thomas E. Hachey and Lawrence J. McCaffrey (Lexington, Ky., 1988), pp. 42–60, analyzes Young Ireland's creation of an activist Irish folklore.

31. Blessing, "The Irish," p. 529.

32. Pre-Famine church problems are the theme of S. J. Connolly, *Priests and People in Pre-Famine Ireland, 1780–1845* (New York, 1983); and David W. Miller, "Irish Catholicism and the Great Famine," *Journal of Social Studies* 9 (Sept. 1975): 81–98.

33. In *The Historical Dimensions of Irish Catholicism* (Washington, D.C., 1984); *The Making of the Roman Catholic Church in Ireland, 1850–1860* (Chapel Hill, 1980); and *The Consolidation of the Roman Catholic Church in Ireland, 1860–1870* (Chapel Hill, 1987), Emmet Larkin details and analyzes Irish Catholicism in the reign of Cullen and his achievement of a "Devotional Revolution."

34. David Montgomery, "The Irish and the American Labor Movement," in *America and Ireland, 1776–1976: The American Identity and the Irish Connection*, ed. David Noel Doyle and Owen Dudley Edwards (Westport, Conn. 1980), p. 211.

35. Steven P. Erie, *Rainbow's End: Irish-Americans and the Dilemmas of Urban Machine Politics, 1840–1985* (Berkeley, 1988), pp. 25–66.

36. Stephen A. Riess, *Touching Base: Professional Baseball and American Culture in the Progressive Era* (Westport, Conn., 1980), pp. 184–87. In Bill James, *The Bill James Historical Baseball Abstract* (New York, 1986), pp. 8–59, the author discusses the Irish domination of baseball from 1870 to 1900, particularly in the 1890s.

37. Dennis Clark, "Sports Cults Among the Latter Day Celts," paper presented at the American Conference for Irish Studies, Syracuse, New York, Apr. 14, 1989.

38. Kenneth Jackson, *The Study of the Ku Klux Klan in the City, 1915–1930*, (New York, 1967), pp. 102–3, 116, 124.

39. Maureen Murphy, "Irish-American Theatre," in *Ethnic Theatre in the United States*, ed. Maxine Schwartz Seller (Westport, Conn., 1983), pp. 221–35, discusses the stage portrait of Irish America in early American theater.

40. Joseph M. Curran, *Hibernian Green on the Silver Screen* (Westport, Conn., 1989), pp. 15–18, discusses negative stereotyping of the Irish in early cinema.

41. Ibid., pp. 18–21.

42. Miller, *Emigrants and Exiles*, pp. 49–50, describes the percentages of Irish employed in various blue-collar occupations around 1900.

43. Malcolm Brown, *The Politics of Irish Literature from Thomas Davis to W. B. Yeats* (Seattle, 1972), pp. 18–47, discusses the Young Ireland contents of Irish nationalism as the *Nation* preached it. R. Vincent Comerford, *Charles Kickham (1828–1882): A Study in Irish Nationalism and Literature* (Dublin, 1979), deals with Charles Kickham's contribution to journalistic and literary nationalism.

44. Quoted in Charles Fanning, ed., *The Exiles of Erin: Nineteenth-Century Irish Fiction* (Notre Dame, 1987), p. 241, an excellent anthology, offering valuable insights into early Irish America. Fanning evaluates John Boyle O'Reilly's *Boston Pilot* school of Irish-American writing in "Finley Peter Dunne and Irish-American Realism," in *Irish-American Fiction*, ed. Daniel J. Casey and Robert E. Rhodes (New York,

1979). Fanning is also the author of a comprehensive and perceptive study of Irish-American fiction from its beginnings, *The Irish Voice in America: Irish American Fiction from the 1760s to the 1980s* (Lexington, Ky., 1990).

45. Charles Fanning, *Finley Peter Dunne and Mr. Dooley: The Chicago Years* (Lexington, Ky., 1978); and Fanning, *Mr. Dooley and the Chicago Irish* (Washington, D.C., 1987).

46. Vinyard, *Irish on the Urban Frontier,* analyzes the success of the Irish in the Midwest and West, using Detroit as her main example. Also see Timothy J. Meagher, ed., *From Paddy to Studs: Irish-American Communities at the Turn of the Century Era, 1880–1920* (Westport, Conn., 1986); Burchell, *San Francisco Irish;* McCaffrey et al., *Irish in Chicago;* and Clark, *Hibernia America.*

47. Doyle, *Irish-Americans,* pp. 59–65.

48. Blessing, "The Irish," p. 532.

49. In *Erin's Daughters in America* Hasia Diner discusses the mobility and professionalization of Irish-American women and their role in the labor movement (pp. 70–105) and the significance of nuns in their progress (pp. 120–38). The importance of nuns is a topic of Eileen Brewer, *Beyond Utility: The Role of the Nun in the Education of American Catholic Girls, 1860–1920* (Chicago, 1987).

50. James Paul Rodechko, *Patrick Ford and His Search for America: A Case Study of Irish-American Journalism, 1870–1913* (New York, 1976).

51. Burchell, *The San Francisco Irish,* pp. 153–54.

52. J. F. Power, *Morte D'Urban* (New York, 1962), p. 189.

53. Wayne G. Broehl, *The Molly Maguires* (Cambridge, Mass., 1964); William A. Gudelunas, Jr., and William J. Shade, *Before the Molly Maguires: The Emergence of the Ethno-Religious Factor in the Politics of the Lower Anthracite Region, 1844–72* (New York, 1976).

54. Shannon, *American Irish,* pp. 389–90, Emmet Larkin, *James Larkin, Irish Labour Leader, 1876–1947* (London, 1989).

55. Montgomery, "The Irish and the American Labor Movement," p. 206.

56. Herbert Hill, "Race and Ethnicity in Organized Labor: The Historical Sources for Resistance to Affirmative Action," in *Ethnicity and the Work Force,* ed. Winston A. Van Horne and Thomas V. Tonneson (Madison, 1985), pp. 1–64.

57. Higham, *Strangers in the Land,* is the most comprehensive study of post–Civil War nativism. Also consult Donald L. Kinzer, *An Episode in Anti-Catholicism: The American Protective Association* (Seattle, 1964); and Jackson, *Ku Klux Klan in the City.* Originally the Ku Klux Klan was a Reconstruction-era white supremacist terror organization partly responsible for Jim Crow laws in the South, which were sanctioned by the United States Supreme Court. Reorganized in 1915, the Klan concentrated its attacks on Catholics and Jews.

58. Curtis, *Anglo-Saxons and Celts,* pp. 1–121; Lebow, *White Britain and Black Ireland* pp. 28–67; Appel and Appel, "Distorted Image" Bolger, *Irish Character in American Fiction.*

59. More than one writer has called anti-Catholicism "the anti-Semitism of the American intellectual" (Michael Novak, *The Rise of the Unmeltable Ethnics* [1922 rpt. New York, 1973], p. 163). For the anti-Catholicism of the American intellectual see

D. W. Brogan, *American Aspects* (New York, 1964), p. 164; and Andrew M. Greeley, *The Irish-Americans: The Rise to Money and Power* (New York, 1981), p. 107.

60. The quest for respectability in Irish-American nationalism is analyzed in Thomas N. Brown, "The Origins and Character of Irish-American Nationalism," *Review of Politics* 68 (July 1956): 327–58.

61 Francis M. Carroll, *American Opinion and the Irish Question, 1910–1923* (New York, 1978); Joseph Edward Cuddy, *Irish-America and National Isolation, 1914–1920* (New York, 1976); and Cuddy, "The Irish Question and the Revival of Anti-Catholicism in the 1920s," *Catholic Historical Review* 67 (Apr. 1981): 236–55.

62. Greeley, *Irish-Americans*, p. 112.

63. The Studs Lonigan trilogy and the O'Neill-O'Flaherty pentalogy or the Washington Park novels are *Young Lonigan* (New York, 1932); *The Young Manhood of Studs Lonigan* (New York, 1934); *Judgment Day* (New York, 1935); *A World I Never Made* (New York, 1936); *No Star Is Lost* (New York, 1938); *Father and Son* (New York, 1940); *My Days of Anger* (New York, 1943); and *The Face of Time* (New York, 1953). Charles Fanning and Ellen Skerrett, "James T. Farrell and Washington Park: The Novel as Social History," *Chicago History* 8 (Summer 1979): 80–91; and Charles Fanning, "The Literary Dimension," in McCaffrey et al., *Irish in Chicago*, pp. 120–44, discuss Farrell as social historian of the Chicago Irish.

64. Erie, *Rainbow's End*, p. 242.

65. Ibid., p. 243. Politics as a cause of Irish economic and social stagnation is one of the main theses of *Rainbow's End*.

66. Ibid., pp. 108–18.

67. Allan J. Lichtman, *Prejudice and the Old Politics: The Presidential Election of 1928* (Chapel Hill, 1969).

68. George Q. Flynn, *American Catholics and the Roosevelt Presidency* (Lexington, Ky., 1968), details the importance of the Irish in the machinery of the New Deal.

69. The transition from power to idealistic politics is the main theme of Thomas N. Brown, "The Political Irish: Politicians and Rebels," in *America and Ireland*, ed. David Noel Doyle and Owen Dudley Edwards, pp. 133–49. An expanding Irish Catholic social conscience is examined in David J. O'Brien, *American Catholics and Social Reform: The New Deal Years* (New York, 1968); and Francis L. Broderick, *Right Reverend New Dealer John A. Ryan* (New York, 1963).

70. Ronald H. Bayor, *Neighbors in Conflict: The Irish, Germans, Jews, and Italians of New York City, 1929–1941* (Baltimore, 1978).

71. Joseph M. Curran, *Hibernian Green on the Silver Screen*, discusses the significance of Cagney in creating the Irish film role urban antihero (pp. 39–48) and the movie priest (pp. 52–58). In *Beyond the Melting Pot: The Negroes, Puerto Ricans, Jews, Italians, and Irish of New York City* (Cambridge, Mass., 1963), pp. 246–47, Nathan Glazer and Daniel Patrick Moynihan write of Cagney: "When it came to portraying the tough American, up from the streets, the image was repeatedly that of an Irishman. James Cagney (a New Yorker) was the quintessential figure: fists cocked, chin out, back straight, bouncing along on his heels."

72. Curran, *Hibernian Green on the Silver Screen*, p. 87.

73. Andrew M. Greeley, *Why Can't They Be Like Us* (New York, 1971), pp. 66–80; and Greeley, *The American Catholic: A Social Portrait* (New York, 1977), pp. 50–67, compare Irish-American educational levels with those of other groups.

74. Greeley, *Why Can't They Be Like Us*, pp. 66–80, and *American Catholic*, pp. 112–124, discuss the liberal values and self-esteem of Irish Americans.

75. Joe Flaherty, *Fogarty and Company* (New York, 1973), pp. 116–17.

76. Garry Wills, *The Kennedy Imprisonment* (Boston, 1982), argues that Joseph Kennedy and his sons were more impressed with upper-class British than Irish Catholic values.

77. Curran, *Hibernian Green on the Silver Screen*, p. 133, n. 4. Curran's source is an interview by James Warner Bellah (typescript), B 11, F16, John Ford Papers, Lilly Library, Indiana University, Bloomington.

78. In *Hibernian Green on the Silver Screen*, p. 120, Curran argues: "The characterization of Willie Conklin (Kenneth MacMillan), the captain of the Emerald Isle Fire Company, is not far removed from the vicious nativist caricatures of the Irish a century ago. Had Coalhouse Walker of Tateh (Mandy Patimkin), the movie's principal Jewish character, been as savagely depicted as Willie Conklin, *Ragtime* would surely have aroused a storm of protest for its white racism or anti-semitism. The Irish, however, have again become fair game for social critics. Once they were pilloried by the WASP elite. Now the success that has made them part of the American establishment has also made them safe and inviting targets for enemies of that establishment."

79. Tom Wolfe, *The Bonfire of the Vanities* (New York, 1988).

80. For information on Gene Kelly and Grace Kelly and the changing Irish film image see Curran, *Hibernian Green on the Silver Screen*, pp. 105–7.

81. T. J. English, *The Westies: Inside the Hell's Kitchen Irish Mob* (New York, 1990).

82. J. Anthony Lukas, *Common Ground* (New York, 1985), is a brilliant examination of the Boston busing issue. Stephan Thernstrom, *The Other Bostonians: Poverty and Progress in the Urban Metropolis, 1860–1970* (Cambridge, Mass., 1970), discusses how the Irish continued to lag behind all other whites except Italians in achieving economic and social mobility in Boston. Greeley, *Irish-Americans*, p. 118, reinforces Thernstrom's thesis. He quotes National Opinion Research Center study of alcohol use that shows that 54 percent of the Boston Irish were white-collar workers and only 26 percent in the managerial and professional classes.

83. Arnold R. Hirsch, *Making the Second Ghetto: Race and Housing in Chicago, 1940–1960* (New York, 1983), describes Irish resistance in Chicago to African-American expansion into white neighborhoods.

84. Lukas's *Common Ground* is an exceptionally good examination of the fears and anxieties of Irish and African Americans in Boston concerning the race issue. An interesting study of the complexities involved in changing neighborhoods in Eileen McMahon, "What Parish Are You From: The Study of the Chicago Parish Community" (Ph.D. dissertation, Loyola Univ. of Chicago, 1989). McMahon describes and discusses the passage of St. Sabina, a prosperous parish on Chicago's South Side, from Irish to African American. She analyzes how the cultural differences and the fear of crime and loss of property value resulted in white flight, defeating the efforts of the

pastor, Father McMahon, and other members of the parish to create an integrated Catholic community.

85. A best-selling novel that became a successful film, Judith Rossner's *Looking for Mr. Goodbar* (New York, 1975), labels Catholics as bigots. The half-Irish, half-Italian Theresa Dunn describes her father and mother to her college English professor as "very prejudiced you know, typical lower-middle class Roman Catholics. . . . I grew up with that stuff you know, the niggers are coming. They don't even like Martin Luther King" (p. 39).

86. Greeley, *Irish-Americans*, p. 118.

87. Greeley compares the Irish to other groups as follows: "26 [sic] percent of families in America reported an annual income in excess of $20,000; of those who describe themselves as British Protestant, 30 percent reported more than $20,000 in income; and 47 percent of the Irish Catholic families reported more than $20,000 in income, a little higher than 46 percent of Jewish families and 43 percent of Italian families. Irish occupational prestige, on a scale of 100, was 42.0 as compared to 39.8 for all American white families, 38.6 for Italian families, and 42.1 for British Protestant families. The mean number of years of schooling of Irish Catholics is 12.6 as compared to the national average of 11.8, 12.7 for British Protestants, and 11.4 for Italian Catholics and 13.7 for Jews. Of the Irish Catholics, 32 percent were professionals or managers, as compared to a national average of 25 percent, an Italian figure of 22 percent, a British Protestant figure of 33 percent, and a Jewish figure of 40 percent" (ibid.).

88. Ibid., p. 113.

89. Greeley has favorably evaluated the social conscience liberalism of Irish-American Catholics in other books, including *The American Catholic* (New York, 1977); *Why Can't They Be Like Us; Ethnicity in the United States: A Preliminary Reconnaissance* (New York, 1974); and the *The Catholic Experience* (New York, 1967).

90. Estimates of the numbers of illegal Irish immigrants vary considerably. "The Consul General of Ireland asserts that there are fewer than 40,000 undocumented Irish in the United States, and the United States Catholic Conference (U.S.C.C.) puts the total at 50,000. The Irish Immigrant Reform Movement (I.I.R.M.), represented at the Boston conference by Sean Minihane, its national chairman, believes that there are at least 150,000 undocumented Irish in the United States" (Richard Bautch, "The New Irish Immigrant," *America*, Mar. 18, 1989, p. 236).

91. In 1991 the Irish received 40% preferential treatment in a United States government lottery that awarded many green cards to illegal immigrant contestants. This will ease but not solve the problem of many Irish young people determined on staying in the country.

3. RELIGION AS CULTURE AND COMMUNITY

1. Annabelle M. Melville, *John Carroll of Baltimore* (New York, 1955).

2. For the Irish historical background of this chapter see Thomas E. Hachey, Joseph M. Hernon, Jr., and Lawrence J. McCaffrey, *The Irish Experience* (Englewood Cliffs, N.J., 1989), and Karl Bottigheimer, *Ireland and the Irish* (New York, 1982).

3. Sean O'Faolain, *King of the Beggars* (London, 1938), p. 29.

4. Robert Kee, *The Green Flag* (New York, 1972), pp. 41–145, presents a good discussion of the events of 1798 in Ireland. For an exceptionally perceptive fictional account see Thomas Flanagan, *The Year of the French* (New York, 1979).

5. Sean O'Faolain, *The Irish* (Harmondsworth, Middlesex, England, 1969), p. 88.

6. Fergus O'Ferrall, *Catholic Emancipation: Daniel O'Connell and the Birth of Irish Democracy, 1820–1830* (Dublin, 1985), convincingly argues that O'Connell in Ireland and Andrew Jackson in the United States created the forces of modern political democracy in the Western world.

7. Ibid., pp. 277–78, discusses the reactions of Beaumont and Tocqueville to clerical democratic views in Ireland. For Tocqueville's observations on Irish Catholicism and its political and social attitudes see Emmet Larkin, ed. and trans., *Alexis de Toqueville's Tour in Ireland, July–August, 1835* (Washington, D.C., 1990), pp. 39–47, 61–67, 78–80.

8. Patrick O'Farrell, *Ireland's English Question* (New York, 1971), p. 306.

9. British no-popery, anti-Irish nativism is analyzed and discussed in Gilbert A. Cahill's "Irish Catholicism and English Toryism," *Review of Politics* 19 (Jan. 1957): 62–76, and Cahill "The Protestant Association and the Anti-Maynooth Agitation of 1845," *Catholic Historical Review* 43 (Oct. 1957): 273–308. E. R. Norman, *Anti-Catholicism in Victorian England* (New York, 1968), also discusses nineteenth-century British anti-Catholic xenophobia.

10. Pre-Famine church weaknesses are studied in S. J. Connolly, *Priests and People in Pre-Famine Ireland, 1780–1845* (New York, 1982); Emmet Larkin, *The Historical Dimensions of Irish Catholicism* (Washington, D.C., 1984); and David W. Miller, "Irish Catholicism and the Great Famine," *Journal of Social Studies* (Sept. 1975): 81–98.

11. Patrick Corish, *The Irish Catholic Experience: A Historical Survey* (Wilmington, Del., 1985), pp. 151–91, discusses reforms in the Irish Catholic church before the Famine and distinguishes between the religious situations in various regions of Ireland.

12. In addition to Corish, K. Theodore Hoppen, *Elections, Politics, and Society in Ireland, 1832–1885* (Oxford, 1984); James O'Shea, *Priest, Politics and Society in Post-Famine Ireland: A Study of County Tipperary, 1850–1891* (Atlantic Highlands, N.J., 1983); and Donal A. Kerr, *Peel, Priest, and Politics* (Oxford, 1982), analyze pre-Famine Irish Catholicism.

13. Desmond Bowen, *Paul Cardinal Cullen and the Shaping of Modern Irish Catholicism* (Dublin, 1983), blames Cullen's ultramontanism for much of the lingering sectarian antagonism and cultural divisiveness in Ireland. Emmet Larkin, *The Making of the Roman Catholic Church in Ireland, 1850–1860* (Chapel Hill, 1980), and *The Consolidation of the Roman Catholic Church in Ireland, 1860–1870* (Chapel Hill, 1987), presents a fuller and more objective look at Cullen's part in Irish religious history, as does Corish's *Irish Catholic Experience*.

14. The most influential explanation of the Jansenist character of Irish Catholicism and its French origins through Maynooth appeared in the first printing of

Sean O'Faolain's, *The Irish: A Character Study* (New York, 1956), pp. 116–19, 146. Tony Gray, *The Irish Answer* (Boston, 1966), p. 297, attributes puritanism to the "French theologians who dominated Maynooth when it was first set up." In his interview with Peter Occhiogrosso in *Once a Catholic* (1987 rpt. New York, 1989), p. 308, Senator Eugene McCarthy said: "Indeed, the Church in America is kind of an Irish Jansenist Church. Actually, the whole Church is pretty Jansenist, even in Ireland." In *The Rise of the Unmeltable Ethnics* (1972 rpt. New York, 1973), p. 56, Michael Novak claims that Jansenism makes Irish piety "chill and bleak and death-centered." Encouraged by the British government, the Irish Parliament established a Catholic seminary at Maynooth in 1794 to keep Irish candidates for the priesthood away from French revolutionary ideas circulating in Continental seminaries.

15. Eugene Hynes, "The Great Hunger and Irish Catholicism," *Societas* 8 (Spring 1978): 137–56, points to the Famine as a force persuading people to follow Catholic guidelines on sex as a way to restrict population. Robert E. Kennedy, Jr., *The Irish: Emigration, Marriage, and Fertility* (Berkeley, 1973), pp. 13–15, 145–51, examines relationships between religion and celibacy in modern Ireland and concludes that economic reasons persuaded the Irish to use Catholic sexual morality to justify and strengthen their determination to postpone marriage until they were financially secure. Kennedy emphasizes that Irish Catholicism encourages marriage while discouraging sex outside that state.

16. In *The Rise of the Unmeltable Ethnics*, p. 11, Novak claims that because of Irish leadership the Catholic church in the United States has become "Protestant, individualistic, and pietistic in character" and that the Irish "easily absorb Calvinism and its ethic of work, decency, and moral indignation." Brian Cleeve, *A View of the Irish* (London, 1983), pp. 19–20, mentions the Maynooth Jansenist factor in Irish Catholic puritanism but insists that British Victorianism is a more important influence.

17. The morality aspect of the Parnell leadership controversy is the subject of Emmet Larkin, "The Roman Catholic Hierarchy and the Fall of Parnell," *Victorian Studies* 4 (June 1961): 315–36; and F. S. L. Lyons, *The Fall of Parnell, 1890–1891* (Toronto, 1960).

18. Lawrence J. McCaffrey, *Daniel O'Connell and the Repeal Year* (Lexington, Ky., 1966), pp. 21–23.

19. Irish and Irish-American literature has focused on the Irish drinking problem and its association with sexual frustration. Hugh Brody, *Innishkillane: Change and Decline in the West of Ireland* (New York, 1974), connects the social inadequacies of rural life, celibacy, and pub culture in Ireland.

20. Most of the general information about the American Catholic church in this chapter comes from two excellent recent studies of the subject: Jay P. Dolan, *The American Catholic Experience* (New York, 1985); and James Hennessey, S. J., *American Catholics: A History of the American Catholic Community in the United States* (New York, 1981). Another important source is a shorter but perceptive examination of the history of American Catholicism, John Cogley, *Catholic America* (New York, 1973).

21. Peter Guilday, *The Life and Times of John England: First Bishop of Charleston, 1786–1842* (New York, 1927).

22. According to *Newsweek*, Sept. 21, 1987, p. 25, the Irish compose 18 percent of the American Catholic population. Andrew Greeley, *That Most Distressful Nation: The Taming of the American Irish* (Chicago, 1972), p. 264, says that the Irish in 1972 constituted 17 percent of American Catholics and had 50 percent of the bishops and 35 percent of the priests. Novak in *The Rise of the Unmeltable Ethnics*, p. 55, says that the Irish are only 17 percent of the American Catholic population but have 57 percent of the bishops.

23. Joseph M. Curran, *Hibernian Green on the Silver Screen* (Westport, Conn., 1989), pp. 48–52.

24. Philip Roth, *The Anatomy Lesson* (New York, 1983), p. 74; Novak's *Rise of the Unmeltable Ethnics* frequently makes the point that though the Irish are Catholic, their Catholicism has been Anglicized and Protestantized. In "The Myth of the Irish: A Failure of American Catholic Scholarship," in *The Changing Face of Catholic Ireland* (London, 1968), pp. 121–34, Desmond Fennell effectively criticizes proponents of the "Celtic Heresy" thesis. He provides strong evidence to show that Catholicism among the Irish is true to the rules and spirit of the Roman church.

25. Tom MacHale, *Farragan's Retreat* (New York, 1971); Edward Hannibal, *Chocolate Days, Popsicle Weeks* (New York, 1970); John R. Powers, *The Last Catholic in America* (New York, 1973), and *Do Patent Leather Shoes Really Reflect Up?* (Chicago, 1975); Caryl Rivers, *Virgins* (New York, 1984).

26. Harry Sylvester, *Moon Gaffney* (New York, 1947); Jimmy Breslin, *World Without End, Amen* (New York, 1973).

27. Eugene O'Neill, *Long Day's Journey into Night* (New London, Conn., 1956); Frank D. Gilroy, *The Subject Was Roses* (New York, 1965).

28. The social and economic positions of the American hierarchy are the subject of James Edmund Roohan, *American Catholics and the Social Question, 1865–1900* (New York, 1976).

29. Probably the most perceptive, informative, and well-written biography of an American Catholic churchman, Marvin O'Connell's *John Ireland and the American Catholic Church* (St. Paul, 1988), is a valuable source for American Catholic history, particularly for the conflict within the hierarchy over the church in America.

30. Henry J. Browne, *The Catholic Church and the Knights of Labor* (New York, 1976), pp. 228–74.

31. In addition to O'Connell, *John Ireland and the American Catholic Church*, Hennessey, *American Catholics*, and Dolan, *The American Catholic Experience*, Robert D. Cross, *The Emergence of Catholic Liberalism in America* (1958 rpt. Chicago, 1967) presents an informative discussion of the factional fight within the American hierarchy.

32. Relations between the American hierarchy and Rome are thoroughly treated in O'Connell, *John Ireland and the American Catholic Church*, and in Gerald P. Fogarty, *The Vatican and the American Hierarchy from 1870 to 1965* (Wilmington, Del., 1985).

33. The Americanization of papal encyclicals is a subject of Garry Wills, *Bare Ruined Choirs* (New York, 1971), pp. 49–56.

34. Francis L. Broderick, *Right Reverend New Dealer John Ryan* (New York, 1963), and Dolan, *The American Catholic Experience*, pp. 321–46, 402–4.

35. John Tracy Ellis, *American Catholics and the Intellectual Life* (Chicago, 1955), pp. 15 and 16, from D. W. Brogan, *U.S.A.: An Outline of the Country, Its People and Institutions* (London, 1941), p. 65. Thomas F. O'Dea, *The American Catholic Dilemma* (New York, 1958), gives strong support to Ellis's thesis. Wilfrid Sheed, in his loving portrait of his parents, *Frank and Maisie* (New York, 1986), provides an accurate description of a shallow, clerical-ridden Catholic intellectualism before and after World War II.

36. Ellis gave a better explanation than O'Dea's concentration on Irish leadership for the problems of Catholic education. He said that the church had never widened its educational perspective beyond the early mission of civilizing poor immigrants and keeping them in the faith and that Catholicism had assimilated the anti-intellectual materialism of the general American environment.

37. Wills, *Bare Ruined Choirs*, p. 37. Many Irish immigrants must have found the same beauty in their churches as did Mary McCarthy, orphaned and living with cruel and ignorant guardian relatives in Minneapolis.

> Looking back, I see that it was religion that saved me. Our ugly church and parochial school provided me with my only aesthetic outlet, in the words of the Mass and the litanies and the old Latin hymns, in the Easter lillies around the altar, rosaries, ornamented prayer books, votive lamps, holy cards stamped in gold and decorated with flower wreaths and a saint's picture. This side of Catholicism, much of it cheapened and debased by mass production, was for me, nevertheless, the equivalent of Gothic cathedrals and illuminated manuscripts and mystery plays. I threw myself into it with ardor.
>
> —Mary McCarthy, *Memories of a Catholic Girlhood*
> (New York, 1957), p. 18.

38. "The whole nature of Gaelic society was opposed to urban living, and where this society lasted longest, notably in Ulster, towns and townscapes are almost without exception post-medieval. . . . The town in Ireland is the mark of the invader" (E. Estyn Evans, *The Personality of Ireland: Habitat, Heritage, and History* [Cambridge, England, 1973], p. 82).

39. James Carroll, *Prince of Peace* (Boston, 1984).

40. William Gibson, *Mass for the Dead* (New York, 1968). For interesting discussions on the role of the parish in American Catholicism see Dolan, *American Catholic Experience*, pp. 158–94; and Ellen Skerrett, "The Catholic Dimension," in Lawrence J. McCaffrey, Ellen Skerrett, Michael Funchion, and Charles Fanning, *The Irish in Chicago* (Urbana, 1987), pp. 22–60.

41. James Joyce, *A Portrait of the Artist as a Young Man* (1916 rpt. New York, 1963), p. 38; William Kennedy, *Billy Phelan's Greatest Game* (1978 rpt. New York, 1983), p. 18; Thomas Fleming, *The Sandbox Tree* (New York, 1970).

42. Edwin O'Connor, *The Edge of Sadness* (Boston, 1961).

43. John Gregory Dunne, *True Confessions* (New York, 1977). *True Confessions* is a good novel, but the 1980 movie version, with script by Dunne and Joan Didion, is even better.

44. J. F. Powers, *Morte D'Urban* (New York, 1962); *Prince of Darkness* (New York, 1947); *The Presence of Grace* (New York, 1956); *Look How the Fish Live* (New York, 1975). In *The Wheat That Springeth Green* (New York, 1988), Powers's latest novel, the author continues to exhibit has satirical genius and his graceful writing style, but he seems more emotionally detached from his subject and takes a more compassionate view of American Catholicism and its clergy.

45. "I think entering the Order was a very interesting thing for many girls. Number one, it was a way of getting away from their families if they didn't want marriage. It was a way of getting a good education. Nuns were wonderful people, the most educated people that I knew. Not a lot of women in the city of Erie were educated like that. And this was before the Peace Corps—if you wanted to enter a life of service without getting married, what else was there?" (interview with Patricia Heidt in Peter Occhiogrosso, *Once a Catholic* [1987 rpt. New York, 1989], p. 185). Despite her problems with Catholicism, Mary McCarthy in *Memories of a Catholic Girlhood* pays tribute to the inspiration and example of nuns who taught her in St. Stephen's parochial school in Minneapolis and in a Sacred Heart order boarding school in Seattle.

46. In *Erin's Daughters in America: Irish-American Women in the Nineteenth Century* (Baltimore, 1983), pp. 100–101, Hasia Diner identifies some Irish-American women labor movement leaders. Kate Kennedy organized women teachers in the San Francisco public schools, as did Margaret Haley and Catherine Goggins in Chicago. Kate Mullaney organized collar laundresses in Troy, New York. Leonora Barry was a full-time organizer for the Knights of Labor. Mary Kenney O'Sullivan began her labor union activities mobilizing women in the bookbinding industry and moved on to become the first full-time organizer of her sex in the American Federation of Labor. Leonora O'Reilly organized women in the garment industry and then became a co-founder of the Women's Trade Union League. Elizabeth Flynn Rogers had the highest position in the Knights of Labor as grand master workman of District 24, which included all members from the Chicago area. Another Chicagoan, Agnes Nestor, was active in the glove makers union.

47. Barry Coldrey, an Australian member of the order, has written an excellent history of the Irish Christian Brothers, *Faith and Fatherland* (Dublin, 1988).

48. Many critics of Father Charles Coughlin emphasize his anti-Semitism and fascism, which indicts his supporters, particularly his Catholic following. But in *Voices of Protest: Huey Long, Father Coughlin, and the Great Depression* (New York, 1982), pp. 269–83, Alan Brinkley convincingly argues that Coughlin's anti-Semitism was veiled and not a major position in his program until 1938, and by that time he was no longer a popular figure. Although he was isolationist and strongly anticommunist, once saying that given the choices of fascism or communism, he would select the former, Coughlin never praised Mussolini and Hitler until 1938, the same time that he began to focus on the Jews as the enemy. Charles Tull, *Father Coughlin and the New Deal* (Syracuse, 1965), pp. 170–71, 247, discusses Irish and German support for Coughlin in the late 1930s and early 1940s. According to

Brinkley (pp. 200–201), even before Coughlin became so radical he had German and Irish working-class support, not because he was radical but because he was conservative on labor issues, favoring the interests of the elite skilled labor unions of which they were members. In *The Catholic Counterculture in America, 1933–1962* (Chapel Hill, 1989), pp. 72–79, James Terence Fisher argues that Coughlin, like Dorothy Day's Catholic Worker movement, reflected the Catholic counterculture's suspicion of capitalism and its emphasis on "medieval corporatism" and "modern distributist theory." Some followers of Coughlin were so unaware of the leftist tilt of the Catholic Worker movement and Coughlin's rightist interpretation of social justice that they beseeched Dorothy Day to defend Coughlin when he fell out of favor. For an understanding of the medieval aspects of the Catholic counterculture see Philip Gleason, *Keeping the Faith* (Notre Dame, 1987), pp. 11–34.

49. Donald F. Crosby, *God, Church, and Flag: Senator Joseph R. McCarthy and the Catholic Church, 1950–1957* (Chapel Hill, 1978), discusses the associations between American Catholicism and McCarthyism. John Cooney, *The American Pope: The Life and Times of Francis Cardinal Spellman* (New York, 1984), pp. 220–30, details the connection between Spellman and the junior senator from Wisconsin.

50. According to a 1954 Gallup Poll, before McCarthy began to lose respect and influence, he had 58 percent of Catholic support, 49 percent from Protestants, and only 15 percent from Jews (John Cogley, *Catholic America* (New York, 1973), p. 112.

51. In *Bare Ruined Choirs*, pp. 141–272, Wills discusses post–Vatican II trends in American Catholicism. Almost all of the present and past Catholics interviewed by Occhiogrosso in *Once a Catholic* lamented the "modernization" or "vulgarization" of the liturgy.

52. Wills, *Bare Ruined Choirs*, pp. 174–87, presents an exceptionally intelligent analysis of the church's puritanism and how it led to the mistake of *Humanae Vitae*.

53. According to a *Time* magazine poll, Sept. 7, 1987, pp. 46–51, 75 percent of American Catholics regard the pope as a significant world leader, but 93 percent believe that disagreeing with him does not mean that they are not good Catholics. Only 27 percent support abortion on demand, but 52 percent believe that certain situations would justify termination of a pregnancy (comparative Protestant percentages on the same issues are 34 and 57). Only 14 percent of Catholics think that abortion should be illegal, which is only 2 percent higher than Protestant opinion on the subject. Fifty-three percent of Catholics believe in permitting priests to marry, and 52 percent favor the ordination of women. Seventy-six percent of American Catholics approve of divorced people remarrying in a church ceremony. A mere 24 percent think that the church's stand on artificial contraception is right, but 68 percent disapprove of homosexual conduct. The *Time* poll corresponds to other public opinion surveys. According to Greeley, *American Catholic*, p. 142, as early as 1965, 77 percent of Catholic women under age forty-five were using means to prevent conception, but only 28 percent were following the church's recommended rhythm system. Chapters 7 and 8 of Greeley's book discuss changes in Catholic attitudes in the United States. According to George Gallup, Jr., and Jim Castelli, *The People's Religion: American*

Faith in the 90s (New York, 1990), among present-day Catholics, 28 percent of the American population, only about half attend Sunday mass. Three-quarters rely on their own consciences rather than the pope's teaching. Like Protestants, they are evenly divided on whether abortion should be legally limited and overwhelmingly opposed (80 percent) to outlawing it in all cases. The Gallup-Castelli findings agree with the research evidence that Andrew Greeley has produced in previous studies and in his new book, *The Catholic Myth: The Behavior and Belief of American Catholics* (New York, 1990). Why do Catholics remain at least nominally in the church if they are so opposed to its authority? Because they enjoy being Catholics, says Greeley. They like remains of its history and mystery and its long historical tradition. In *American Catholics*, p. 329, Hennessey records a drop in mass attendance on Sundays from 75 percent in 1957 to 54 percent in 1975 (Gallup Poll) or from 71 percent in 1966 to 50 percent in 1975 (National Opinion Research Center).

54. According to Hennessey, *American Catholics*, p. 323, enrollment in Catholic elementary and secondary schools fell from 5.6 million in 1965 to less than 3.2 million in 1980. In that same time span, the number of elementary schools decreased from 10,879 to 8,149 and secondary schools from 2,413 to 1,527. The decline of Catholic schools probably is more reflective of the expense of maintaining them, with a reduction in the number of religious orders and mounting salaries for lay teachers, than of the laity's rejection of their value.

55. *Chicago Tribune*, Nov. 15, 1988.

56. William D. Montalbano, "Vatican Tells Theologians Dissent Won't Be Tolerated," *Chicago Sun Times*, June 27, 1990.

57. A brief history of the stand of American bishops against choice appeared in Charles W. Madigan, "Catholic Church Gets Tough on Abortion," *Chicago Tribune*, July 8, 1990, pp. 1, 8.

58. For examples of journalists' concern see the editorial "The Cardinal Gets Tougher," and A. M. Rosenthal, "The Cardinal's Crusade," and Frank Lynn, "The Stakes Are Raised for Catholic Politicians," *New York Times*, June 17, 1990, sec. E; Mike Royko, "Cardinal Takes Aim at the Wrong Target," *Chicago Tribune*, June 18, 1990; and Jeff Greenfield, "Cardinal's Threat Raises Complex Issues," *Chicago Sun Times*, June 18, 1990. An exceptionally interesting, intelligent, and thoughtful discussion of the abortion issue, Catholic politicians, and some members of the hierarchy is Garry Wills, "Mario Cuomo's Trouble with Abortion," *New York Review of Books*, June 28, 1990, pp. 9–13.

59. The declining numbers of clericals are discussed in Dolan, *American Catholic Experience*, pp. 436–38; and Hennessey, *American Catholics*, p. 329.

60. Vincent L. Woodward et al., "Gays in the Clergy," *Newsweek*, Feb. 23, 1987, pp. 58–61. James G. Wolf, *Gay Priests* (New York, 1989), is a friendly sociological treatment of homosexual priests in the American Catholic church.

61. Woodward, "Gays in the Clergy."

62. Thomas J. Fleming, *The God of Love* (New York, 1963); *Romans, Countrymen and Lovers* (New York, 1969); *Sandbox Tree*; *The Good Shepherd* (New York, 1974); and *Promises to Keep* (New York, 1978).

63. On November 16, 1988, the American hierarchy became a little bolder in resisting Roman intrusion by rejecting a papal attempt to diminish the teaching authority of the National Conference of Bishops (*Chicago Tribune*, Nov. 17, 1988).

4. POWER WITH OR WITHOUT PURPOSE?

1. John Paul Bocock, "The Irish Conquest of Our Cities," *Forum* 17 (1894): 195.

2. Alan J. Ward, *Ireland and Anglo-American Relations, 1899–1921* (London, 1969), p. 94. Spring Rice was evaluating Irish politicians in relationship to their success in keeping the United States neutral in the early stages of World War I and free of a military alliance with Britain and France.

3. James P. Walsh, ed., *The Irish: America's Political Class* (New York, 1976).

4. Bocock, "Irish Conquest," p. 195.

5. Daniel Patrick Moynihan, "The Irish," in Nathan Glazer and Daniel Patrick Moynihan, *Beyond the Melting Pot: The Negroes, Puerto Ricans, Jews, Italians, and Irish of New York City* (Cambridge, Mass., 1963), p. 229.

6. Thomas J. Fleming, *All Good Men* (New York, 1963), p. 30

7. Edward R. F. Sheehan, *The Governor* (New York, 1970), pp. 196–97.

8. Ibid., p. 80.

9. James Carroll, *Mortal Friends* (Boston, 1978).

10. William V. Shannon, *The American Irish* (New York, 1974), pp. 231–32. Curley spoke for himself in *I'd Do It Again* (New York, 1976).

11. Joseph Huthmacher, "Urban Liberalism and the Age of Reform," *Mississippi Valley Historical Review* 49 (1962): 231–41; John B. Buenker, *Urban Liberalism and Progressive Reform* (New York, 1973); Robert Dahl, *Who Governs? Democracy and Power in an American City* (New Haven, 1961); and Elmer E. Cornwell, "Bosses, Machines, and Ethnic Groups," *Annals* 353 (May 1964): 27–39.

12. Steven P. Erie, *Rainbow's End: Irish-Americans and the Dilemmas of Urban Machine Politics, 1840–1985* (Berkeley, 1988).

13. Ibid., p. 243. In discussing the Irish Catholic rejection of the Anglo-Protestant "value of economic achievement," Erie relies on Edward Levine's analysis of Chicago Irish politics, *The Irish and Irish Politicians* (Notre Dame, 1966).

14. Mary Deasy, *O'Shaughnessey* (New York, 1957); and John O'Hara, *Ten North Frederick* (New York, 1955). Unlike most Irish politicians in American literature, O'Shaughnessey is a most unpleasant person.

15. Ramona Stewart, *Casey* (Boston, 1968).

16. Bocock, "Irish Conquest," p. 187.

17. Alfred Connable and Edward Silberfarb, *Tigers of Tammany* (New York, 1967), pp. 173–96.

18. Marjorie Fallows, *Irish-Americans: Identity and Assimilation* (Englewood Cliffs, N.J., 1979), pp. 112–16, discusses Irish-American politics. For specific cities see Dennis Clark, *The Irish in Philadelphia* (Philadelphia, 1973); Earl F. Niehaus, *The Irish in New Orleans, 1880–1860* (New York, 1976); R. A. Burchell, *The San Francisco*

Irish, 1848–1880 (Berkeley, 1980); Michael F. Funchion, "Irish Chicago," and Michael Green, "Irish Chicago: The Multi-Ethnic Road to Machine Success," in *Ethnic Chicago*, ed. Peter a'A. Jones and Melvin G. Holli (Grand Rapids, Mich., 1981); and Timothy J. Meagher, ed., *From Paddy to Studs: Irish-American Communities at the Turn of the Century Era, 1880–1920;* (Westport, Conn., 1986). Previous to Kelly-Nash, Anton Cermak, the Bohemian ethnic mayor, began to bring some order to Chicago Democratic politics. In 1933, he was accidentally killed when an assassin shooting at President Roosevelt missed and hit him. Edward Kelly took his place as mayor while Patrick Nash took command of the organizational aspects of Chicago's Democratic party.

19. For a detailed examination of Irish politics in Chicago see Michael F. Funchion, "The Political and Nationalist Dimensions," in Lawrence J. McCaffrey, Ellen Skerrett, Michael Funchion, and Charles Fanning, *The Irish in Chicago* (Urbana, 1987), pp. 61–97.

20. Shannon, *American Irish*, pp. 74–82. Connable and Silverfarb, *Tigers of Tammany*, pp. 197–230. Stewart's novel *Casey* is based on Croker's life.

21. William D. Miller, *Mr. Crump of Memphis* (Baton Rouge, 1964); Alan Brinkley, *Voices of Protest: Huey Long, Father Coughlin, and the Great Depression* (New York, 1982), pp. 8–81.

22. Charles Fanning, *Finley Peter Dunne and Mr. Dooley: The Chicago Years* (Lexington, Ky., 1978), pp. 107–37; and Fanning, *Mr. Dooley and the Chicago Irish* (Washington, D.C., 1987), pp. 205–55.

23. Joseph Dinneen, *Ward Eight* (New York, 1976).

24. Terry Nichols Clark, "The Irish Ethic and the Spirit of Patronage," *Ethnicity* 2 (Dec. 1975): 305–59.

25. Cecil Woodham-Smith, *The Great Hunger: Ireland 1845–49* (London, 1962): 407–13.

26. Richard Hofstadter, *Social Darwinism in American Thought* (New York, 1955).

27. Huthmacher, "Urban Liberalism and the Age of Reform"; Buenker, *Urban Liberalism and Progressive Reform;* Dahl, *Who Governs?;* and Elmer E. Cornwell, "Bosses, Machines, and Ethnic Groups;" favorably evaluate Irish political machines. Buenker and Huthmacher disagree with "status revolution" historians such as George Mowry and Richard Hofstadter, who blame the "boss-immigrant machine complex" for impeding the thrusts "of the reformer-individualistic Anglo-Saxon complex."

28. Erie, *Rainbow's End*, pp. 67–106. In *Power and Society: Greater New York at the Turn of the Century* (New York, 1983), David C. Hammack presents an excellent analysis of the conflicts and relationships between the upper classes and Tammany and how the former, Swallow Tail Democrats, limited the latter.

29. O'Connor, *The Last Hurrah* (Boston, 1956) pp. 43–44.

30. William L. Riordan, *Plunkitt of Tammany Hall* (New York, 1963), pp. 91–93.

31. For examinations of the power struggle between Powers and Jane Addams and other reformers see Jane Addams, "Why the Ward Boss Rules," *Outlook* 58

(1898): 879–882; and Allen F . Davis, "Jane Addams and the Ward Boss," *Journal of the Illinois State Historical Society* 53 (1960): 247–65.

32. In the novel, pp. 269–70, the choice was between Columbus; Roosevelt; Monsignor Tancredi, a parish priest; and Charlie di Mascola, a ward boss.

33. In *Irish American Nationalism* (Philadelphia, 1966), pp. 133–51, Thomas N. Brown discusses the emphasis on power in Irish-American politics. In "The Political Irish: Politicians and Rebels," in *America and Ireland, 1776–1976* (Westport, Conn., 1980), ed. David Noel Doyle and Owen Dudley Edwards, pp. 133–49, he analyzes its passage to idealism.

34. Alan J. Lichtman, *Prejudice and Old Politics: The Presidential Election of 1928* (Chapel Hill, 1969) is an excellent study of Smith's defeat.

35. George Q. Flynn, *American Catholics and the Roosevelt Presidency* (Lexington, Ky., 1968), pp. 50–55, 98–99, 230, 234, 237, details Roosevelt's rewards to Catholics for their long support of the Democratic party.

36. Alan Brinkley, *Voices of Protest*, pp. 128–33; and Charles J. Tull, *Father Coughlin and the New Deal* (Syracuse, 1965), pp. 202–4, discuss Catholic anti-Coughlin responses.

37. Shannon, *American Irish*, pp. 327–48.

38. Maureen Howard, *Facts of Life* (Boston, 1978), pp. 67–68.

39. Thomas C. Reeves, *The Life and Times of Joe McCarthy* (New York, 1982), is the most comprehensive study of the senator from Wisconsin. Donald F. Crosby, *God, Church, and Flag: Senator Joseph R. McCarthy and the Catholic Church, 1950–57* (Chapel Hill, 1978), examines the responses of American Catholics to McCarthyism.

40. Paul Blanshard, *The Irish and Catholic Power* (Boston, 1953), p. 289.

41. Thomas J. Fleming, *King of the Hill* (New York, 1965); Thomas J. Fleming, *Rulers of the City* (New York, 1977).

42. Erie, *Rainbow's End*, pp. 119–23.

43. O'Connor, *Last Hurrah*, p. 374.

44. Erie, *Rainbow's End*, pp. 16–17, 110, 141, 154–55, 224–25, 245–46.

45. Daley and the machine he controlled have attracted a considerable bibliography, including William F. Gleason, *Daley of Chicago* (New York, 1970); Eugene Kennedy, *Himself: The Life and Times of Richard J. Daley* (New York, 1978); Levine, *The Irish and Irish Politicians*; Mike Royko, *Boss* (New York, 1971); Len O'Connor, *Clout* (Chicago, 1975); Milton Rakove; *Don't Make No Waves—Don't Back No Losers* (Bloomington, 1975); and Rakove, *We Don't Want Nobody Nobody Sent* (Bloomington, 1979).

46. The provincial limitations of Chicago's Irish politics are discussed in Funchion, "Political and Nationalist Dimensions," in McCaffrey et al., *Irish in Chicago*, p. 93.

47. Kennedy, *Himself*, pp. 156–58, 160, 169, 171–75, 178–87, discusses the role of Chicago's mayor in the election of John F. Kennedy. For my analysis of the 1960 presidential campaign and election I am indebted to Herbert S. Parmet, *JFK: The Presidency of John F. Kennedy* (Harmondsworth, Middlesex; England, 1984),

pp. 3–60; Theodore H. White, *The Making of the President 1960* (New York, 1960); and my own experience as a campaign worker.

48. The Catholic issue in the 1960 presidential campaign is the subject of Timothy Sarbaugh, "John Fitzgerald Kennedy, the Catholic Issue, and Presidential Politics, 1959–60" (Ph.D. dissertation, Loyola Univ., Chicago). On the Houston meeting see Parmet, *JFK*, pp. 42–45.

49. In 1937, Monsignor Maurice S. Sheehy, assistant rector of the Catholic University of America, wrote to a friend that the year before, 103 out of 106 American bishops voted for FDR (Tull, *Father Coughlin and the New Deal*, p. 158).

50. Kennedy collected between 61 percent (IBM computer evaluation) and 78 percent (Gallup Poll) of the Catholic vote. Though probably less than Roosevelt gathered in 1936, it was a significant reversal of the Catholic drift to Eisenhower in 1956. It is estimated that only 50 percent of German-American Catholics voted for Kennedy, and no doubt some of the Irish-American middle class, particularly in the Mid-Atlantic States, who became more conservative as they became more prosperous, cast Republican ballots.

51. *U.S. News and World Report*, Apr. 16, 1979, p. 33.

52. Nat Hentoff, "The Constitutionalist," a profile of Justice William J. Brennan, Jr., *New Yorker*, Mar. 12, 1990, p. 45.

53. Stephen J. Markman and Alfred S. Regnery, "The Mind of Justice Brennan: A 25 Year Tribute," *National Review*, May 18, 1984, pp. 31, 30, 38.

54. My comments on Brennan are based on the Hentoff and Markman-Regnery articles and David Kaplan's essay "A Master Builder," *Newsweek*, July 30, 1990, p. 19.

55. Theodore H. White, *America in Search of Itself: The Making of the President, 1956–1980* (New York, 1981), p. 144.

56. *Washington Post*, Nov. 6, 1980.

57. Ibid., Nov. 8, 1984.

58. *New York Times*, Nov. 6, 1980, Nov. 8, 1984.

59. *Chicago Sun Times*, Nov. 11, 1984.

60. Ibid., Nov. 7, 1988.

61. *New York Times* and *Wall Street Journal*, Nov. 10, 1988; *Washington Post*, Nov. 9, 1988; *Time*, Nov. 21, 1988. In his November 20, 1988, syndicated column in the *Chicago Sun Times*, Andrew M. Greeley pointed out that although American Catholics have been disenchanted with Democratic presidential candidates, over the past ten years between 60 and 65 percent of them have voted for Democrats in congressional elections.

62. Peggy Noonan, *What I Saw at The Revolution: A Political Life in the Reagan Era* (New York, 1990), p. 15. In her book, Noonan explains why she left her ancestral political home, the Democratic party of her Irish Catholic grandparents and parents, to work for a Republican president.

63. Erie, *Rainbow's End*, pp. 259–66.

64. The discussion of recent Chicago politics is based on newspaper coverage in the *Chicago Tribune* and the *Chicago Sun Times* and on Chicago television news.

5. "FROM A LAND ACROSS THE SEA"

1. Elizabeth Gurley Flynn, one of the foremost leaders of the Communist party in the United States, was baptized but not raised as a Catholic. Describing her ancestors as "immigrants and revolutionists," Flynn was inspired by the nationalist tradition of rebellion. Before she was ten, "I knew of the great heroes—Robert Emmet, Wolfe Tone, Michael Davitt, Parnell and O'Donovan Rossa" (Elizabeth Gurley Flynn, I Speak My Own Piece [New York, 1939], pp. 13–33). William J. Brennan, Jr., a devout Catholic, also was influenced by Irish nationalism. In his interview with Nat Hentoff (New Yorker, May 18, 1984, p. 45), Justice Brennan said he believed " 'in the age old dream,' that eventually no one will be denied his or her inherent dignity and rights." He said, "The dream, though always old, is never old, like the poor Old Woman in Yeats' play 'Cathleen ni Houlihan.' " Brennan then went on to give a brief excerpt from the play: " 'did you see an old woman going down the path?' asks Bridget. 'I did not,' replies Patrick, who came into the house just after the old woman left it, 'but I saw a young girl and she had the walk of a queen.' " Brennan then smiled and added, "That passage has often meant a great deal to me. I've used it often over the last thirty years." A Newsweek article, July 30, 1990, p. 20, also discusses Brennan's admiration for Cathleen ni Houlihan. Cathleen was Yeats's representation of Ireland. The dream was national freedom.

2. For an exceptionally perceptive analysis of Irish Catholic society in the eighteenth century see the "Proem" of Sean O'Faolain's King of the Beggars (Dublin, 1980), pp. 13–38.

3. Thomas Flanagan's Year of the French (New York, 1979) is a novel about the rebellion in Mayo. But it captures the mood of 1798 all over Ireland and presents excellent portraits of real and fictional actors on the Irish stage, representing a variety of views within the Catholic, Protestant, and Nonconformist communities.

4. The Anglo-Irish Protestant unionist historian William Edward Harpole Lecky's profile of O'Connell in The Leaders of Public Opinion in Ireland (London, 1871) appreciated O'Connell's genius, his work in improving the lot of the Catholic masses, and his sincerity. He complained, however, "But when to the great services he rendered to his country we oppose the sectarian and class warfare that resulted from his policy, the fearful elements of discord he evoked, and which he alone could in some degree control, it may be questioned whether his life was a blessing or curse to Ireland" (p. 320). Young Ireland's criticism of O'Connell's alliance between nationalism and Catholicism is well expressed throughout Charles Gavan Duffy, Young Ireland (London, 1896).

5. The best study of the Catholic emancipation agitation and its impact on Irish history and politics is Fergus O'Ferrall, Catholic Emancipation: Daniel O'Connell and the Birth of Irish Democracy, 1820–1830 (Dublin, 1985).

6. For a survey of Irish history covered in this section see Thomas E. Hachey, Joseph M. Hernon, Jr., and Lawrence J. McCaffrey, The Irish Experience (Englewood Cliffs, N.J., 1989). For histories and interpretations of Irish nationalism see D. George Boyce, Nationalism in Ireland (Baltimore, 1982); Malcolm Brown, The Politics of Irish Literature from Thomas Davis to W.B. Yeats (Seattle, 1972); Owen Dudley Ed-

wards, "Ireland," in *Celtic Nationalism*, ed. Owen Dudley Edwards (New York, 1968); Thomas E. Hachey and Lawrence J. McCaffrey, eds., *Perspectives on Irish Nationalism* (Lexington, Ky., 1988); John Hutchinson, *The Dynamics of Cultural Nationalism: The Gaelic Revival and the Creation of the Irish Nation State* (Boston, 1987); and Robert Kee, *The Green Flag* (New York, 1982).

7. Thomas N. Brown, "Nationalism and the Irish Peasant," *Review of Politics* 15 (Oct. 1953): 445, reprinted in the American Committee for *Irish Studies Reprint Series*, ed. Emmet Larkin and Lawrence J. McCaffrey (Chicago, 1971); and Lawrence J. McCaffrey, ed., *Irish Nationalism and the American Contribution* (New York, 1976).

8. Lawrence J. McCaffrey, *Daniel O'Connell and the Repeal Year* (Lexington, Ky., 1966), pp. 71-76.

9. Charles Kickham, *Sally Cavanagh* (Dublin, 1869), p. 251.

10. William Butler Yeats, "Remorse for Intemperate Speech," in *The Collected Poems of W.B. Yeats* (New York, 1961).

11. Thomas Flanagan, "Rebellion and Style: John Mitchel and the Jail Journal," *Irish University Review* 1 (Autumn 1970): 4–5. Flanagan borrowed this quote from William Dillon's two-volume *Life of John Mitchel* (London, 1888).

12. James Paul Rodechko, *Patrick Ford and His Search for America: A Case Study of Irish-American Journalism, 1870–1913* (New York, 1976), p. 34.

13. In *The Chicago School* (Princeton, 1987), chap. 7, Stow Persons describes how sociologists at the University of Chicago before World War II worked out the "marginal man" theory to explain the rise of ethnic nationalisms in the United States. According to this theory, some ethnics desiring to become integrated into the dominant culture learn its values but are either rejected by the establishment or feel uncomfortable in a new setting. Some remain suspended between their old and new cultures. Others return to the former and emphasize its significance and greatness, thus becoming nationalists. This explanation fits many early Irish-Americans.

14. This speech from the *Irish World*, Nov. 13, 1880, appears in this context in Thomas N. Brown's *Irish-American Nationalism* (Philadelphia, 1966), p. 24.

15. Brown's *Irish-American Nationalism* and "The Origins and Character of Irish-American Nationalism," *Review of Politics* 18 (July 1956): 327–58, present the case for Irish-American nationalism as a search for respectability; Kerby A. Miller, *Emigrants and Exiles: Ireland and the Irish Exodus to North America* (New York, 1985), argues that it is the product of an exile psychology and an expression of Irish failure and poverty in the United States. These two views are not necessarily contradictory. They indicate different kinds of generational, geographic, and community alienation.

16. McCaffrey, *Daniel O'Connell and the Repeal Year*, p. 72.

17. Eighteenth-century sources of Irish republicanism are well discussed in Marianne Elliott, *Partners in Revolution: The United Irishmen and France* (New Haven, 1982).

18. Quoted from James Loughlin, *Gladstone, Home Rule and the Ulster Question, 1892–93* (Atlantic Highlands, N.J., 1987), p. 189.

19. The connections between assertiveness and declining deference among Irish Catholics and American influences are discussed in R.V. Comerford, *The Fenians in Context: Irish Politics and Society, 1845–1882* (Atlantic Highlands, N.J.,

1985); Brian Griffin, "Social Aspects of Fenianism in Connacht and Leinster, 1858–70," *Eire-Ireland* 22 (Spring 1986): 16–39; and Tom Garvin, *The Evolution of Irish Nationalist Politics* (Dublin, 1984), pp. 59–68.

20. For book-length discussions of Fenianism see Comerford, *Fenians in Context*; William D'Arcy, *The Fenian Movement in the United States, 1858–1886* (Washington, D.C., 1947); Maurice Harmon, ed., *Fenians and Fenianism* (Seattle, 1970); and T. W. Moody, ed., *The Fenian Movement* (Cork, 1968).

21. The blocked mobility motivation for joining and promoting the IRB is an important theme in Comerford's *Fenians in Context*. He and Griffin, "Social Aspects of Fenianism in Connacht and Leinster," emphasize the recreational aspects of the republican movement.

22. Finley Peter Dunne, "The Annual Freedom Picnic," in *Mr. Dooley and the Chicago Irish*, ed. Charles Fanning (Washington, D.C., 1987), p. 286.

23. Joseph M. Hernon, Jr., *Celts, Catholics and Copperheads: Ireland Views the American Civil War* (Columbus, Ohio, 1968) includes a variety of Irish nationalist reactions to the war between the States.

24. For an excellent fictional insight into Fenianism and the 1867 insurrections see Thomas Flanagan, *The Tenants of Time* (New York, 1988).

25. Brian Jenkins, *Fenians and Anglo-American Relations During Reconstruction* (Ithaca, 1969) discusses the relationship between Fenianism and Anglo-American diplomacy.

26. Flanagan, *Tenants of Time*, p. 328.

27. Sean O'Faolain, *Come Back to Erin* (New York, 1940).

28. Comerford, *Fenians in Context*, pp. 195–222.

29. Rodechko, *Patrick Ford and His Search for America*, discusses the life and opinions of Patrick Ford.

30. For information on John Boyle O'Reilly see Francis G. MacManamin, *The American Years of John Boyle O'Reilly, 1870–1880* (New York, 1976), and William Leonard Joyce, *Editors and Ethnicity: A History of the Irish-American Press, 1848–1883* (New York, 1976).

31. Brown, *Irish-American Nationalism*, pp. 85–98, is the best analysis of New Departure strategy and the first interpretation of the Irish-American role in authoring it.

32. T. W. Moody, *Davitt and Irish Revolution, 1847–1882* (Oxford, 1981).

33. Comerford, *Fenians in Context*, pp. 223–48.

34. For discussions of the land war see Paul Bew, *Land and the National Question in Ireland, 1858–82* (Dublin, 1978); Samuel Clark, *Social Origins of the Land War* (Princeton, 1979); Charles Townshend, *Political Violence in Ireland: Government and Resistance Since 1848* (New York, 1983); and W. E. Vaughn, *Landlords and Tenants in Ireland, 1848–1904* (Dublin, 1984).

35. O'Donovan Rossa, through the agency of the Irish World, originally established the skirmishing fund.

36. Tom Corfe, *The Phoenix Park Murders: Conflict, Compromise and Tragedy in Ireland, 1879–1882* (London, 1968).

37. The role of A. M. Sullivan in Irish-American nationalism and the Cronin murder are topics in Michael F. Funchion, *Chicago's Irish Nationalists, 1881–1890* (Chicago, 1976).

38. James Joyce, *A Portrait of the Artist as a Young Man* (1916 rpt. New York, 1963), pp. 28–40.

39. The best analysis of the disillusionment entering Irish-American nationalism in the 1880s and continuing into the 1890s is in Brown, *Irish-American Nationalism*, pp. 153–82. Joseph Patrick O'Grady, *Irish-America and Anglo-American Relations, 1880–1888* (New York, 1976), discusses nationalist intrusion into Irish-American politics.

40. Joseph Edward Cuddy, *Irish-America and National Isolationism, 1914–1920* (New York, 1976).

41. Alan J. Ward, *Ireland and Anglo-American Relations, 1899–1921* (London, 1969); Francis M. Carroll, *American Opinion and the Irish Question, 1910–1923* (New York, 1978).

42. Marie Veronica Tarpey, *The Role of Joseph McGarrity in the Struggle for Irish Independence* (New York, 1976).

43. Patrick Pearse first expressed the goal "Ireland Gaelic as well as free" as the objective of revolutionary republicanism.

44. For the Irish Republican Army see J. Bowyer Bell, *The Secret Army: A History of the IRA, 1916–1970* (London, 1972); and Timothy Patrick Coogan, *The IRA* (London, 1970). Patrick Bishop and Eamonn Mallie, *The Provisional IRA* (London, 1987) brings the IRA story up to date.

45. Joshua B. Freeman, "Catholics, Communists, and Republicans: Irish Workers and the Organization of the Transport Workers Union," in *Working Class America: Essays on Labor, Community, and American Society*, ed. Michael H. Frish and Daniel J. Walkowitz (Urbana, 1983), pp. 256–83; and Freeman, *In Transit: The Transport Workers Union in New York City, 1933–1966* (Oxford, 1990).

46. There are many good studies on Northern Ireland, including Sally Belfrage, *Living in War: A Belfast Year* (New York, 1987); Patrick Buckland, *A History of Northern Ireland* (Dublin, 1981); John Conroy, *Belfast Diary: War as a Way of Life* (Boston, 1987); John Darby, *Conflict in Northern Ireland: The Development of a Polarized Community* (New York, 1976); Rosemary Harris, *Prejudice and Tolerance in Ulster: A Study of Neighbors and Strangers in a Border Community* (Manchester, 1972); Dervla Murphy, *A Place Apart* (Old Greenwich, Conn., 1978); Padraig O'Malley, *The Uncivil Wars: Ireland Today* (Boston, 1983); and Richard Rose, *Governing Without Consensus: An Irish Perspective* (London, 1971).

47. Andrew Wilson, "Irish-America and the Ulster Conflict, 1968-85" (Ph.D. diss., Loyola Univ. of Chicago, 1991) is the most thorough study of Irish-America and the Northern Ireland situation.

48. This point is briefly but well made in John McCarthy, "Irish-American Conservatives and the IRA," *Four Quarters* 3: (Fall 1989): 6–8.

49. William V. Shannon, "The Lasting Hurrah," *New York Times Magazine*, Mar. 14, 1976, p. 78.

50. Andrew J. Wilson, "Irish-America and the Hunger Strikes," *Recorder* 2 (Summer, 1987): 14–30. But even the American response to the self-imposed martyrdom of Sands could not match the emotional outpouring that took place in 1920, when three captive Irish republicans died after hunger strikes. Then one hundred thousand Irish-Americans protested in Boston Common. In 1981, only about one hundred demonstrated their anger outside British consulate in Boston (*Newsweek*, May 18, 1981, p. 53). In *Biting at the Grave: The Irish Hunger Strikes and the Politics of Despair* (Boston, 1990), Padraig O'Malley offers a well-written, factually detailed, and carefully analyzed account of the hunger strike. He explains why the Irish nationalist martyr tradition and the psychology of an oppressed people produced such an extreme form of protest. He also describes Catholic elements in the hunger strike: redemptive sacrifice and the use of mothers, like the Blessed Virgin, consoling their martyred sons. Protestants in Ireland and Catholics in Britain considered the hunger strike suicide and insisted that the Catholic church in Ireland condemn it as such. But the hunger strikers believed that they were giving their lives for a noble cause. Irish Catholic bishops and priests accepted the sincerity of their motivation.

51. Jack Holland, *The American Connection: U.S. Guns, Money, and Influence in Northern Ireland* (New York, 1987; and Sean Cronin, *Washington's Irish Policy, 1916–1989: Independence, Partition, and Neutrality* (Dublin, 1986) along with Wilson, *Irish-America and the Ulster Conflict*, discuss the American dimension of the Northern Ireland crisis.

52. The Birmingham Six have been released from prison. In 1984, the British government appointed John Stalker, retired chief deputy of the Greater Manchester police force, to investigate accusations against the RUC. Two years later, he was removed. He has written a book, *Stalker* (London, 1988), claiming that his dismissal stemmed from his discovery that eleven RUC officers were guilty of subverting justice in Northern Ireland. Stalker's book gives credence to charges by Dublin and Northern Ireland Catholics that the British government has covered up the anti-Catholic activities of the security forces.

6. SOMEPLACE OR NO PLACE?

1. For a good example of Irish communal liberalism see Thomas P. O'Neill with William Novak, *Man of the House: The Life and Political Memoirs of Speaker Tip O'Neill* (New York, 1987).

2. Mary Gordon, *The Other Side* (New York, 1989).

3. John Gregory Dunne, *Harp* (New York, 1989), p. 184.

Recommended Reading

THE IRISH HERITAGE

Because the Irish-American personality derives from the experience in Ireland as well as the United States, some knowledge of the former is necessary to understand the latter. Thomas E. Hachey, Joseph M. Hernon, Jr., and Lawrence J. McCaffrey, *The Irish Experience* (Englewood Cliffs, N.J., 1989), is a broad survey of Irish history from its beginnings to 1989. Roy Foster, *Modern Ireland, 1600–1972* (New York, 1989), offers an exceptionally well-written view of modern Irish history that takes exception to several previously accepted opinions on the subject. F. S. L. Lyons's *Ireland Since the Famine* (New York, 1971) covers a shorter period of time than *The Irish Experience* or *Modern Ireland*, but it is nicely written, presents a great deal of information, and analyzes it in an intelligent way.

Since 1970, two History of Ireland Series, the Gill and Helicon, have published volumes relevant to the Irish background of immigrants to the United States, including Gearóid Ó Tuathaigh, *Ireland Before the Famine, 1798–1848* (Dublin, 1972); Joseph Lee, *The Modernization of Irish Society, 1848–1918* (Dublin, 1973); John A. Murphy, *Ireland in the Twentieth Century* (Dublin, 1975); and Donal McCartney, *The Dawning of Democracy: Ireland, 1800–1870* (Dublin, 1987). Lee's *Ireland, 1912–1985* (Dublin, 1990) is a major revisionist look at twentieth-century Ireland. For interesting analyses of the impact of the past on Irish attitudes and values see Oliver MacDonagh's *States of Mind: A Study of Anglo-Irish Conflict, 1780–1880* (Boston, 1983); Sean O'Faolain's, *The Irish* (Harmondsworth, Middlesex, England, 1969); and Patrick O'Farrell's *Ireland's English Question* (New York, 1972) and *England and Ireland Since 1800* (New York, 1975).

In many ways, American Catholicism in the nineteenth century was incorporated in an Irish spiritual empire in the English-speaking world. Irish-American devotionalism, loyalty to Rome, financial generosity to the church, and belief in the separation of church and state reflected the values

211

of Irish Catholicism. In three articles published between 1967 and 1975 in the *American Historical Review*, Emmet Larkin triggered research interest in nineteenth-century Irish Catholicism. These three essays have been combined in *The Historical Dimensions of Irish Catholicism* (Washington, D.C., 1984). Larkin has done detailed studies of nineteenth-century Irish Catholicism in *The Making of the Roman Catholic Church in Ireland, 1850–1860* (Chapel Hill, 1980); *The Consolidation of the Roman Catholic Church in Ireland, 1860–1870* (Chapel Hill, 1987); *The Roman Catholic Church and the Home Rule Movement in Ireland, 1870–1874* (Chapel Hill, 1990); *The Roman Catholic Church and the Creation of the Modern Irish State, 1878–1886* (Philadelphia, 1975); *The Roman Catholic Church and the Plan of Campaign, 1886–1888* (Cork, Ireland, 1978); and *The Roman Catholic Church in Ireland and the Fall of Parnell, 1888–1891* (Chapel Hill, 1979). Much scholarly interest in nineteenth-century Irish Catholicism was stimulated by Larkin's June 1972 *American Historical Review* article, "The Devotional Revolution in Ireland, 1850–1875," in which he argued that pre-Famine Irish Catholicism featured an ignorant, not too devout laity; a poorly educated, rebellious clergy; and a quarreling hierarchy. Larkin claimed that Famine deaths and emigration prepared the way for religious reform by eliminating many of the most ignorant members of the laity and reducing the disproportion between numbers of priests and people. According to Larkin, after the Famine, Paul Cardinal Cullen led a "Devotional Revolution" that made Irish Catholics the most generous, loyal, and churchgoing members of their faith in the world.

Pre-Famine Irish Catholic church problems are analyzed in S. J. Connolly's *Priests and People in Pre-Famine Ireland, 1780–1845* (New York, 1982). Patrick Corish's excellent overview *The Irish Catholic Experience: A Historical Survey* (Wilmington, Del., 1985); James O'Shea's thorough local study, *Priest, Politics and Society in Post-Famine Ireland: A Study of County Tipperary, 1850–1891* (Atlantic Highlands, N.J., 1983); and K. Theodore Hoppen's thought-provoking, revisionist *Elections, Politics, and Society in Ireland, 1823–1885* (Oxford, 1984). These studies indicate that the condition of the church before the Famine differed in various parts of Ireland depending on the economic and social conditions of the people and the quality and quantity of the clergy. They and Larkin's latest "Introduction" to *The Historical Dimensions of Irish Catholicism* (Washington, D.C., 1984) have modified the "Devotional Revolution" into an evolution.

Irish Americans developed their political style and values as well as their Catholicism in the context of historical experiences. The surveys of Irish history listed above discuss how various nationalist and land agitations tutored the Irish in the skills of mass-pressure politics. Among first-rate studies of nineteenth-century Irish nationalism and its political dimension, the following three are relevant for Irish America: Sean O'Faolain's *King of the Beggars* (Dublin, 1986); Fergus O'Ferrall's *Catholic Emancipation: Daniel O'Connell and the Birth of Irish Democracy, 1820-30* (Dublin, 1985); and R. Vincent Comerford's *The Fenians in Context* (Atlantic Highlands, N.J., 1985).

Although other subjects are catching up, nationalism, the third prominent feature of the Irish-American profile, has had the most attention in Irish historiography. The following works are recommended: D. George Boyce, *Nationalism in Ireland* (Baltimore, 1982); Robert Kee, *The Green Flag* (New York, 1972); and Thomas E. Hachey and Lawrence J. McCaffrey, eds., *Perspectives on Irish Nationalism* (Lexington, Ky., 1988).

Economic and social conditions in Ireland sent millions of people to the United States. K. H. Connell, *The Population of Ireland, 1750-1845* (Oxford, 1950), is an interesting population and social examination of pre-Famine Ireland that argues that dependence on the potato caused the Irish population explosion. More recent studies have concluded that the relationship between the potato, early marriages, and many children was more complicated than Connell suggested. Joel Molkyr, *Why Ireland Starved: A Quantitative and Analytical History of the Irish Economy, 1800-1852* (Boston, 1982), is almost incomprehensible to those who do not know the specialized language of economic and quantitative historians, but it does contain valuable data that reject the notion that social and economic conditions in Ireland made the Famine inevitable. Perhaps the best studies of the Famine are Cormac O'Gráda, *Great Irish Famine* (Atlantic Highlands, N.J., 1988); and the eight chapters on "The Great Hunger, 1845-1851" by James S. Donnelly, Jr., in W. E. Vaughn, ed., *A New History of Ireland V: Ireland Under the Union, 1: 1801-1870* (Oxford, Clarendon Press, 1989). In less than two hundred well-written pages, O'Gráda synthesizes the best available research on the subject and interprets it in an exciting and interesting manner. Donnelly's effort also does an excellent job in synthesizing previous research. His study results in a strong condemnation of British policy in Ireland. Other Famine studies are Mary E. Daly, *The Famine in Ireland* (Dublin, 1986); R. Dudley Edwards and T. Desmond Williams, eds., *The Great Famine: Studies in Irish History, 1845-1852* (New York, 1956); the well-written best-seller, Cecil Woodham Smith, *The Great Hunger: Ireland, 1845-1849* (New York, 1962); and Thomas Gallagher, *Paddy's Lament: Ireland 1846-47, Prelude to Hatred* (Orlando, Fla., 1987). Janet Ann Nolan's *Ourselves Alone: Female Emigration from Ireland, 1825-1920* (Lexington, Ky., 1989) articulately and intelligently discusses the social changes caused by the Famine that produced an emigration of women from Ireland. Kerby Miller's *Emigrants and Exiles: Ireland and the Irish Exodus to North America* (New York, 1985) presents the factors behind Irish Catholic and Protestant emigrations as well as the problems immigrants encountered in the New World. Contrary to the thesis of this book, Miller strongly maintains that the Irish-American story is one of exile and alienation rather than success and adaptation.

An interesting way to approach Irish history is through the imagination and intuition of good fiction. Perhaps the three best Irish historical novels are Thomas Flanagan's *Year of the French* (New York, 1972) and *Tenants of Time* (New York, 1988), and Sean O'Faolain's *Nest of Simple Folk* (London, 1989). Flanagan's first novel uses the Mayo aspect of the 1798 revolution to discuss its issues and personalities. His second covers Irish nationalist history from the Fenian rising in 1867 to the fall of Parnell in the early 1890s. A *Nest of Simple Folk* also starts with the Fenians but goes up to Easter Week, 1916.

IRISH AMERICA

Among the many interpretations of Irish America are John B. Duff, *The Irish in America* (Belmont, Calif., 1971); Marjorie Fallows, *Irish-Americans: Identity and Assimilation* (Englewood Cliffs, N.J., 1977); Andrew M. Greeley, *The Irish-Americans: The Rise to Money and Power* (New York, 1981); William D. Griffin, *A Portrait of the Irish in America* (New York, 1981) and *The Book of Irish-Americans* (New York, 1990); Lawrence J. McCaffrey, *The Irish Diaspora in America* (1976 rpt. Washington, D.C., 1984); Joseph P. O'Grady, *How the Irish Became American* (New York, 1973); William V. Shannon, *The American Irish* (1963 rpt. New York, 1974); and Carl Wittke, *The Irish in America* (New York, 1970). Wittke's book is rich in detail. Shannon offers informative and perceptive essays on important Irish-American individuals, politics, literature, sports, and religion. Greeley provides a sociological perspective, insisting that Irish America evolved into a prosperous, progressive, and intellectual community, and that it is still alive and well. Fallows also combines historical and social science approaches into an informative and lively book. O'Grady and Duff present brief examinations of the Irish-American story that are useful in ethnic history courses. Griffin's first book offers a pictorial study of Irish America. More than most of the surveys, McCaffrey emphasizes the impact of the Irish experience on the Irish in America and believes that they brought as much to as they took from the United States. He agrees with Greeley and others that Irish America is a success story, but he is not sanguine about its present condition or future. Patrick Blessing, "The Irish," in *Harvard Encyclopedia of American Ethnic Groups*, ed. Stephan Thernstrom (Cambridge, Mass., 1980), is an exceptionally informative short survey of Irish America. Two volumes that contain sagacious essays on various aspects of Irish America are *America and Ireland, 1776–1976,* ed. David Noel Doyle and Owen Dudley Edwards (Westport, Conn., 1880), and *The Irish in America,* ed. P. J. Drudy (New York, 1985). Of the two, Drudy's collection is more consistent in quality.

Terry Coleman's *Going to America* (1972 rpt. New York, 1973) and Philip Taylor's *The Distant Magnet* (New York, 1971) concern the process of emigration. Coleman focuses on the departure from Liverpool and the hardships of the long transatlantic crossing. Most of the emigrants he discusses were Irish. Taylor reviews the entire scope of European emigration, describing the voyage to America and discussing the problems immigrants encountered in the United States. Audrey Lockhart's *Some Aspects of Emigration from Ireland to the North American Colonies Between 1660 and 1775* (New York, 1976) provides valuable information on Irish Catholic indentured servants and transported convicts in the eighteenth-century colonization of the New World. W. F. Adams's *Ireland and Irish Immigration to the New World from 1815 to the Famine* (New York, 1967) reflects some Anglo-American Protestant antipathies to Irish Catholics, but it is thorough on Irish emigration before the Great Famine. George W. Potter's *To the Golden Door* (Westport, Conn., 1974) also deals with pre-Famine immigrants.

In 1851, Reverend John O'Hanlon, an Irish priest who had been on the American mission in St. Louis, Missouri, prepared a guide for emigrants going to the United States, telling them what to bring with them and what to expect when they arrived. Fearing that living in cities would weaken their religious ties, he advised them to farm in the United States. Some of O'Hanlon's advice and other interesting information about the immigrant experience is in Edward J. Maguire, ed., *Reverend John O'Hanlon's The Irish Emigrant's Guide for the United States* (New York, 1976). Janet A. Nolan's *Ourselves Alone: Women's Emigration from Ireland, 1885–1920* is an exceptionally well-written and perceptive examination of conditions that limited the role and opportunities of Irish women and motivated them to set sail for the United States. Ide O'Carroll's *Models for Movers: Irish Women's Emigration to America* (Dublin, 1989) argues that an oppressive patriarchy and a rigid Catholicism have forced women to leave Ireland. But her oral interviews do not always support her thesis. Although it is a gold mine of information, *To the Golden Door* is too concerned with and probably exaggerates Irish economic and social progress. Unfortunately, Potter died before completing his book, and it contains no information about sources for his information and interpretations.

John F. Maguire was the proprietor of the *Cork Examiner* and a prominent nationalist politician in the British Parliament. His *Irish in America* (New York, 1974), originally published in 1868, is still a valuable study of the conditions and attitudes of early Irish Catholics in the United States. Arnold Schrier's *Ireland and the American Emigration* (New York, 1970) uses letters back home to analyze aspects of the immigrant experience. Miller's *Emigrants and Exiles* also relies heavily on immigrants' letters, but they sometimes distort as well as reveal. Only a portion of emigrants corresponded with relatives in Ireland, and they often expressed homesickness and alienation that might have been temporary and probably not typical of the majority of the Irish in the United States.

Oscar Handlin's classic portrait of the first Irish ghetto in the United States, *Boston's Immigrants: A Study in Acculturation* (1941 rpt. New York, 1968) pioneered serious scholarship in urban Irish-American history. Stephan Thernstrom's *Poverty and Progress* (Cambridge, Mass., 1964) discusses slow and small Irish economic and social mobility in Newburyport, Massachusetts, 1850–80. In a more recent book, *Other Bostonians: Poverty and Progress in the American Metropolis, 1860–1970* (Cambridge, Mass., 1973), Thernstrom shows that Boston's Irish were no more successful than those in Newburyport. Thernstrom has been criticized for creating a negative stereotype of Irish Americans, but his findings demonstrate that the New England Irish were exceptions to the general Irish American success story. Other local studies of Irish America are R. A. Burchell, *The San Franciso Irish, 1848–1880* (Berkeley, 1980); Dennis Clark, *The Irish in Philadelphia* (Philadelphia, 1973) and *Erin's Heirs: Irish Bonds of Community* (Lexington, Ky., 1991); David M. Emmons, *The Butte Irish: Class and Ethnicity in an American Mining Town, 1875–1925* (Urbana, 1989); Lawrence J. McCaffrey, Ellen Skerrett, Michael Funchion, and Charles Fanning, *The Irish in Chicago* (Urbana, 1987); Grace MacDonald, *History of the Irish in Wisconsin in the Nineteenth Century* (New York, 1976); Brian C. Mitchell, *The Paddy Camps: The Irish of Lowell, 1821–61* (Urbana, 1988); Earl F. Niehaus, *The Irish in New Orleans* (New York, 1976); Jo Ellen McNergney Vinyard, *The Irish on the Urban Frontier: Detroit, 1850–1880* (New York, 1976); and Douglas V. Shaw, *The Making of an Immigrant City: Ethnic and Cultural Conflict in Jersey City, 1850–1877* (New York, 1976). Emmons demonstrates how much can be learned about an ethnic group by studying them in a small urban area. Vinyard's book makes a strong case that the Irish on the urban frontier, from Buffalo west, achieved more social mobility than those in the East. Local studies support her thesis as do the essays in Timothy J. Meagher, ed., *From Paddy to Studs: Irish-American Communities at the Turn of the Century Era, 1880–1920* (Westport, Conn., 1986). Contributors to the Meagher volume discuss Irish social mobility after 1880 and conclude that Irish Americans made more progress in the West than in the East. Alice Lida Cochran's *Saga of an Irish Immigrant Family: The Descendants of John Mullanphy* (New York,

1976) chronicles Irish pioneers in the frontier village of St. Louis and concludes that midwestern Irish were more successful than those in the East. Dennis Clark's well-written, innovative, and imaginative *Hibernia America: The Irish and Regional Cultures* (Westport, Conn., 1986) is an ambitious and mostly successful effort to compare the success and assimilation of Irish Americans in various parts of the United States. The results suggest that eastern ghettoization retarded both but that Irishness faded outside urban neighborhoods. California sunshine seemed to burn off ethnicity. Hasia Diner's *Erin's Daughters in America: Irish-American Women in the Nineteenth Century* (Baltimore, 1983) reveals that Irish-American achievements have gender as well as regional variations and that women for a long time did better than men. Other useful portraits of Irish-American women are Eileen Brewer, *Beyond Utility: The Role of the Nun in the Education of American Catholic Girls, 1860–1920* (Chicago, 1987), and Nolan, *Ourselves Alone.*

To compare the Irish-American experience with other branches of the Irish diaspora see John Archer Jackson, *The Irish in Britain* (London, 1963); Lynn Lees, *Exiles of Erin: Irish Migrants in Victorian London* (Ithaca, 1979); John Hickey, *Urban Catholics: Urban Catholicism in England and Wales from 1829 to the Present Day* (London, 1967); Patrick O'Ferrall, *The Irish in Australia* (Notre Dame, 1989); and Robert O'Driscoll and Lorna Reynolds, eds., *The Untold Story: The History of the Irish in Canada* (Toronto, 1988).

In an essay in *The Untold Story*, "Data: What Is Known About the Irish in North America," and in *Being Had: Historians, Evidence and the Irish in North America* (Toronto, 1985) and *Small Differences: Irish Catholics and Irish Protestants, 1815–1922* (Kingston and Montreal, 1988) Donald Harmon Akenson argues that leading historians of the Irish in the United States have exaggerated their urbanization. In making this charge, Akenson distorts census information. By 1870, the Irish were the most urbanized American group, and by 1900 almost 75 percent of them were living in cities with populations over twenty-five thousand. Few of those living in communities under twenty-five thousand were engaged in the agricultural economy. Akenson's comparison of the Canadian and American Irish situations is not germane. His work is an example of quantitative history gone wrong.

The two most important volumes that deal with the anti-Catholic component of American nativism are Ray Allen Billington, *The Protestant Crusade, 1800–1860* (1938 rpt. Chicago, 1964), and John Higham, *Strangers in the Land: Patterns of American Nativism, 1860–1925* (1955 rpt. Chicago, 1965). Other informative studies of American nativism are Donald L. Kinzer, *An Episode in Anti-Catholicism: The American Protective Association* (Seattle, 1964); and Kenneth Jackson, *The Ku Klux Klan in the City* (New York, 1967). Anglo-Saxon racism is the main theme in L. P. Curtis, Jr,

Anglo-Saxons and Celts: A Study in Anti-Catholic Prejudice in Victorian England (Bridgeport, Conn., 1968); and Richard Ned Lebow, *White Britain and Black Ireland: The Influence of Stereotypes on Colonial Policy* (Philadelphia, 1976). Irish people with simian features appeared in American as well as British newspaper and magazine cartoons. They are presented and discussed in John J. Appel and Selma Appel, "The Distorted Image" (New York Anti-Defamation League of B'Nai Brith) a slide collection. Stephan Garrett Bolger, *The Irish Character in American Fiction, 1830–1860* (New York, 1976), analyzes negative portraits of the Irish in early and mid-nineteenth-century American literature. The Irish often reacted to prejudice with prejudice. Their role in the infamous 1863 New York draft riot is the subject of chapters 10 through 12 in Joel Tyler Headley's *The Great Riots of New York, 1712–1873*, introduction by Thomas Rose and James Rodgers (Indianapolis, 1970). Ronald H. Bayor, *Neighbors in Conflict: The Irish, Germans, Jews, and Italians of New York City, 1929–1941* (Baltimore, 1978) discusses Depression-triggered Irish anti-Semitism in New York during the 1930s and 1940s. In *Common Ground* (New York, 1985), Anthony J. Lukas brilliantly portrays both Irish and African-American ghettos in Boston and how the Irish experience created so much defensiveness and paranoia that they lashed out with hatred during the school busing crisis of the 1970s. Arnold R. Hirsch's *Making the Second Ghetto: Race and Housing in Chicago, 1840–1960* (New York, 1983) describes Irish resistance to African-American efforts to move out of their overcrowded, poverty-ridden enclaves into white neighborhoods.

The two best general studies of the American Catholic church, including the Irish dimension, are Jay P. Dolan, *The American Catholic Experience* (New York, 1985); and James Hennessey, S.J., *American Catholics: A History of the American Catholic Community in the United States* (New York, 1981). Three brief but good surveys are John Cogley, *Catholic America* (New York, 1973); John Tracy Ellis, *American Catholicism* (Chicago, 1956); and Andrew M. Greeley, *The Catholic Experience* (New York, 1967). Specific information about Irish-American Catholicism can be found in Thomas N. Brown and Thomas McAvoy, *The United States of America*, vol. 6 of *A History of Irish Catholicism* series, ed. Patrick J. Corish (Dublin, 1970); Jay P. Dolan, *The Immigrant Church, New York's Irish and German Catholics, 1815–1865* (Baltimore, 1975); and Ellen Skerrett, "The Catholic Dimension," in McCaffrey et al., *Irish in Chicago*. In "The Myth of the Irish: A Failure of American Catholic Scholarship," in *The Changing Face of Catholic Ireland*, ed. Desmond Fennell, Fennell makes a good case that the so-called Irish puritan, authoritarian, and anti-intellectual aspects of American Catholicism owe much more to Roman and British than to Irish influences.

The best biography of an important Irish-American prelate is Marvin O'Connell's *John Ireland and the American Catholic Church* (St. Paul, 1988). Other significant profiles of Irish-American bishops are Peter Guilday, *The Life and Times of John England: First Bishop of Charleston, 1786–1842* (New York, 1927); John Tracy Ellis, *The Life of James Cardinal Gibbons, Archbishop of Baltimore, 1834–1921*, 2 vols. (Milwaukee, 1952); Richard Shaw's *Dagger John: The Unquiet Life and Times of Archbishop John Hughes of New York* (New York, 1977); and James P. Gaffey, *Citizen of No Mean City: Archbishop Patrick Riordan of San Francisco, 1841–1914* (Wilmington, N.C., 1976).

Relations between the American hierarchy and Rome are thoroughly discussed in O'Connell's biography of Ireland and in Gerald P. Fogarty, *The Vatican and the American Heirarchy from 1870 to 1965* (Wilmington, Del., 1985). Robert D. Cross, *The Emergence of Catholic Liberalism in America* (1958 rpt. Chicago, 1967), discusses the conflict over Americanism in the American Catholic church. O'Connell's biography of Ireland contains additional information on the subject. James Edmund Roohan, *American Catholics and the Social Question, 1865–1900* (New York, 1976), examines the defensive social conservatism of the hierarchy in the East, pointing to regional differences in Irish-American Catholicism. That contrast also is a major theme in David Noel Doyle's *Irish-Americans, Native Rights, and National Empires: The Structure, Divisions, and Attitudes of the Catholic Minority in the Decade of Expansion, 1890–1901* (New York, 1976). Irish-American social liberalism is examined in Francis L. Broderick, *Right Reverend New Dealer John A. Ryan* (New York, 1963), and David J. O'Brien, *American Catholics and Social Reform: The New Deal Years* (New York, 1968). Philip Gleason, *Catholicism in America* (New York, 1970) and *Keeping the Faith: American Catholicism Past and Present* (Notre Dame, 1987); and James Terence Fisher, *The Catholic Counter Culture in America, 1933–1962* (Chapel Hill, 1989), contain useful information about Irish-American Catholicism. Garry Wills's *Bare Ruined Choirs* (Garden City, N.Y., 1972) describes the values and worship of pre- and post-Vatican II American Catholicism. John Tracy Ellis's *American Catholics and the Intellectual Life* (Chicago, 1956) touched off a national discussion of the failure of American Catholic education to produce intellectuals, and Thomas O'Dea's *American Catholic Dilemma* (1958 rpt. New York, 1962) added fuel to the controversy. In explaining this failure, Ellis discussed an immigrant church concentrating on the basic needs of its flock for survival and respectability and the impact of American pragmatism and anti-intellectualism on Catholics in the United States. O'Dea added the authoritarian character of Irish-American Catholicism. In *Religion Culture and Values: A Cross-Cultural Analysis of Motivational Factors in Native Irish and*

American Irish Catholicism (New York, 1976), a quantitative study, Bruce Francis Biever concludes that although American Catholicism is structurally based on an Irish model and the American Irish have many of the same religious and moral values as Catholics in Ireland, they are much less likely to accept the authority of the church or clergy on matters that are not strictly spiritual. Like other Americans, they fear the power of institutionalized religion and insist on democratic and pluralistic controls over the church. Biever's book, originally a 1965 University of Pennsylvania Ph.D. dissertation, does not research the obvious decline in Irish-American Catholic enthusiasm since then. In *Once a Catholic* (New York, 1987), Peter Occhiogrosso interviews present and former Catholics, many of them Irish, about the impact of Catholic values on their lives.

Literature has provided perceptive insights into Irish American Catholicism. The virtue of charity failures of Irish Americans' sexual neuroses are subjects of Harry Sylvester's *Moon Gaffney* (New York, 1947), and Tom McHale's two satires, *Principatio* (New York, 1970) and *Farragan's Retreat* (New York, 1971), and Jimmy Breslin's *World Without, Amen* (New York, 1971). Priests have been the subject of James F. Powers's short stories and novels, *Prince of Darkness* (Garden City, N.Y., 1947), *Presence of Grace* (Garden City, N.Y., 1956), *Look How the Fish Live* (New York, 1975), *Morte D'Urban* (New York, 1962), and *The Wheat That Springeth Green* (New York, 1989). In the first four books, Powers relentlessly criticized and satirized the worldliness of the clergy, their compromises with the luxurious American life, and their anti-intellectualism and social conservatism. He wanted a more dedicated, less affluent clergy that sympathized with the unfortunate. In *The Wheat That Springeth Green*, Powers seems to have become more tolerant of clerical imperfection. Edwin O'Connor's *Edge of Sadness* (Boston, 1961), the story of a physically and spiritually recovering alcoholic cleric, is the best literary portrait of an Irish-American priest. In *Prince of Peace* (Boston, 1984), James Carroll portrays the role of the Catholic church in American Cold War anticommunism, especially in regard to the Vietnam War. John Gregory Dunne's *True Confessions* (New York, 1977), made into a movie in 1980, shows that the role of the Catholic clergy has political dimensions and that they sometimes use questionable means to obtain worthwhile ends. One of the most perceptive studies of the negative effects of pietistic Irish Catholicism on family life is Elizabeth Cullinan's *House of Gold* (Boston, 1969). In *The God of Love* (New York, 1963), *Romans, Countrymen and Lovers* (New York, 1969), *The Sandbox Tree* (New York, 1970), *The Good Shepherd* (New York, 1974), and *Promises to Keep* (New York, 1978), Thomas Fleming analyzes the impact of Catholicism on Irish-American life. He concludes that at the beginning it sheltered and comforted, but in the long run its authoritarianism and puritanism contradicted the American spirit and held the Irish back. Mary McCarthy's *Memories of a Catholic Girlhood* (New York, 1957) pays tribute to the influence of the history and mystery of Catholicism in the development of one of America's great writers. William Gibson, one of the foremost playwrights in the United States, discusses the importance and comfort of Catholic liturgy in Irish-American life in *Mass for the Dead* (New York, 1968).

James P. Walsh, ed., *The Irish: America's Political Class* (New York, 1976), offers a variety of essays on Irish-American politics. Daniel Patrick Moynihan's famous essay "The Irish" in Nathan Glazier and Daniel Patrick Moynihan, *Beyond the Melting Pot: Jews, Italians, and Irish of New York City* (Cambridge, Mass., 1963), pays tribute to Irish skill in acquiring political power but argues that because of peasant parochial conservatism they were reluctant to apply it to solve urban problems. Other scholars disagree with Moynihan. In *Urban Liberalism and Progressive Reform* (New York, 1973), John B. Buenker argues that Irish political machines did much to alleviate urban poverty and bring ethnics into the mainstream of American politics. This thesis is supported by Robert Dahl's *Who Governs? Democracy and Power in an American City* (New Haven, 1961).

Perhaps the most comprehensive study of Irish-American politics, Steven P. Erie's *Rainbow's End: Irish-Americans and the Dilemmas of Urban Machine Politics, 1840–1985* (Berkeley, 1988), rejects the claim that politics speeded Irish-American social mobility or that Irish politicians were champions of ethnic America. According to Erie, political employment locked the Irish into blue-collar and lower-middle-class jobs and Irish politics focused on the Irish, not other ethnics. Erie's book is a corrective to exaggerations about Irish-American politics, but it falsely assumes that there were many and better alternatives for the Irish to politically related jobs, and it undervalues Irish political service to others. Although the Irish, like other American politicians, catered to their own constituents, they were more generous in dispensing favors and services and more concerned about non-Irish ethnics than were Anglo-Protestants.

Alfred Connable and Edward Silberfarb, *Tigers of Tammany* (New York, 1967), discusses the first great Irish-American political organization. William L. Riordan, *Plunkitt of Tammany Hall* (New York, 1963), details the daily activities of an Irish machine politician. David C. Hammack, *Power and Society: Greater New York at the Turn of The Century* (New York, 1982), offers valuable information concerning the interplay between Irish Tammany politicians and economic elites in New York in the late nineteenth and early twentieth centuries. He concludes that the power of the latter far exceeded their numbers. In *Tammany Hall and the New Immigrants: The Progressive Years*

(New York, 1976), Thomas McLean Henderson discusses Jewish and Italian challenges to Irish political power in New York. Those two groups forced Irish politicians to be more concerned with social welfare issues, but they directed their new social consciousness at the Jews and ignored the Italians. Italian anger led to an anti-Irish coalition that elected Fiorello La Guardia mayor and caused the decline of Irish influence in Tammany. George Q. Flynn's *American Catholics and the Roosevelt Presidency* (Lexington, Ky., 1968) explains the importance of the Irish in the operation of the New Deal. Milton Rakove's *Don't Make No Waves—Don't Back No Losers* (Bloomington, 1975) and *We Don't Want Nobody Nobody Sent* (Bloomington, 1979) are interesting and highly entertaining examinations of Mayor Richard J. Daley's competently led Chicago political machine. For a detailed study of Chicago Irish politics see Michael F. Funchion, "The Political Dimension, in McCaffrey et al., *Irish in Chicago*. Edward M. Levine's *The Irish and Irish Politicians* (South Bend, 1966) analyzes the style and the values of Chicago Irish politicians. Mayor Daley has inspired a number of interesting studies. Among the best are William F. Gleason, *Daley of Chicago* (New York, 1970); Mike Royko, *Boss* (New York, 1970); and Eugene Kennedy, *Himself: The Life and Times of Richard J. Daley* (New York, 1978).

James Michael Curley, a political legend in Boston, inspired several political novels. He recounted his own career in *I'd Do It Again* (New York, 1976), in which he describes himself as a progressive force in Boston politics and honestly describes his skill at dirty trick politics. *I'd Do It Again* gives evidence to the charge that the Boston Irish practiced a politics of revenge. Although Curley was a liberal on social issues, with an empathy for almost all races, religions, and ethnic groups, he never forgave Yankee Protestants for the prejudice and poverty they inflicted on his people.

The best portrait of Father Charles Coughlin is in Alan Brinkley's *Voices of Protest: Huey Long, Father Coughlin, and the Great Depression* (New York, 1982). Charles J. Tull, *Father Coughlin and the New Deal* (Syracuse, 1965), also provides valuable information on the clerical demagogue.

Thomas C. Reeves, *The Life and Times of Joe McCarthy* (New York, 1982), is the most comprehensive biography of the senator from Wisconsin. Donald F. Crosby, *God, Church, and Flag: Senator Joseph R. McCarthy and the Catholic Church, 1950–57* (Chapel Hill, 1978), analyzes American Catholic responses to McCarthyism. Herbert S. Parmet, *Jack: The Struggles of John F. Kennedy* (New York, 1980), and *JFK: The Presidency of John F. Kennedy* (New York, 1983), is an excellent two-part study of the first Irish-American Catholic president. Garry Wills, *The Kennedy Imprisonment* (Boston, 1982), is critical of Kennedy and insists that Joseph Kennedy and his sons were more impressed with upper-class Anglo-Saxon Protestant than with Irish Catholic values. *Man of the House: The Life and Political Memoirs of Speaker Tip O'Neill with William Novak* (New York, 1987) presents the Irish communal political values of one of the most powerful Irish-American politicians of recent times. In *What I Saw at the Revolution: A Political Life in the Reagan Era* (New York, 1990), Peggy Noonan, a speechwriter for Ronald Reagan and George Bush, explains her own defection from the Democratic party.

Some of the best insights into the Irish political personality are found in fiction. The most famous Irish political novel is Edwin O'Connor's *Last Hurrah* (Boston, 1956). Other recommended literary studies of Irish-American politicians are Joseph Dinneen, *Ward Eight* (New York, 1968); Ramona Stewart, *Casey* (Boston, 1968); Mary Deasy, *O'Shaughnessey* (New York, 1957); John O'Hara, *Ten North Frederick* (New York, 1955); Thomas J. Fleming, *All Good Men* (New York, 1961), *King of the Hill* (New York, 1965), and *Rulers of the City* (New York, 1977); James Carroll, *Mortal Friends* (Boston, 1978); R. F. Sheehan, *The Governor* (New York, 1970); and Edwin O'Connor, *All in the Family* (Boston, 1966). Brian Casey in Wilfrid Sheed's *People Will Always Be Kind* (New York, 1973) is a fascinating politician, a combination of John F. Kennedy and Eugene McCarthy. In 1958, John Ford directed a good film version of *The Last Hurrah*, but Irish-American politics has not attracted much attention from playwrights. William Alfred's *Hogan's Goat* (New York, 1968), a play about Irish politics in late nineteenth-century Brooklyn, is an exception.

Irish Nationalism and the American Contribution, ed. Lawrence J. McCaffrey (New York, 1976), contains two brilliant essays by Thomas N. Brown, "Nationalism and the Irish Peasant, 1800–1848" (reprinted from *Review of Politics* 15 [Oct. 1953]), and "The Origins and Character of Irish-American Nationalism" (reprinted from *Review of Politics* 18 [July 1956]). Brown discusses how nationalism in Ireland was weakened by local allegiances and peasants' concerns about land and traditional loyalty and deference to landlords. He emphasizes that loneliness in the United States, the pressures and hostility of Anglo-American Protestant nativism, poverty, and the search for respectability created an Irish consciousness in America that solidified in passionate Irish-American nationalism. Donald Harmon Akenson, *The United States and Ireland* (Cambridge, Mass., 1973), has relevant information on the American influence on Ireland's struggle for independence. In *Emigrants and Exiles*, Kerby Miller stresses alienation as the source of Irish-American nationalism. R. V. Comerford's *The Fenians in Context* is the best and most up-to-date study of Fenianism. It focuses on Ireland but brings in the American dimension. Other useful examinations of Irish republicanism in the 1850s and 1860s are Leon O Broin, *Fenian Fever* (New York, 1971); Maurice Harmon, ed., *Fenians and Fenianism* (Seattle, 1970); and

T. W. Moody, *The Fenian Movement* (Cork, 1968). William D'Arcy, *The Fenian Movement in the United States, 1858–1886* (New York, 1971), offers a detailed examination of the American wing of the republican movement. Brian Jenkins' *Fenians and Anglo-American Relations During Reconstruction* (Ithaca, 1969) discusses how the United States government encouraged Fenianism to pressure Britain into paying reparations for damages inflicted by a Confederate blockade runner, the *Alabama*, built in Britain, and to accept the American naturalization of former British subjects. After its diplomatic victory, the United States ceased encouraging Irish republicanism. In *Irish-American Nationalism*, probably the best book on the subject, Thomas N. Brown credits Irish-American nationalists for authoring the New Departure, featuring a war on landlordism to mobilize peasant enthusiasm in Ireland as a prelude to revolution. He also relates how divisions within the Clan na Gael, the Parnell–Kitty O'Shea scandal, the Cronin murder, and political activities by nationalist leaders damaged the nationalist cause in the United States. The correspondence of John Devoy, a considerable force in the Clan na Gael for a long time, is published in *Devoy's Post Bag, 1871–1928*, 2 vols., ed. William O'Brien and Desmond Ryan (Dublin, 1948). Patrick Ford and John Boyle O'Reilly, along with Devoy, were prominent journalists active in Irish-American nationalism. Ford was more socially radical than most Irish-American nationalists, advocating wars on Irish landlordism and American industrial capitalism. Industrial violence in the 1880s, however, caused Ford to temper his views. he stopped attacking Catholic clericalism and capitalism, advising Irish Americans to improve their their condition by adopting the middle-class work ethic and thrift. Ford's life and values are the subjects of James Paul Rodechko, *Patrick Ford and His Search for America: A Case Study of Irish-American Journalism, 1870–1913* (New York, 1976). In *The American Years of John Boyle O'Reilly, 1870–1890* (New York, 1976), Francis G. McManamin describes how in the United States the former Fenian O'Reilly switched to constitutional nationalism. In addition to his advocacy of Ireland's freedom, O'Reilly defended Irish and Catholic interests, pushed for social reform, championed ethnic and religious minorities, and worked to ease conflicts between Yankees and Irish in Boston. C. C. Tansill's *America and the Fight for Irish Freedom, 1886–1922* (New York, 1957) concentrates on Irish America's financial contributions to efforts for independence in Ireland.

Studies of the Irish-American impact on Anglo-American relations include Joseph Patrick O'Grady, *Irish-Americans and Anglo-American Relations, 1880–1888* (New York, 1976); Joseph Edward Cuddy, *Irish-America and National Isolationism, 1914–1920* (New York, 1976); Alan J. Ward, *Ireland and Anglo-American Relations, 1899–1921* (London, 1969); and Francis M. Carroll, *American Opinion and the Irish Question, 1910–1923* (New York, 1978).

Joseph McGarrity was the strongest post-1922 Irish-American proponent of the use of physical force to push Irish sovereignty beyond the Free State definition and to end partition. His life is featured in Marie Veronica Tarpey's *The Role of Joseph McGarrity in the Struggle for Irish Independence* (New York, 1976). Jack Holland, *The American Connection: U.S. Guns, Money, and Influence in Northern Ireland* (New York, 1987); Dennis Clark, *Irish Blood: Northern Ireland and the American Conscience* (Port Washington, N.Y., 1977); and Sean Cronin, *Washington's Irish Policy, 1916–1986: Independence, Partition, and Neutrality* (Dublin, 1986), provide information on the American dimension of the situation in Northern Ireland.

Wayne G. Broehl, *The Molly Maguires* (Cambridge, Mass., 1964), deals with the most famous group of Irish labor radicals. Broehl makes it clear that the Mollies were as much motivated by hostility to English and Welsh bosses and foremen as by their miserable working conditions and exploitation by the coal company. In *Before the Molly Maguires: The Emergence of the Ethno-Religious Factor in the Politics of the Lower Anthracite Region, 1844–1872* (New York, 1976), William A. Gudelunas, Jr., and William G. Shade argue that ethnoreligious loyalties rather than economic issues or social conditions decided political affiliations in the Schuylkill County, Pennsylvania, coal region. *American and Ireland, 1776–1976*, ed. Doyle and Edwards, contains an important essay by David Montgomery, "The Irish and the American Labor Movement." In the late nineteenth century there was a major dispute in the American hierarchy concerning the legitimacy of labor unions. Conservative prelates such as Michael Corrigan, archbishop of New York, opposed them. Liberals such as John Ireland, archbishop of St. Paul, and James Cardinal Gibbons favored them. The conflict within the hierarchy is the subject of Henry J. Browne, *The Catholic Church and the Knights of Labor* (New York, 1976). In "Race and Ethnicity in Organized Labor: The Historical Source for Resistance to Affirmative Action," in *Ethnicity and the Work Force*, ed. Winston A. Van Horne and Thomas V. Tonneson (Madison, 1985), Herbert Hill insists that Irish and Jewish leaders in the AFL did much for white ethnic labor and little or nothing for African- or Hispanic-American workers. Joshua B. Freeman, *In Transit: The Transport Workers Union in New York City, 1933–1966* (New York, 1990), discusses how Irish immigrants in New York, radicalized by James Connolly's influence on revolutionary republican nationalism in Ireland, cooperated with communists to organize the powerful transport Workers Union.

Rodechko's portrait of Patrick Ford and McManamin's study of John Boyle O'Reilly are two examinations of Irish-American journalism. In *Editors and Ethnicity: A History of the Irish-American Press, 1848–1883* (New York, 1976), William Leonard Joyce explains the role of Irish-American newspapers as keeping the Irish Irish while at the same time making them American, building bridges between the Irish "retrospect" and the American "prospect." He believes O'Reilly's *Boston Pilot* was the best example of this effort.

It is surprising that the Irish athletic prowess in the late nineteenth and early twentieth centuries has received little attention from social and cultural historians. Profiles of great Irish athletes have appeared in histories of various sports and in essays, but there has been no full-scale attempt to interpret the relationship between the Irish-American experience and the games they have played. Anyone interested in pursuing this effort could use as a model Joseph M. Curran's examination of the Irish contribution to American cinema. His *Hibernian Green on the Silver Screen: The Irish and American Movies* (Westport, Conn., 1989) is a short but elegant and encompassing story of the Irish presence and image on film, which documents the political, social, economic, and religious passage of Irish America from working to middle class.

Irish America has not matched the literary genius of Ireland, but it has produced writers and playwrights of significance. Maureen Murphy's "Irish-American Theatre," in *Ethnic Theatre in America*, ed. Maxine Schwartz Seller (Westport, Conn., 1983) describes how early American theater presented the Irish character and personality. Many experts rate Eugene O'Neill as America's greatest playwright. In *Eugene O'Neill, Irish and American: A Study in Cultural Context* (New York, 1976), Harry Cornelius Cronin concludes that although O'Neill rejected Catholicism, he presented life from an Irish Catholic perspective. *Long Day's Journey into Night* (1956 rpt. New Haven, 1969) and *Moon for the Misbegotten* (New York, 1952) are particularly Irish in mood and content. A more recent prize-winning play, Frank Gilroy's *The Subject Was Roses* (New York, 1965), has strong Irish-American subject matter.

Charles Fanning is the leading scholar of Irish-American literature. His *Irish Voice in America: Irish-American Fiction from the 1760s to the 1980s* (Lexington, Ky., 1990) is a perceptive, well-written, and thorough survey of Irish-American literature and its importance in general American fiction. Fanning has specialized in Chicago Irish writers, producing a highly regarded biography, *Finley Peter Dunne and Mr. Dooley: The Chicago Years* (Lexington, Ky., 1978), and a study of Dunne, James T. Farrell, and others in "The Literary Dimension," in McCaffrey et al., *Irish in Chicago*. Fanning has also edited two anthologies: *Mr. Dooley and the Chicago Irish: The Autobiography of a Nineteenth-Century Ethnic Group* (Washington, D.C., 1987) and *The Exiles of Erin: Nineteenth-Century Irish-American Fiction* (Notre Dame, 1987).

Daniel J. Casey and Robert E. Rhodes, *Irish-American Fiction: Essays in Criticism* (New York, 1979), contains studies of several Irish-American authors by prominent scholars. Casey and Rhodes also have produced an anthology of Irish-American writing: *Modern Irish-American Fiction: A Reader* (Syracuse, 1989).

In this essay I have recommended several novels on Irish-American Catholicism and politics. There are other fictional representations that provide valuable insights into the Irish-American community. Some good examples are the Fanning anthology of Dunne's Mr. Dooley Chicago essays. James T. Farrell's Studs Lonigan trilogy and the O'Neill-O'Flaherty pentalogy feature the Chicago Irish a generation and more after Dunne's Bridgeporters. They have advanced in class and moved to Washington Park but are still handicapped by insecurities. Farrell's *Father and Son* (New York, 1940) must be included with Pete Hamill's *Gift* (1973 rpt. New York, 1974) and William Gibson's *Mass for the Dead* as excellent studies of the relationships between Irish-American fathers and sons. Edward McSorley's *Our Own Kind* (New York, 1946), one of the most underrated and neglected Irish-American novels, is about the McDemott family in early twentieth-century Providence, Rhode Island. It is a realistic and sympathetic look at a working-class family. Mary Deasy wrote several novels about the Irish living in the Ohio River Valley. One of her finest, *The Hour of Spring* (New York, 1976), covers three generations of Joyces from their origins in County Kerry to Coroli (Cincinnati), Ohio. Jack Dunphy's *Murderous McLaughlins* (New York, 1988) is a loving tribute to a vanished Irish-America in Philadelphia, featuring a close relationship between a grandmother and grandson similar to the one in Farrell's Danny O'Neill series.

For readers interested in a more comprehensive bibliography of Irish America, Seamus P. Metress's *Irish-American Experience: A Guide to the Literature* (Washington, D.C., 1981) provides the names of authors and books on a variety of subjects and places. Patrick Blessing's *The Irish in America: A Guide to the Literature and Manuscript Collections*, soon to be published by the Catholic University of America Press will supersede Metress's work. It is exceptionally thorough on Irish America and its Irish background.

Since the original 1992 publication of *Textures of Irish America*, I have become acquainted with a number of valuable studies of the Irish-American experience, most new, a few a bit older. *The Irish in America*, ed. Michael Coffey, text by Terry Golway (New York, 1997), contains interesting essays, some by famous scholars and writers. Donald H. Akenson's *The Irish Diaspora: A Primer* (Toronto, 1994) has too much confidence in the value of comparing diasporic experiences, but offers interesting information, and effectively re-buts Kerby A. Miller's alienation and exile theses. He shows that Irish Catholic and Gaelic values did not hinder a rather fast economic and social advance of the Irish in the United States, Canada, Australia, and New Zealand. In *Out of Ireland* (Washington, D.C., 1995), the basis of a quality Public Broadcasting Documentary, Miller and coauthor Paul Wagner qualify the Miller exile-alienation thesis by emphasizing that very few of the Irish who came to America returned and that many who did so were disappointed and realized that the United States was their true home.

The long neglected examination of Irish and Irish-American women continues to attract considerable scholarly attention. In her well-written, thoughtful essay, " 'She Never Then After Forgot Him': Irish Women and Emigration to the United States in Irish Folklore," *Mid-America* 74 (October, 1992), Grace Neville explains how radical changes in post-Famine marriage patterns and women's status in Irish society gave them far more reason than men to emigrate. Women's motives for leaving Ireland and the problems they encountered in the United States are subjects of Rita M. Rhodes's *Women and the Family in Post-Famine Ireland: Status and Opportunity in a Patriarchal Society* (New York, 1992). Maureen Fitzgerald's "Charity, Poverty, and Child Welfare," *Harvard Divinity Bulletin* 25:4 (1996) and Sue Ellen Hoy's "Walking Nuns: Chicago's Irish Sisters of Mercy," in *At the Crossroads: Old Saint Patrick's and the Chicago Irish,* ed. Ellen Skerrett (Chicago, 1997) emphasize the importance of nuns in alleviating social misery in urban America. Their work surpassed the efforts of Anglo-Protestant reformers.

Although the quality of the essays ranges from excellent to trivial to the in-between, many of the leading scholars of the American Irish have contributed to Ronald H. Bayor and Timothy Meagher, eds., *The New York Irish* (Baltimore, 1996). What is good in this collection is very good. Other recommended recent studies on the New York Irish are Robert Ernst, *Immigrant Life in New York City, 1825–1963* (Syracuse, 1994) and Ann M. Shea and Marion R. Casey, *The Irish Experience in New York City: A Select Bibliography* (Syracuse, 1995). The Orange riots in New York are the subject of Michael A. Gordon's *The Orange Riots: Irish Political Violence in New York City, 1870 and 1871* (Ithaca, N.Y., 1993). Gordon explains lower working-class Irish Catholic conduct as resentment against nativist elites frustrating their economic and social mobility. But he underestimates how much of the sectarian animosity present in Orange and Green conflicts emigrated from Ireland. The western Irish are treated in essays published in *The Irish in the West* (Manhattan, Kans., 1993), eds. Timothy J. Sarbaugh and James P. Walsh. All but two of the contributions originally appeared in *Journal of the West* 31 (April 1992).

Irish-American Catholicism has inspired a number of significant additions to the historiography of Irish America. Charles R. Morris's *American Catholic: The Saints and Sinners Who Built America's Most Powerful Church* (New York, 1997) is by far the best overall history of American Catholicism. It features comprehensive coverage, valuable, well-organized information, thoughtful and objective analysis, and graceful writing. John T. McGreevey's *Parish Boundaries: The Catholic Encounter With Race in the Twentieth-Century Urban North* (Chicago, 1996) focuses on conflict and tensions between African Americans and the Irish and other Catholic ethnics. McGreevey pays tribute to the role of ethnic parishes as community when nativists oppressed Catholics, but he laments their evolution into defensive fortresses against neighborhood and school integration. Another study of clashes between African and Irish Americans is Eileen McMahon's *What Parish Are You From? A Chicago Community and Race Relations* (Lexington, Ky., 1995). McMahon describes the difficult transition of Chicago's St. Sabina's parish from Irish to Black. Ellen Skerrett is the leading authority on the Irish-American parish. One example of her work is the previously mentioned *At the Crossroads: Old Saint Patrick's and the Chicago Irish*. Another is *Catholicism, Chicago Style* (Chicago, 1993) which she coauthored with Edward R. Kantowicz and Steven M. Avella. Colleen McDannell's "Going to the Ladies Fair: Irish Catholics in New York City, 1870–1900," in *The New York Irish* is an interesting and intellectually creative look at parish life. Her essay celebrates the leadership role of women in organizing and operating fairs that did so much to finance parish buildings and activities. McDannell emphasizes that investments in parishes indicated how much they meant to the laity as a symbol of their loyalty to the church and their spirituality. Conservative William Henry Cardinal O'Connell of Boston was one of the most influential and controversial members of the American hierarchy in the first half of the twentieth century. James M. O'Toole's biography *Militant and Triumphant: William Henry O'Connell and the Catholic Church in Boston, 1859–1944* (Notre Dame, Ind., 1992) exposes O'Connell as nasty, hypocritical, and a not particularly efficient administrator who covered up clerical scandals including one involving his own nephew. For a long period of time Irish Americans, isolated by prejudice and their own defensiveness, existed in a Catholic subculture. It is discussed by James Terence Fisher in *The Catholic Counter Culture in America, 1833–1962* (Chapel Hill, N.C., 1987) and by Paula M. Kane in *Separatism and Subculture: Boston Catholicism, 1900–1920* (Chapel Hill, N.C., 1994).

Jack Beatty's *The Rascal King: The Life and Times of James Michael Curley (1874–1958)* (Reading, Mass., 1992) is a valuable addition to the literature on Irish-American politics. It is comprehensive in detail, objective and perceptive in analysis, and beautifully written. Beatty reveals the rogue in Curley while at the same time giving readers a sense of the charm and charisma that attracted Boston's Irish electorate. Another worthy contribution to an understanding of Boston's Irish politics is Thomas H. O'Connor, *The Boston Irish: A Political History* (Boston, Mass., 1995). Some, but not enough, of the essays in *The Irish in New York* discuss Irish politics in the city but in "Labor's Decline within New York City's Democratic Party from 1844 to 1884," in William Pencak, Selma Berrol, and Randall M. Miller, eds., *Immigration to New York* (Philadelphia, 1961), Anthony Granowicz argues that Irish influence within Tammany actually declined during the nineteenth century as leaders appeased more influential members of the community. In a Signet Classic reprint of *Plunkett of Tammany Hall: A Series of Very Plain Talks on Very Practical Matters* (New York, 1995), Peter Quinn's introductory essay is a brilliant, exceptionally well-written analysis of the issues, the environment, the constituency, and the personalities that produced the Irish political style. Roger Biles has written two important books on Irish machine politics in Chicago: *Big City Boss in Depression and War: Mayor Edward J. Kelly of Chicago* (DeKalb, Ill., 1984); and *Richard J. Daley: Politics, Race, and the Governing of Chicago* (DeKalb, Ill., 1995). Biles indicates that despite graft and corruption, Kelly was a strong, efficient urban manager who beautified his city and was largely responsible, through his personal commitment to civil rights, for bringing African Americans into the Democratic coalition. Biles credits Daley with a managerial expertise that did make Chicago work but far more for its white ethnic than for its black citizens. William Kennedy's interesting, gracefully written study of his native city, *O Albany*, spends a considerable amount of time on politics, especially the O'Connell machine. Thomas C. Reeves's *A Question of Character: A Life of John F. Kennedy* (New York, 1991) does not hesitate to point out the character flaws that limited the effectiveness of the Kennedy presidency, but it does note that his administration showed signs of a growing maturity before its abrupt termination.

Andrew Wilson's *Irish America and the Ulster Conflict, 1865–1995* (Washington, D.C. and Belfast, 1995) is the best book on the Irish-American impact on the troubles in Northern Ireland and thus a major contribution to an understanding of the subject. In addition to using a variety of primary and secondary sources, Wilson's nicely written, well-organized effort makes effective use of oral interviews. Irish nationalism in New York is the topic of " 'In Time of Peace, Prepare for War': Key Themes in the Social Thought of New York's Irish Nationalists, 1890–1916," by David Brundage in *The New York Irish*. Cultural nationalism expressed in the Irish language is discussed in Kenneth E. Nilsen's "The Irish Language in New York, 1850–1900," also in *The Irish in New York*.

Charles Fanning's "The Heart's Speech No Longer Stifled: New York

Irish Writing since the 1960s," is probably the best essay in *The Irish in New York*. It certainly offers a valuable supplement to his *The Irish Voice in America: Irish-American Fiction from the 1760s to the 1880s*. Another major addition to an understanding of Irish-American culture is William H. A. Williams, *'Twas Only an Irishman's Dream: The Image of Ireland and the Irish in American Popular Song Lyrics, 1800–1920s* (Urbana and Chicago, 1996). Williams claims that the improving image of the Irish and their homeland in popular songs was an important ingredient in their march toward acceptability and respectability. *Textures of Irish America* stresses the importance of entertainment and sports, especially baseball, in the Irish-American community and their role in the change that moved the Irish from the most hated to the most popular ethnic group in the country. Doris Kearns Goodwin's *Wait Till Next Year* (New York, 1997) is a moving profile of her Irish-American Catholic family, and the importance of the Brooklyn Dodgers in the close relationship between father and daughter. Irish-American Catholic writers continue to make important contributions to American literature and Peter Quinn's *The Banished Children of Eve* (New York, 1994) is a major historical novel. In compelling, graceful prose Quinn presents fascinating and complex Irish, Anglo-Protestant, and African-American characters and provides his readers with a perceptive analysis of the social and economic environment that resulted in the New York Draft Riot of 1863.

Index

Abortion: in American Catholicism, 82, 83–84, 119, 173
Addams, Jane, 101
Adrian IV (pope), 56
African Americans: and relations with Irish America, 15, 22, 34, 36, 41, 43–44, 63, 133–34, 160, 168
Akenson, Donald, 183n. 13
Alabama claims, 143, 146
Alcohol abuse: among Irish, 57–59; among Irish Americans, 17–18, 63
Allen, W. P., 145
All Good Men (Fleming), 90, 98, 109, 110
Alliance party (Northern Ireland), 158
America (New York), 107
American Broadcasting Company: 1980 and 1988 *Washington Post* presidential election poll of, 120–21
American Civil War, 17, 22, 23, 139, 143, 168
American Conference for Irish Studies, 177
American Enlightenment and nativism, 2, 18, 49, 89–90, 93
American Federation of Labor (AFL), 34, 39, 168
American Irish (Shannon), 91
Americanism: in Catholic church, 65–66, 82–88, 176–78

American party (Know-Nothings), 20, 21
American Protective Association, 35
American Protestant Vindicator, 19
American Revolution, 51, 136–37
Amnesty Association, 148
Anderson, Congressman John, 120, 121
Anglo-American Protestants: responses of to Irish Catholics, 2, 4, 17, 18, 27, 34, 35, 36, 37, 51, 89, 127. *See also* Anti-Catholic nativism
Anglo-Irish Agreement (Hillsborough), 162–63
Anglo-Irish Protestants: responses of to Irish Catholics, 50–53, 54, 127, 148
Anglo-Irish Treaty (1921), 37, 153, 154
Anglo-Irish War (1919–1921), 6, 35, 37, 38, 153
Anti-Catholic nativism: American, 3, 5, 6, 13, 17–22, 23, 27, 28, 34, 35, 47, 48, 49, 78, 88–89, 93, 94, 98, 103, 114–15, 125, 133, 136, 137–38, 139, 153, 164–65, 168, 169–71; British, 13, 48, 54
Anti-Communism: and American Catholics, 79, 104, 106–9, 115, 171

 Sanford Sternlicht, *Series Editor*

Irish Studies presents a wide range of books interpreting important aspects of Irish life and culture to scholarly and general audiences. The richness and complexity of the Irish experience, past and present, deserves broad understanding and careful analysis. For this reason, an important purpose of the series is to offer a forum to scholars interested in Ireland, its history, and culture. Irish literature is a special concern in the series, but works from the perspectives of the fine arts, history, and the social sciences are also welcome, as are studies that take multidisciplinary approaches.

Selected titles in the series include: